Teaching Guide

BOOK 4 • LESSONS 91 – 120

Reading Eggs Teaching Guide – Book 4

ISBN: 978-1-76020-087-9

Published by Blake Education Pty Ltd
ABN 50 074 266 023
Locked Bag 2022
Glebe NSW 2037

Ph: (02) 8585 4085
Fax: (02) 8585 4058

Email: info@blake.com.au
Website: www.blake.com.au

Publisher: Katy Pike
Series editor: Sara Leman and Megan Smith
Editors: Sandra Iannella and Stacey Belgre
Designed and typeset by The Modern Art Production Group
Printed by Green Giant Press

Introduction

Reading Eggs

Since the launch of the website in 2008, Reading Eggs has grown to be an integral part of how children learn to read in many schools and homes across Australia and the world. Millions of children have successfully used the program and it's a key learning tool in more than 10 000 schools worldwide. The program has continued to grow and improve with many additional lessons, features, books and teaching resources. The Reading Eggs website now has a vast range of literacy resources including teaching tools, posters, lesson plans, worksheets and more than 2000 e-books, making it the most comprehensive reading program on the web.

Reading Eggs Teaching Guide

The four books in this series cover the 120 Reading Eggs lessons that are the core of the learn-to-read program. Each lesson has now been fully cross-referenced to all other components in the program and to the Australian Curriculum. Whether it's handwriting lessons for the Interactive Whiteboard, apps for student practice on their iPads, whole class alphabet activities, comprehension teaching posters, memorable songs, flashcards or more books to read, you will find a vast range of resources to use in your classroom. Every lesson comes with four student worksheets that focus on a specific skill including phonemic awareness, phonics, sight words, vocabulary, comprehension and handwriting.

Reading Eggs Lessons 91 - 120

This book covers lessons 91 – 120. Each lesson is supported by two pages of teaching notes with learning objectives, curriculum links, classroom activities and a Reading Eggs lesson sequence that links to the four student worksheets. Also included for each lesson are the related Reading Eggs activities, interactives, songs, apps and e-books that can be used to reinforce the content and skills covered in each lesson.

My program

From lesson 11 onwards, the additional *My Program* books appear, with four books for every lesson. These carefully levelled books are a balance of fiction and nonfiction titles, each with their own short comprehension quiz. *My Program* books provide students with the real reading practice they need to improve their reading fluency, vocabulary and comprehension skills. In later lessons, other parts of the program including the Skills Bank spelling lessons, Driving Tests and Storylands appear as part of each student's *My Program* board.

Contents

Reading Eggs Teaching Guide Books 1 to 4 Overview

Lesson	Phonic Letters and Sounds	Phonically Decodable Words	High Frequency Sight Words
Reading Eggs Teaching Guide Book 1 Overview			
1 - the letter m	m		
2 - the letter s	s		
3 - words I and am, and the letter i	a, m, am, i	Sam	I, am
4 - the letter t	t		
5 - the word and sound at	a, t, at	bat, cat, fat, pat, rat, sat, mat, hat	at, a, I, am
6 - the letter b	b	bat	
7 - the letter c	c	cat	
8 - the letter f	f, at	cat, bat, fat, mat, sat	
9 - the word a	a, m, t, at, am	am, Sam, cat, bat, fat, mat	I, a, am
10 - Review	a, b, c, f, i, m, s, t, am, at	am, Sam, at, bat, cat, fat, mat, sat	I, am, at, a
11 - the letter n	n	cat, sat, bat	I
12 - the letter p	p, am	pat	am
13 - the sound ap	a, p, ap	Sam, pats, cat, bat, fat, sat, zap, map, cap, tap, nap, rap, lap, gap	I, am, a
14 - the letter h	h	hat, ham	
15 - the letter r	r	rat, ram, rap	
16 - the sound an	a, n, an	ran, fan, can, van, pan, ant, Sam, bat, cat, rat	I, am, a, an, can, man
17 - the letter z	z	zap	
18 - the letter e, the sound ee	e, ee	bee, tree, see, seed, weed, Zee, three, tee	see
19 - the words see and the	s, ee	Sam, can, see, man, fan, pan, tap, cap, hat, bat, cat, sat, rat, mat, fat, zap, map	see, the, I, can, man, at, am
20 - Review	n, p, h, r, z, e, ap, an, ee	see, can, hat, man, bee, bat, Sam	see, the, can, man, you, I
21 - the letter v	v	van	see, the
22 - and		see, ant, band, rat, hat, sand, hand, land, mat, bee, bat, cat, Sam	and, see, the
23 - the letter d	d	Dan, dad	you
24 - the words in and had		rat, cat, hat, sat, fat, map	in, had, I, can, see, the, a
25 - the letter j	j	jam	see, you, the, can
26 - the sound ad	ad	dad, bad, had, pad, mad, sad, cats, rats, bees, ants	had, I, can, see
27 - the letter o	o	on	
28 - the word is		bee, ant, bad, sad, cap, bat	is, good, a, has, see, the, can, bad, an, I, am
29 - the word on	on	zap, mat, sat, bee, ant	on, the, and, is, a, see, can, you, had, an
30 - the letter q	q	queen	I, am, a, an, at, can, see, the, you, and, in, had, is, on, good, bad
Reading Eggs Posters			
Reading Eggs Teaching Guide Book 2 Overview			
31 - the letter g	g	pig, bag	had, see, the, bad, on, is, good
32 - the letter l	l	lap, lad	
33 - the words he and she		cat, sat, tap, can, jam, van, man, Dan, zap, mat, fat, bee, see	he, she, on, had, the, can, see, is, you, and, in, a, I
34 - the letter k	k		
35 - the words as and has		cat, bat, mat, hat, can, map, rat, man, fan, ham	as, has, is, it, on, a, the, on
36 - the letter y	y	yoyo	had, has, can, is, she, he
37 - the words yes and you		hat, cat, ant, man, van, map, has, and, bat, Dan, can, fat, rat, bad, see, bee	yes, you, has, a, and, it, as, I, am, an, in, he, see, the, can
38 - the letter x	x	box, fox, wax, mix, six	yes, see
39 - the letter w	w	web, win, wig	
40 - Review	am, at, an, ap, ad	van, sad, dam, zap, hat, man, gap, ran, jam, bat, pad, ham, ram, cat, can, see, hid, in, tin, sits, pin, fin	he, she, as, has, yes, you, man, the, can, see, in, and, a
41 - the letter u	u	fun, sun, run	

Reading Eggs Teaching Guide Books 1 to 4 Overview Continued

Lesson	Phonic Letters and Sounds	Phonically Decodable Words	High Frequency Sight Words
42 - the alphabet	Alphabet	cat, mat, rat, ham, map, tap, hat, gap, zap, sat, bat, van, fan, can, man, ran, tan, pan, lap, cap, nap, jam, Sam, ant, fun, sun, fox, box, pin, fin, bee	words, it, the, see, you, yes
43 - the sound id	id	hid, lid, kid, Sid, did, bin, rid, hit, bat	has, a, the, can, see, I, am, yes, it, in, he
44 - the sounds ix and in	ix	six, fix, mix, tin, win, pin, fin, din, bin	in, him, I, can, see, you, yes, a
45 - the sound it	it	hit, sit, bit, fit, spin, lit, pit, wit	it, can, you, on, I, we, and
46 - the sound ig	ig	big, wig, dig, fig, gig, pig, rig	like, said, I, it, my, the, has
47 - the word this		wag, bin, kid, pig, big, wig, fig	this, is, yes, the, it, can, he
48 - the sound ip	ip	lip, zip, pip, rip, dip, hip, nip, sip, tip, wip	little, black, blue, big
49 - the sound il	ill	hill, will, sill, pill, bill, kill, till, mill, dill, fill, gill, jill	
50 - the sound ing	ing	king, ring, sing, wing	bird, two, cannot, has, the, can, this, and
51 - the word go		six	go, by, you, can, see, the
52 - the sound ot	ot	cot, dot, hot, pot, lot, got, jot, rot, not	look, got
53 - the sound og	og	dog, log, fog, cog, bog, hog, jog, rock, sock, shop	of, this, got, lots, the, had, to, go, at, and
54 - the sound op	op	cop, hop, mop, pop, top, shop, stop	play, got, can, the, we, all, in
55 - the sound o	o	lots, dog, hog, log, fog, jog, cog, bog, pop, mop, hop, top, sock, cot, put, dot, hot, not, nod	got, he, lots, of, the, on
56 - the word are		not	are, happy, said, not, this, you, yes, like, no, to
57 - the words his and her		dog	his, her, we, said, like, it, she, this, is, the, he, all
58 - the sound ock	od, ock, ox	fox, cod, rod, nod, god, pod, dock, lock, clock, boxes, sock, rock	
59 - the sound od, y at the end	ox, y at the end	puppy, muddy, bossy, messy, silly, sorry, pod, rod, cod, fox, box, rocks, socks, pot, cot, hot, dot, rot, got	very
60 - Review	ock, ot, og, od, op, ox	clock, dock, rock, sock, lock, pod, rod, cod, dog, cog, jog, hog, log, fog, dot, cot, hot, pot, rot, lot, top, mop, hop, pop, fox, box	
Reading Eggs Posters			
Reading Eggs Teaching Guide Book 3 Overview			
61 - the word me			me, be
62 - the sound up	ut, up	cup, pup, cut, up, but, gut, hut, jut, nut, put	three, green
63 - the sound ug	un, ug	bug, dug, hug, jug, mug, rug, tug, bun, sun, fun, gun, pun, run	
64 - the word to	uck	muck, duck, fluffy, luck, mud, bud	to
65 - the sound uck	uck	fluff, truck, puck, tuck, yuck, stuck	
66 - the word there		leaf, ant, green, duck, mud, sun	there, that, this, hello
67 - the word have		mug, log, cup, green, duck, bug, chin	have
68 - the word they		leq, dog, cat, sun, run	they
69 - the word do		jump, run	do, can, cannot
70 - Review	us	bus, bug, bun, cab, cup, cut, duck, hot, jog, muck, nun, not, pup, rug, run, slug, sun	
71 - the word come		band	come, my, here, goes, day, play
72 - the sound ed	ed, eg, ing	bed, red, leg, peg, beg, egg	baby, open, hello
73 - the sound et	ed, et	bed, fed, wed, red, led, ted, pet, net, jet, vet, wet, hen, ten, pen, leg, egg	
74 - the sound eg	en, et	pet, bet, get, jet, met, set, vet, wet, yet, den, pen, hen, ten, when, men, zen	where
75 - the word where		pen, ten, peg, men, hen, shop	where, when, down, up, go, now
76 - the sound en	eg	leg, beg, keg, peg, peck	
77 - the word who		peck, shell	who, lives, here, into
78 - the word what		wing, tail, log, bed, net, her	what
79 - the sound ell	ell	bell, tell, yell, fell, well, shell, sell, hell	who, what, where
80 - Review		egg, net, bed, red, jet, peg, ten, pen	seven

Lesson	Phonic Letters and Sounds	Phonically Decodable Words	High Frequency Sight Words
81 - the word with	short vowels	pen, pig, leg, log, mug, mop, hat, hug, bed, box	have, with, what, you
82 - the sound ie	ie, ile	pie, tie, lie, smile, crocodile	going, where, want
83 - the sound i-e	ie, ine, ike	lie, line, mine, like, hike	shoe, car, table
84 - the sound ine	ine, ide, ike	dine, pine, fine, spine, shrine	too, off, over, this
85 - the sound sh	sh	shell, shop, sheep, ship, shed	shop, bike
86 - the sound sh	sh	shelley, sheep, shop, shopping	buy, tried, these, new
87 - the sound ie	long i	kite, bite, bike, hike, hide, ride	white, nine, girl, boy
88 - the sound ch	ch	chat, chick, cheese, chin, chips, chest	says, ask, why
89 - the sound th	th	throw, thanks, thin, that, thud, thick, thorn, think	none, two, stayed, home
90 - the sound ch	ch	chimp, chicken, cheese, chilli	these, made, together
Reading Eggs Teaching Guide Book 4 Overview			
91 - the soft c sound	soft c	city, celery, cement, bicycle, park, shark, dark, bark	one, two, three, four, five
92 - the sound ice	ice	mice, rice, dice, slice, line, bike, nine, fine, lime, vine	fly, look, white, fine, nine
93 - the soft g sound	soft g	cage, page, sage, stage, rage	today, park, Saturday
94 - the sound ake	ake	cake, lake, rake, bake, take, snake, shake, make, wake	snake, giraffe, wheel, shark
95 - the sond a-e	long a, ane	cane, mane, lane, plane, cage, ape, game	flew, bowl, brother, everywhere, what, about, another
96 - the sound ace	ace	space, lace, face	clouds, sky, stars, above
97 - the vowels	vowels	life, space	hours, outside, white, purple, yellow, orange
98 - the vowel sounds	long vowel words	make, snake, five, ape	these, out, eight, blue
99 - the sound y	y on the end	itchy, hairy, floppy, rusty, party, creepy	sleep, party, work, easy, flew, plane, high
100 - Review		five, mice, cage	up, down, night, day, in, out, five, nine, eight
101 - the sound oo (short)	oo	cook, book, wool, foot, look, took	dressed, delicious, winner
102 - the sound oo (long)	oo	roof, zoo, noon, moon, cool, spoon, pool, hoop, wood, baboon, cockatoo, coop	moose, cocoon, kangaroo, raccoon, baboon
103 - the sound ole	ole	pole, sole, mole, hole, stole, woke, poke, joke, bone, stone, cone	wombat, ground, kangaroo, mole, phone, poke
104 - the sound o-e	long o, e sounds	rode, code, vote, rose, boat, coat, goat, float, tadpole, flagpole	tangled, seaweed, wavy, bubbly, foam
105 - blends	blends	frog, clam, slam, swam, grub, crab, plug, grab, slug, shell	phone
106 - more blends	blends	crab, clam, frog, fly, green, trunk, lunch, crash, tree	crash, butterfly, hungry
107 - the sound ea	ea	pea, seal, leaf, dream, peach, beach, beast, eat, peace	peace, sitting, scary
108 - the sound u-e	long u words	cube, flute, tune, duke, June, tube	worried, perfect, flute, choose, tongue,
109 - the sound er	er	helper, brother, sister, cleaner, badger, bigger, better, plumber, builder	garden, leaky
110 - adjectives	blends	strong, pretty, dry, crunchy, glossy, flower, ground, cloud, drank, crunchy, squishy	wept, weak, cloud, pretty, adjectives
111 - blends	blends	wanted, trip, crashed, stuck, three	happy, boat, leaf, clock
112 - syllables	syllables	exercise, somewhere, drink, growing, eaten	keeping, drinking, sunlight
113 - end blends	end blends	flamingo, rabbit, duckling, stamp, thump	stinky, wanted, running, wants, keeping
114 - the sound oa	oa	flowers, raincoat, house	picture
115 - the sound /er/	ir	sunlight, seedling, warm, leaf, fingernail	
116 - the sound igh	igh	moonlight, goodnight, sandpaper, icecube, caring	family, forest
117 - nouns	nouns	raincoat, coast, better, bathroom, friends	shirt, goat
118 - the sound or	or	boots, long pants, jumper, coat, cloudy	windy, snow, sunny, rainy, horse
119 - verbs	verbs	remember, imagine, insect, sideways, flap	whistle, squeal, swoop, scuttle, scared
120 - the sound ay	ay	their, apple, spelling, feet, crabs	library, cling, eight, walk

Lesson 91 the soft c sound

Learning objectives

Children will:

- identify words with the soft c sound.
- recognise when the soft c sound applies.
- read and write words with the soft c sound.

Australian Curriculum Content Descriptions

Sound and letter knowledge

ACELA1439 listen to the sounds a student hears in the word, and write letters to represent those sounds; identify and manipulate sounds (phonemes) in spoken words

ACELA1459 recognise that letters can have more than one sound for example 'u' in cut, put, use; recognise sounds that can be produced by different letters for example the /s/ sound in sat, cent, scene

Expressing and developing ideas

ACELA1435 learn that word order in sentences is important for meaning

ACELA1438 build word families using onset and rime

ACELA1758 know that spoken words are written down by listening to the sounds heard in the word and then writing letters to represent those sounds

ACELA1778 learn an increasing number of high-frequency sight words recognised in shared texts and in texts being read independently; know that regular one-syllable words are made up of letters and common letter clusters that correspond to the sounds heard, and how to use visual memory to write high-frequency words

Interpreting, analysing and evaluating

ACELY1649 navigate a text correctly, starting at the right place and reading in the right direction, returning to the next line as needed, matching one spoken word to one written word

ACELY1659 combine knowledge of context, meaning, grammar and phonics to decode text

Word families

circle, cent, city, cell, cement, circus, celery, cycle, bicycle, celebrate, cinema, cylinder, cellar, cymbals, centre

Vocabulary words

wheel, one, two, three, park, school, bike, fell, hurt, knee

Extra assistance

Students have been introduced to the idea that one letter can make two different sounds. The distinction between letters (graphemes) and sounds (phonemes) is important. It can be helpful to make a wall chart to revise and remind students about the alternative sounds for each letter, the rules for their pronunciation and some example words:

Letter	Sounds	Rules	Examples
Cc	hard c - k	before a, o, u	cat, cod, cup
	soft c - s	before e, i, y	cell, city, cycle

Classroom activities

Which Hat?

Place two hats on the floor with the labels soft *c* – /s/ and hard *c* - /k/. Discuss the sounds. Have a pile of objects or pictures of objects that start with *c*. Each student chooses one and works out which hat it must go in. Discuss their choice with the class.

Reading Eggs Lesson sequence	TEACH Content and skills	PRACTISE Children will:	APPLY
Hear: *Animated Lesson*	Introduce the rule: when *c* comes before *e* or *i* or *y* it says /s/.	identify words which have a soft *c* in them.	**Worksheet 1** Phonics
Write: *Bird Words*	Recognise correct word order for a sentence.	choose the correct words to make a sentence.	**Worksheet 2** Vocabulary
Find: *Snowman, What's Missing?, Word Family, Dragon Fire*	Recognise a given word. Identify the missing sound in a word. Identify the correct onset letter to complete the word.	find the given word in a group. Choose the correct sound to make the word. Choose the correct initial letter to make the word.	**Worksheet 3** Sight words
Vocabulary: *Today's Topic Words, Rockpool*	Build vocabulary skills: Recognise key vocabulary.	match pictures to words. Read and follow instructions.	**Worksheet 4** Check
Read: *Book*	Read aloud book.	listen, follow the reading and read along.	**Reading Eggs nonfiction book** Bicycles

Classroom activities

Mind the Gap!

Write this sentence on the board: I ride my bicycle to ____

Read the sentence together and brainstorm a list of possible answers. Students should copy the sentence into their book and finish it with their choice of word and matching illustration.

Related Reading Eggs Activities, Interactives, Songs and Books

Spelling Bank

Kangaroos

Lesson 84

Focus sound words: cent, succeed, cell, cellar, cycle, cyclone

Challenge: exercise, celebrate

Reading Eggs Puzzle Park

More Than One

Transport

Colour Code

Fingers

Driving Tests

Reading Eggs Posters

Alternate Sounds c

Reading Eggs Library Books

My Program Books

Teacher Toolkit

- Spelling Activities
- Grammar Lessons
- Comprehension Lessons
- Targeting Comprehension Interactively
- Targeting Text Interactively

Reading Eggs Apps

Eggy Sight words

Eggy Snap

Eggy Vocab

Critter Card

Leggy the centipede

Soft c

Name

Phonics

Lesson 91 • Worksheet 1

1 Add **soft c** and say the word.

____elery 	____ement 
____ycle 	____ity 
____ircle	____ircus 

2 Circle the **soft c** words.

Leggy likes to cycle in circles.

The circus is coming to the city.

Colour a circle each time you find a **soft c** word.

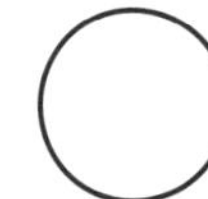 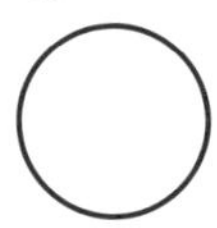 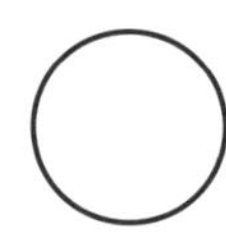 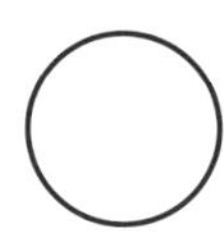

Name

Vocabulary

Soft c

Lesson 91 · Worksheet 2

1 Join Ride the kite bike to the word **bicycle**.

bicycle	circle	bicycle
bicycle		bubble
colour	bicycle	bicycle

2 Trace and copy.

Sight words

Lesson 91 • Worksheet 3

Name

Trace and write the words.

Name

Check

Soft c

Lesson 91 · Worksheet 4

1 Match each word to a number.

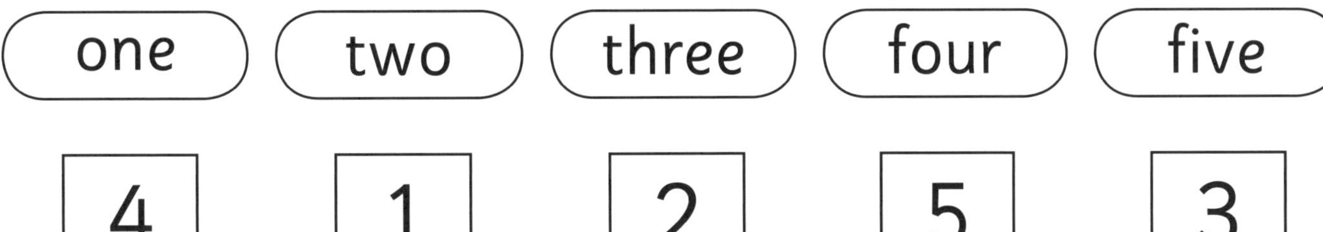

2 Guess the word by its shape. Write each word in a box.

cycle city circle

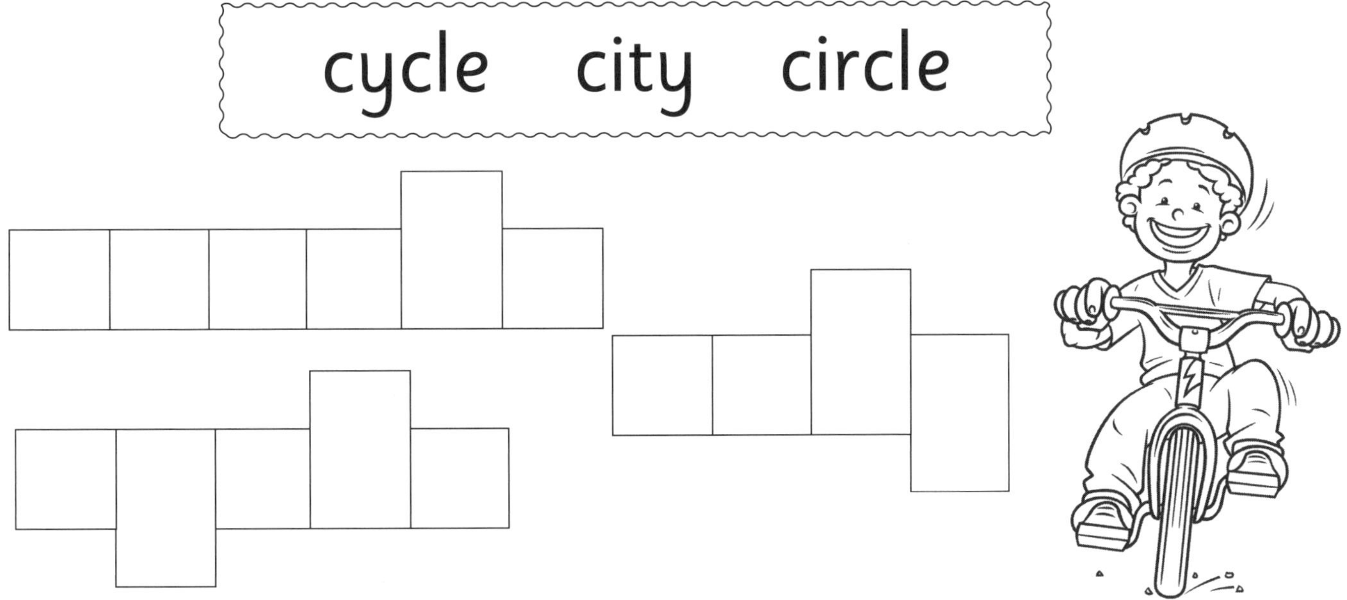

3 Colour the correct word. Cross out the wrong word.

I have two wheels on my bisycle / bicycle.

Let's see the funny sircus / circus clowns!

Lesson 92 the sound **ice**

Learning objectives

Children will:

- identify the rime ice.
- read and write ice words.
- revise other i-e word families.
- make compound words.

Australian Curriculum Content Descriptions

Sound and letter knowledge

ACELA1439 listen to the sounds a student hears in the word, and write letters to represent those sounds; identify and manipulate sounds (phonemes) in spoken words; identify onset and rime in one-syllable spoken words

ACELA1458 recognise sound-letter matches including common vowel and consonant digraphs and consonant blends

ACELA1459 recognise that letters can have more than one sound for example 'u' in cut, put, use; recognise sounds that can be produced by different letters for example the /s/ sound in sat, cent, scene

Expressing and developing ideas

ACELA1435 learn that word order in sentences is important for meaning

ACELA1438 build word families using onset and rime

ACELA1758 know that spoken words are written down by listening to the sounds heard in the word and then writing letters to represent those sounds

ACELA1778 learn an increasing number of high-frequency sight words recognised in shared texts and in texts being read independently; know that regular one-syllable words are made up of letters and common letter clusters that correspond to the sounds heard, and how to use visual memory to write high-frequency words

Interpreting, analysing and evaluating

ACELY1649 navigate a text correctly, starting at the right place and reading in the right direction, returning to the next line as needed, matching one spoken word to one written word

ACELY1659 combine knowledge of context, meaning, grammar and phonics to decode text

Word families

nice, lice, mice, rice, dice, slice

Vocabulary words

football, shoelace, sandbox, lighthouse

Extra assistance

Compound words use two words to make a new word. For example, a ground where you play is a playground. Learning compound words can be lots of fun for students. Have them illustrate compound words in a way that shows the two parts of the word, eg drawing a shoe with laces and writing the word shoe on the heel or toe and laces on the laces. Ask them to draw the two parts of a compound word and their buddy has to guess the word. Give them a sentence using the two parts of the word and ask them to come up with the compound word, eg This ball is for kicking with your foot.

Classroom activities

Word Pairs

Give each student a word on a card – each word is half of a compound word. Ask the children to find a partner and make a word, then sit together. Ask one person to write their word on the board. The other person sticks their word cards at the bottom of the board. After all the words are written, ask if anyone can see any other compound words that could be made using the word cards. Add them to the list.

Reading Eggs Lesson sequence	TEACH Content and skills	PRACTISE Children will:	APPLY
Hear: *Animated Lesson*	Introduce the sound *ice*.	identify the *ice* sound and make *ice* words.	**Worksheet 1** Word families 1
Write: *Scrapbook, Look, Listen and Spell, Rocket Launch, Write the Banner*	Identify the parts of a compound word. Identify sounds in a word and write or make the word. Recognise correct word order for a sentence.	choose two words to make a given compound word. Sound out a word and select letters and/or rimes to spell it correctly. Choose the correct words to make a sentence.	**Worksheet 2** Vocabulary
Find: *Word Family, Bowling*	Identify the correct onset letter to complete the word. Identify the rime in the word.	choose the correct initial letter to make the word. Match a word to its rime.	**Worksheet 3** Word families 2
Vocabulary: *Power Words*	Build vocabulary skills: Recognise key vocabulary.	match pictures to words.	**Worksheet 4** Check
Read: *Book*	Read aloud book.	listen, follow the reading and read along.	**Reading Eggs Story book** Five white mice

Classroom activities

Say it Right!

Have a set of pictures of things using the *i-e* split digraph. Hold up a picture and say the word incorrectly, using the wrong consonant sound in the digraph, eg *mine* for *mice*. Students need to call out the right word.

Related Reading Eggs Activities, Interactives, Songs and Books

Spelling Bank

Fish

Lesson 45

Focus sound words: line, mine, mice, dice, bite, kite, five

High frequency sight words: like, ride, white

Challenge: excite, fireworks

Reading Eggs Puzzle Park

Animal Fun

Squares

What is it?

Song Lines

Driving Tests

Reading Eggs Posters

Split Digraph i-e

Compound Words

Reading Eggs Library Books

My Program Books

Teacher Toolkit

- Spelling Activities
- Grammar Lessons
- Comprehension Lessons
- Targeting Comprehension Interactively
- Targeting Text Interactively

Reading Eggs Apps

Eggy Sight words

Eggy Snap

Eggy Phonics 2

Eggy Vocab

Critter Card

Icy mice

ice

Lesson 92 • Worksheet 1

Name

Word families 1

1 Join each word to a picture.

2 Use the word wheels to make words. Write the words.

m n ine p f

s m ite k b

Name

Vocabulary

Lesson 92 · Worksheet 2

1 Join the two words together. Write each new word.

foot + ball = ____________________

sand + box = ____________________

light + house = ____________________

shoe + lace = ____________________

2 Join each word to a picture.

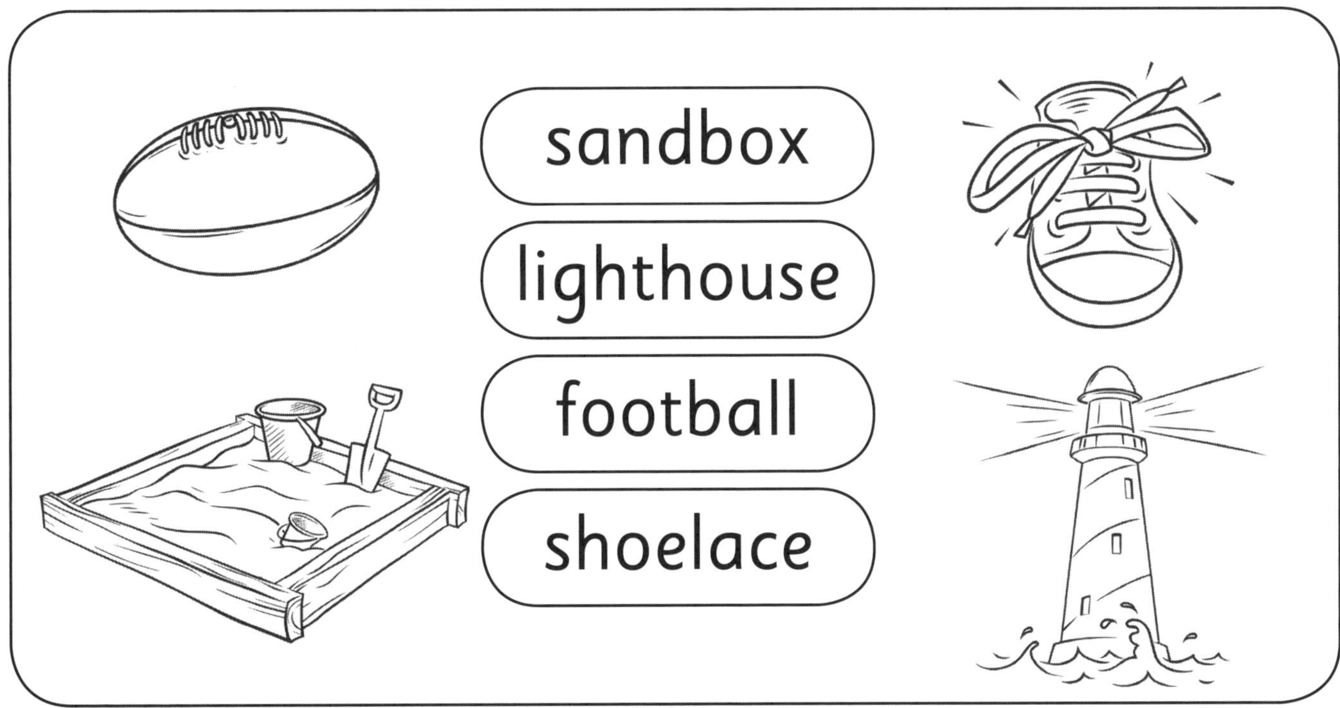

Word families 2

Lesson 92 · Worksheet 3

Name

1 Put the letters through the word machine.
Write the words you make.

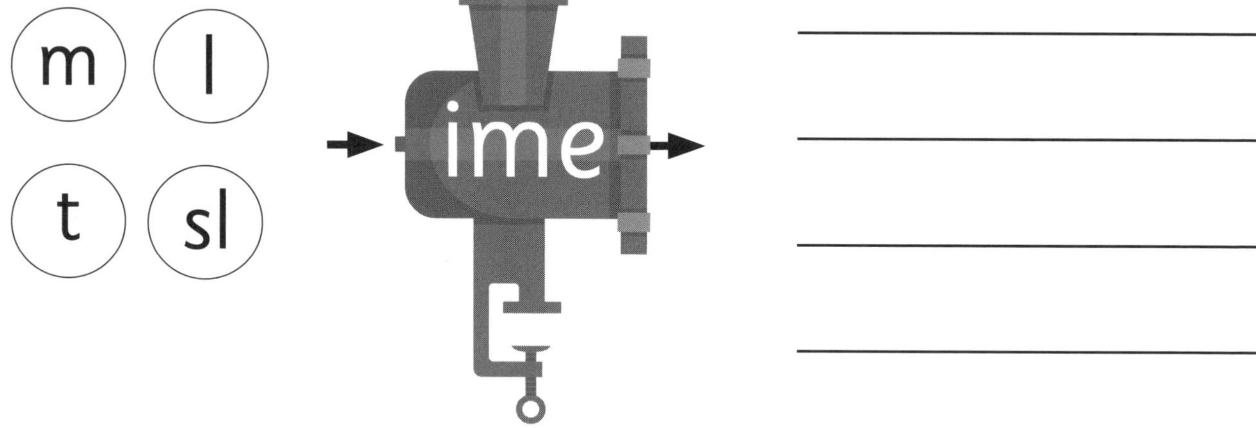

2 Colour the **ipe** words.

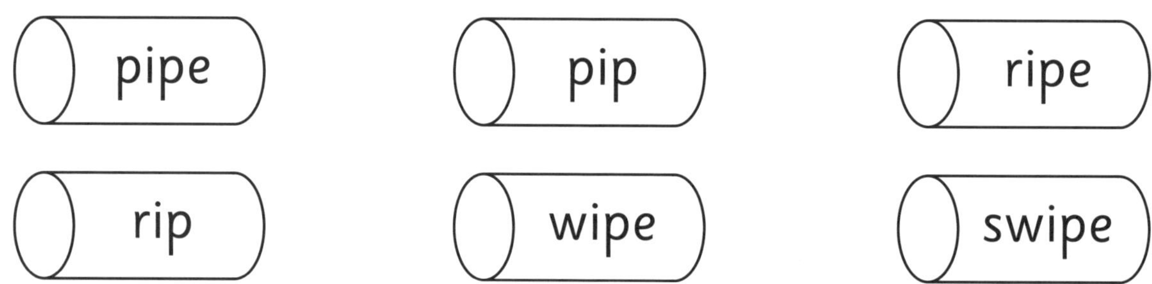

3 Say the word for the picture. Find the word that rhymes.

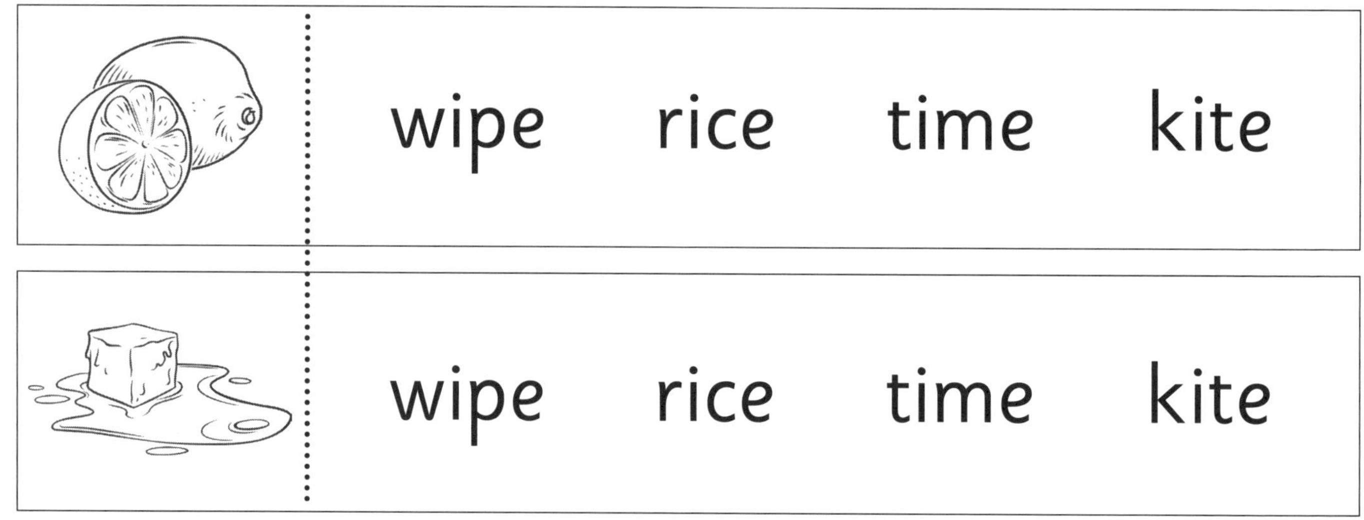

Name

Check

ice

Lesson 92 • Worksheet 4

1 Complete each sentence.

bites   bedtime   hide

Five white mice __________ in the vine.

Five white mice say no more __________!

And now it's ______________!

2 Draw.

five mice flying kites	a line of nice limes

Lesson 93 the soft g sound

Learning objectives

Children will:

- identify words with the soft g sound.
- recognise when the soft g sound applies.
- read and write words with the soft g sound.

Australian Curriculum Content Descriptions

Sound and letter knowledge

ACELA1439 listen to the sounds a student hears in the word, and write letters to represent those sounds; identify and manipulate sounds (phonemes) in spoken words

ACELA1459 recognise that letters can have more than one sound for example 'u' in cut, put, use; recognise sounds that can be produced by different letters for example the /s/ sound in sat, cent, scene

Expressing and developing ideas

ACELA1435 learn that word order in sentences is important for meaning

ACELA1438 build word families using onset and rime

ACELA1758 know that spoken words are written down by listening to the sounds heard in the word and then writing letters to represent those sounds

ACELA1778 know that regular one-syllable words are made up of letters and common letter clusters that correspond to the sounds heard, and how to use visual memory to write high-frequency words

Interpreting, analysing and evaluating

ACELY1649 navigate a text correctly, starting at the right place and reading in the right direction, returning to the next line as needed, matching one spoken word to one written word

ACELY1659 combine knowledge of context, meaning, grammar and phonics to decode text; recognise most high-frequency sight words when reading text

Word families

Gemma, gem, gelato, gentle, germ, giraffe, giant, ginger, gym, page, cage, age, stage, rage, magic

Vocabulary words

today, Saturday

Extra assistance

When pronunciation rules (such as that for the soft *g*) are not 100% applicable, it can be frustrating for ESL students to learn when to apply them. It is important to explain to all English language learners that there are often exceptions to the rules (such as *get, gill, begin* and *girl*). Make (or find online) lists of exceptions to the rules you are learning in class to post around the room or make a booklet of rules and their exceptions for each student to use as a reference.

Classroom activities

Brainstorm

Ask the class to make suggestions for a list of words that start with the soft *g* sound. Then add words that end with *age*. Next, add words that have a soft *g* in the middle, such as *magic*. Ask students to illustrate one word each and create a visual word family list together.

Reading Eggs Lesson sequence	TEACH Content and skills	PRACTISE Children will:	APPLY
Hear: *Animated Lesson*	Introduce the rule: when *g* comes before *e*, *i* or *y* it sometimes says /j/. Listen to the mnemonic song *Gemma giraffe loves gemstones.*	identify words which have a soft *g* in them.	**Worksheet 1** Phonics
Write: *Bird Words*	Recognise correct word order for a sentence.	choose the correct words to make a sentence.	**Worksheet 2** Sight words
Find: *Word Family, Shooting Stars, Driving Trucks*	Identify the correct onset letter to complete the word. Recognise a given word.	choose the correct initial letter to make the word match the picture. Find the given word in a group.	**Worksheet 3** Word families
Vocabulary: *Today's Topic Words, Define It*	Build vocabulary skills: Recognise key vocabulary. Identify words by their definitions.	match pictures to words. Choose the correct word to match the definition.	**Worksheet 4** Check
Read: *Book Ends, Book*	Read sentences using basic vocabulary. Read aloud book.	choose a word to finish the sentence. Listen, follow the reading and read along.	**Reading Eggs Story book** Gemma Giraffe

Classroom activities

Bingo!

Give students a laminated board with ten squares on it. Ask them to write a word in each square from the lists of soft *g* and *c* words (use whiteboard markers). Say words from the list. Students put a cross on that word on their board. First one to ten calls out 'bingo' and wins!

Related Reading Eggs Activities, Interactives, Songs and Books

Spelling Bank

Kangaroos

Lesson 86

Focus sound words: germ, cage, huge, angel, giant, gentle, magic

Challenge: giraffe, engine

Reading Eggs Puzzle Park

What is it?

Arrows

Do it

Name it

Driving Tests

Music Café

Gemma giraffe loves gemstones

Reading Eggs Library Books

My Program Books

Reading Eggs Posters

Alternate Sounds g

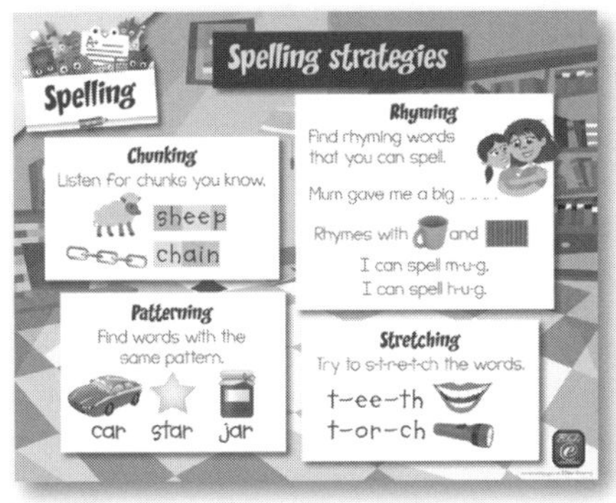

Critter Card

Gemma giraffe

Teacher Toolkit

- Spelling Activities
- Grammar Lessons
- Comprehension Lessons
- Targeting Comprehension Interactively
- Targeting Text Interactively

Reading Eggs Apps

Eggy Sight words

Eggy Snap

Eggy Vocab

Soft g

Name

Phonics

Lesson 93 • Worksheet 1

1 Add **soft g** and say the word.

____em	____iant
____ym	____elato
____iraffe	____enie

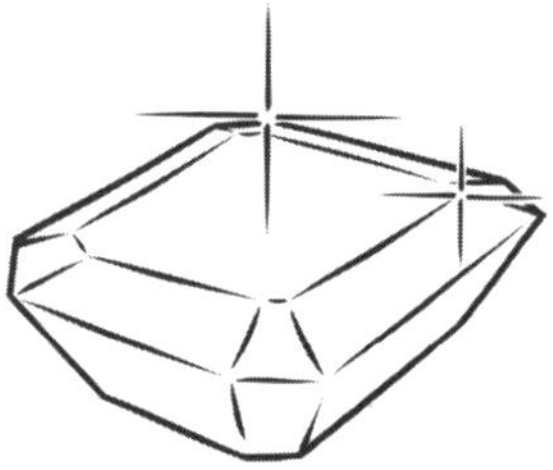

2 Circle the **soft g** words.

Gemma giraffe likes to go to the gym.

Sam has got a giant green gelato.

Colour a gem each time you find a **soft g** word.

 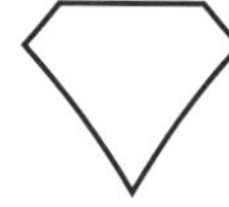 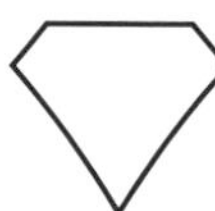 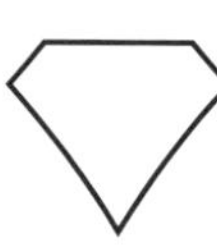 

Name

Read and write

Lesson 93 • Worksheet 2

1 Trace and write the words.

2 Colour **Saturday** red, colour **today** green.

Saturday | Saturday | today

today | today | Saturday

3 Guess the word by its shape. Write each word in a box.

Saturday today day

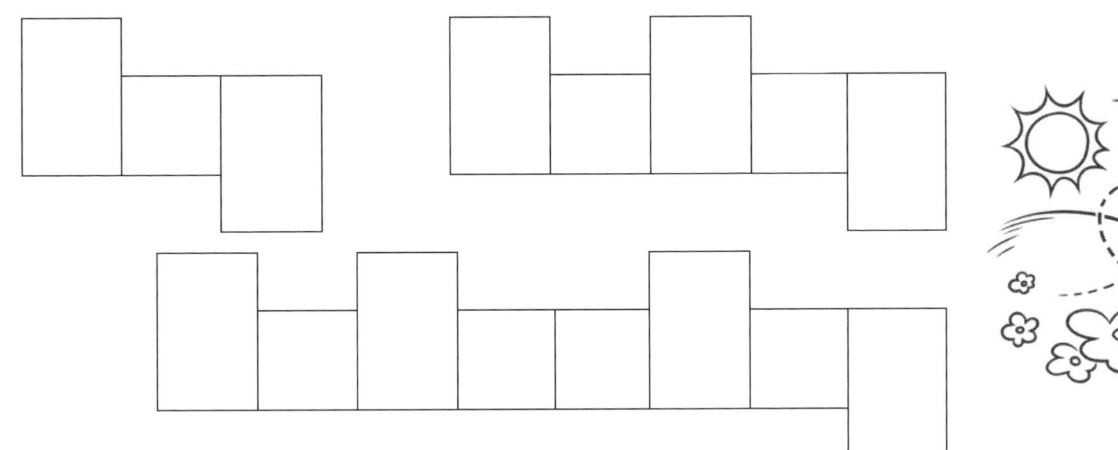

Soft g

Lesson 93 • Worksheet 3

Name

Word families

1 Complete the words. Use Gemma giraffe's letters.

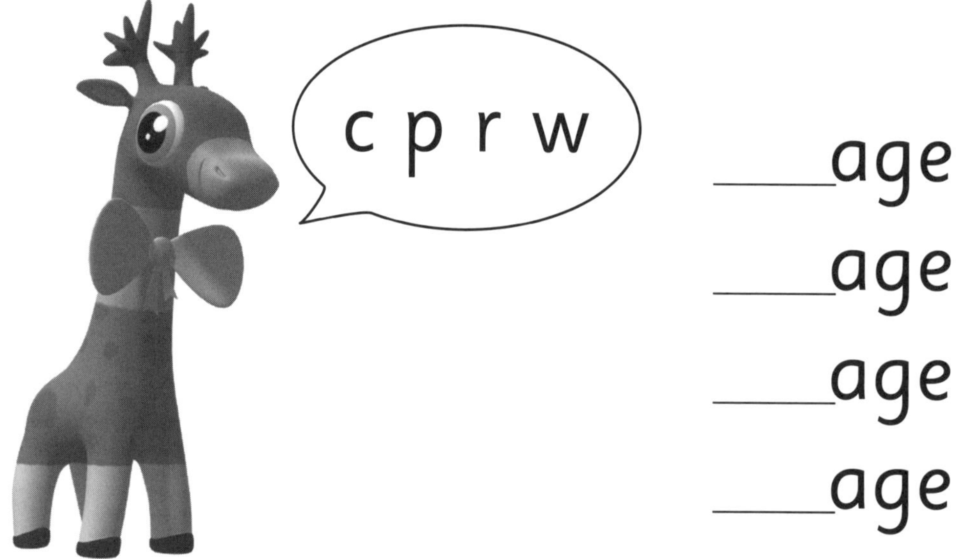

____age

____age

____age

____age

2 Colour the **age** words green, colour the **ice** words yellow.

page	rice	mice	cage
stage	sage	nice	dice

3 Draw the two mice in the cage.

Name

Check

Soft g

Lesson 93 · Worksheet 4

1 Colour the **soft g** words.

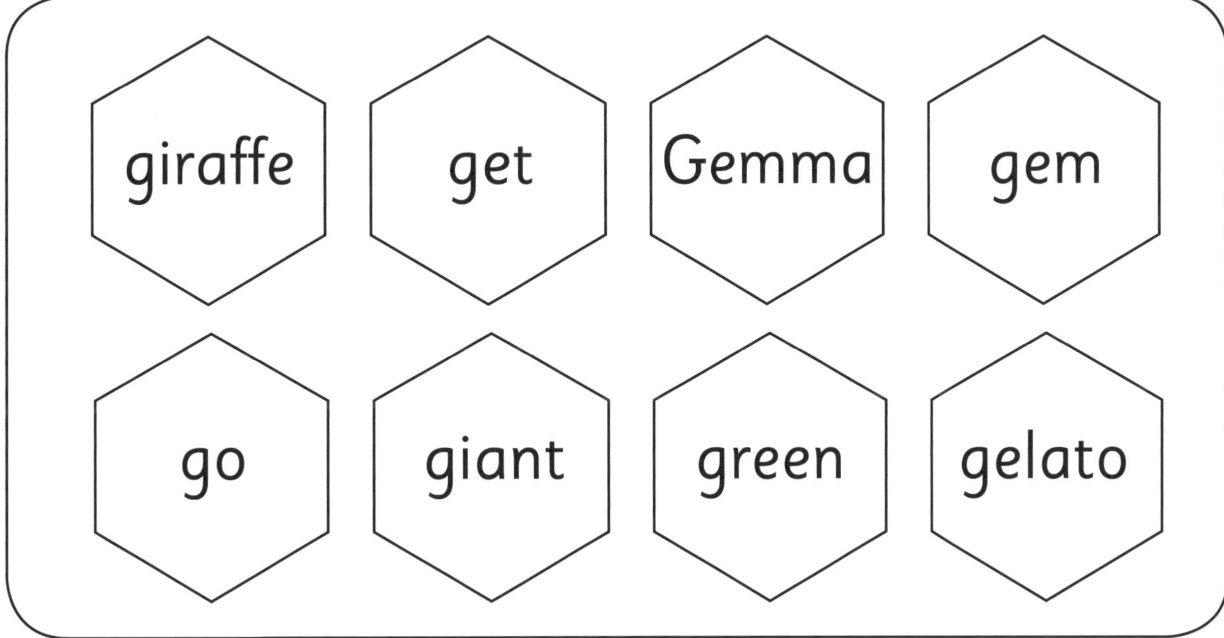

2 Write each word.

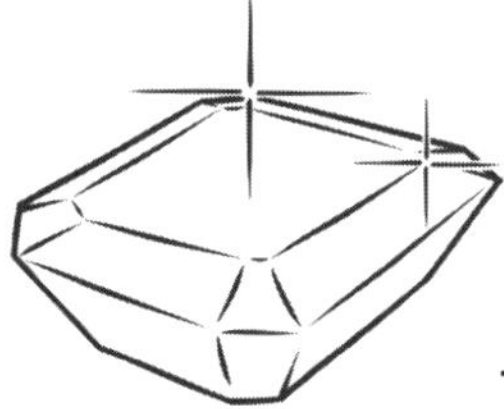

______________ ______________

3 Complete the sentences.

cage gelato Today

__________ is Saturday.

There are three mice in a __________.

Gemma loves yummy __________.

Lesson 94 the sound **ake**

Learning objectives

Children will:

- identify the split digraph a-e.
- read and write words ending with ake.

Australian Curriculum Content Descriptions

Sound and letter knowledge

ACELA1439 identify rhyme and syllables in spoken words; identify onset and rime in one-syllable spoken words

ACELA1457 recognise and produce rhyming words; replace sounds in spoken words

ACELA1459 recognise that letters can have more than one sound

Expressing and developing ideas

ACELA1435 learn that word order in sentences is important for meaning

ACELA1438 build word families using onset and rime

ACELA1457 recognise words that start with a given sound, end with a given sound, have a given medial sound, rhyme with a given word; recognise and produce rhyming words

ACELA1458 say words with the same rime as a given word; recognise sound-letter matches including common vowel and consonant digraphs and consonant blends

ACELA1778 write one-syllable words containing known blends; learn an increasing number of high-frequency sight words recognised in shared texts and in texts being read independently; know that regular one-syllable words are made up of letters and common letter clusters that correspond to the sounds heard, and how to use visual memory to write high-frequency words

Interpreting, analysing and evaluating

ACELY1659 combine knowledge of context, meaning, grammar and phonics to decode text; recognise most high-frequency sight words when reading text

Word families

Jake, bake, cake, lake, take, wake, rake, snake, shake, late, date, plate

Vocabulary words

yummy, duck, rooster

Extra assistance

The long *a* sound is made in this instance by the split digraph *a-e*. It is important to stress to students that this is two letters functioning as a single unit to make one sound. It is not an *a* and a silent or magic *e*. The *e* makes the *a* say its name – *ay*, as in *cake*, not *cat*. Be sure to give them time to practise their pronunciation of the long *a* sound and compare it with the short *a* sound. Use pairs of words to contrast: *can* and *cane, fate* and *fat, wage* and *wag*.

Classroom activities

Throw it Away!

Sit in a circle with a box in the middle. Students each hold two items, pictures or words on cards. They take turns telling what their item or picture or word is. If the object ends with *ake* or *ate* they throw it into the box. Discuss the objects with the class.

Reading Eggs Lesson sequence	TEACH Content and skills	PRACTISE Children will:	APPLY
Hear: *Animated Lesson*	Introduce the sound *a-e* through *ake* words.	select the letters which make the *a-e* sound. Make *ake* words and sentences.	**Worksheet 1** Word families
Write: *Write the Banner*	Recognise correct word order for a sentence.	choose the correct words to make a sentence.	**Worksheet 2** Read and write
Find: *Word Family, What's Missing?*	Identify the correct onset letter to complete the word. Identify the missing sound in a word.	choose the correct initial letter to make the word. Choose the correct letter to make the word.	**Worksheet 3** Vocabulary
Vocabulary: *Today's Topic Words, City Zoo, Word Dominoes, Rhyme Time*	Build vocabulary skills: Recognise key vocabulary. Identify rhyming words.	match pictures to words. Find images of rhyming words.	**Worksheet 4** Check
Read: *Book*	Read aloud book.	listen, follow the reading and read along.	**Reading Eggs Story book** Let's bake a cake

Classroom activities

Sentence Shuffle

Write and jumble an enlarged version of the sentence: *Jake can bake a cake.* Read it with the children and ask them to work out the correct order. Suggest clues such as capital letters and full stops. Discuss the sentence when they are done.

Related Reading Eggs Activities, Interactives, Songs and Books

Spelling Bank

Fish

Lesson 44

Focus sound words: bake, cake, late, mate, ate

High frequency sight words: make

Reading Eggs Puzzle Park

Animal Fun

Animal Colours

Number Nuts

What is it?

Driving Tests

Reading Eggs Posters

Split Digraph a-e

Reading Eggs Library Books

My Program Books

Teacher Toolkit

- Spelling Activities
- Grammar Lessons
- Comprehension Lessons
- Targeting Comprehension Interactively
- Targeting Text Interactively

Reading Eggs Apps

Eggy Sight words

Eggy Snap

Eggy Phonics 2

Eggy Vocab

Critter Card

Jake snake

ake

Lesson 94 • Worksheet 1

Name

Word families

1 Write the words on the correct plate.

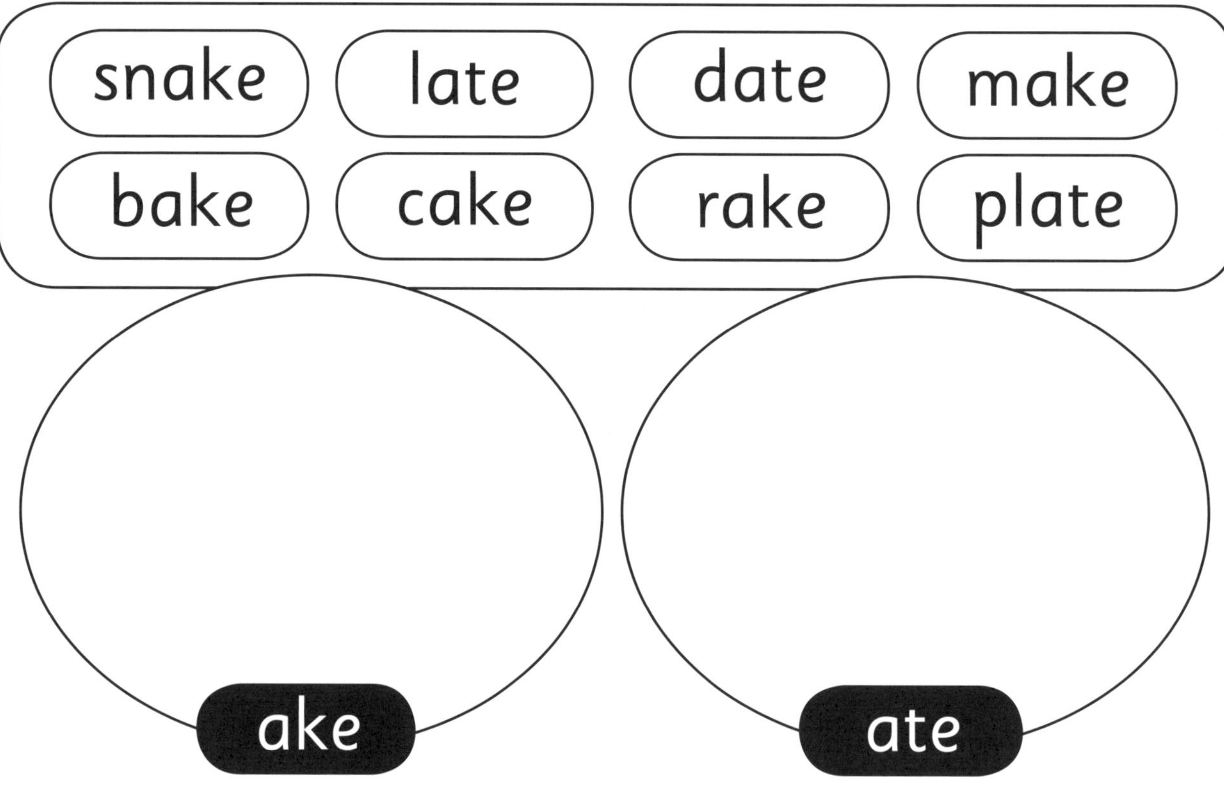

2 Label the pictures.

Name

Read and write

Lesson 94 • Worksheet 2

1 Draw.

a cake in a chocolate lake

a snake on a plate

2 Read the clue. Write the word.

You use me to collect leaves.

I am a

r________________ .

You put your food on me.

I am a

pl________________ .

You can swim in me.

I am a

l________________ .

I taste yummy!

I am a

c________________ .

Vocabulary

Name

Lesson 94 • Worksheet 3

1 Match each word to a picture.

2 Colour the correct word. Cross out the wrong word.

Jake wants to bake a (rake) (cake).

"Quack!" said Fluff the (snake) (duck).

Let's have a swim in the (lake) (rooster).

I will tidy the leaves with this (rake) (lake).

Name

Check

Lesson 94 • Worksheet 4

1 Find the words.
Colour **rake** red, **bake** blue, **lake** yellow and **cake** green.

c	a	k	e	r	a	k	e
l	a	k	e	b	a	k	e
r	a	k	e	l	a	k	e
b	a	k	e	c	a	k	e

2 Make a word with the letters on the fridge.

_____ake

_____ate

_____ake

_____ate

_____ake

3 Draw a picture for this sentence.

Jake the snake has a cake on a plate.

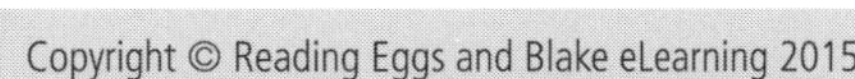

Lesson 95 the sound ***a-e***

Learning objectives

Children will:

- identify the rimes that can be made with a-e.
- read and write a-e words.

Australian Curriculum Content Descriptions

Sound and letter knowledge

ACELA1439 listen to the sounds a student hears in the word, and write letters to represent those sounds; identify onset and rime in one-syllable spoken words

ACELA1457 replace sounds in spoken words; recognise words that start with a given sound, end with a given sound, have a given medial sound, rhyme with a given word

ACELA1458 say words with the same rime as a given word; recognise sound-letter matches including common vowel and consonant digraphs and consonant blends

ACELA1459 recognise that letters can have more than one sound; recognise sounds that can be produced by different letters

Expressing and developing ideas

ACELA1435 learn that word order in sentences is important for meaning

ACELA1438 build word families using onset and rime

ACELA1758 know that spoken words are written down by listening to the sounds heard in the word and then writing letters to represent those sounds

ACELA1778 write one-syllable words containing known blends; know that regular one-syllable words are made up of letters and common letter clusters that correspond to the sounds heard, and how to use visual memory to write high-frequency words

Interpreting, analysing and evaluating

ACELY1659 combine knowledge of context, meaning, grammar and phonics to decode text; recognise most high-frequency sight words when reading text

Word families

ape, shape, tape, cape, grape, save, cave, wave, gave, rave, fame, same, lame, tame, game, flame, name, dame, ate, skate, date, gate, stage, page, cage, sale, whale, bale, cane, mane, lane, plane, take, cake, rake

Vocabulary words

pour, flew, bowl, brother, everywhere

Extra assistance

To create a word family using the *a-e* split digraph divide the class into pairs and give them a piece of paper and a specific *a-e* rime, eg *ape, ave, ame, ate, ale, ane, ake*. Ask each pair to run through the consonants as onset letters and then to see if they can come up with any other words ending with their rime. Put the papers together to make one big *a-e* word family list.

Classroom activities

Mind the Gap!

Write this sentence on the board: Sophie wanted to make a ____ . Read the sentence together and brainstorm a list of possible answers. Students should copy the sentence into their book and finish it with their choice of word and matching illustration.

Reading Eggs Lesson sequence	TEACH Content and skills	PRACTISE Children will:	APPLY
Hear: *Animated Lesson*	Review the sound *a-e* with a variety of consonants.	make *a-e* words.	**Worksheet 1** Word families 1
Write: *Look, Listen and Spell, Bird Words*	Identify sounds in a word and write the word. Recognise correct word order for a sentence.	sound out a word and select letters to spell it correctly. Choose the correct words to make a sentence.	**Worksheet 2** Vocabulary
Find: *Word Family, Snowman, Bowling, Dragon Fire*	Identify the correct onset letter to complete the word. Recognise a given word. Identify the rime in the word.	choose the correct initial letter to make the word. Find the given word in a group. Match a word to its rime.	**Worksheet 3** Word families 2
Vocabulary: *Pack the Shelves*	Build vocabulary skills: Identify the correct word to complete the sentence.	choose the word which completes the sentence.	**Worksheet 4** Check
Read: *Book*	Read aloud book.	listen, follow the reading and read along.	**Reading Eggs Story book** Frankie Lends a Hand

Classroom activities

Word Pairs

Give half the class a consonant on a card. Give the other half of the class an *a-e* rime on a card. Ask the children to find a partner with a card that makes a word and sit together. Ask each consonant person to write their word on the board. Have the pairs swap cards and play again – they must make a different word this time!

Related Reading Eggs Activities, Interactives, Songs and Books

Driving Tests

Test 11

Sight words: name

Letter and sounds: race, place, crane , lane, brave, wave, make, lake, late, date, rage, stage

Reading Eggs Puzzle Park

More Than One

Hidden Words

Song Lines

What is it?

Spelling Bank

Reading Eggs Posters

Split Digraph a-e

Context Clues

Reading Eggs Library Books

My Program Books

Teacher Toolkit

- Spelling Activities
- Grammar Lessons
- Comprehension Lessons
- Targeting Comprehension Interactively
- Targeting Text Interactively

Reading Eggs Apps

Eggy Sight words

Eggy Snap

Eggy Phonics 2

Eggy Vocab

Critter Card

Red tape ape

a-e

Lesson 95 · Worksheet 1

Name

Word families 1

1 Say the word for each picture. Complete each word in the family.

gr________ fr________ g________
c________ g________ m________
t________ s________ d________

2 Join each sound to the **ave** machine. Write each word you make.

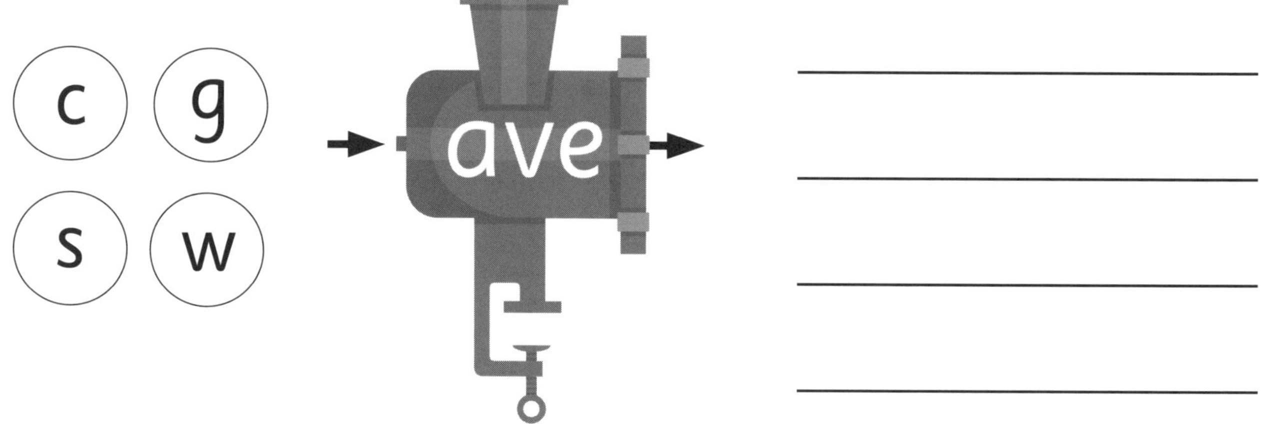

3 Colour the **long a** words.

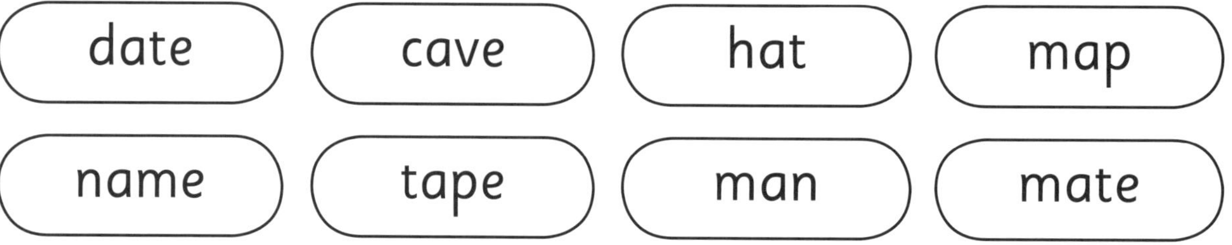

Name

Vocabulary

Lesson 95 • Worksheet 2

1 Match each picture to a word.

2 Number the pictures in order 1 – 4.

Making a cake

Mix it all up.	Put it in the oven.	Put the eggs in.	Pour it into a tin.
☐	☐	☐	☐

a-e

Lesson 95 • Worksheet 3

Name

Word families 2

1 Say the word for each picture. Complete each word in the family.

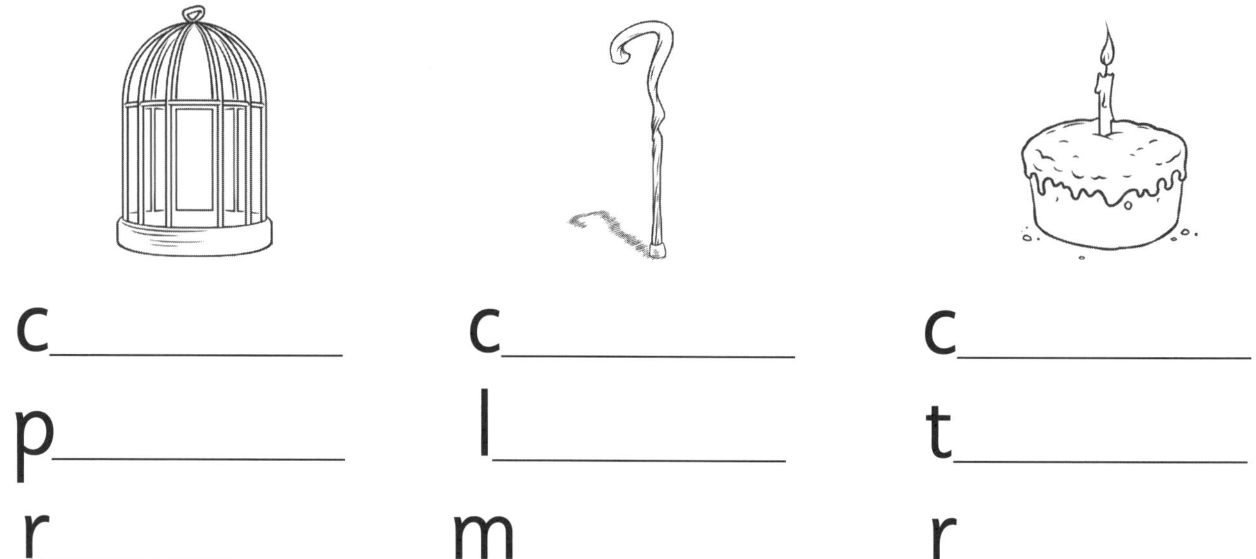

2 Join each sound to the **ale** machine. Write each word you make.

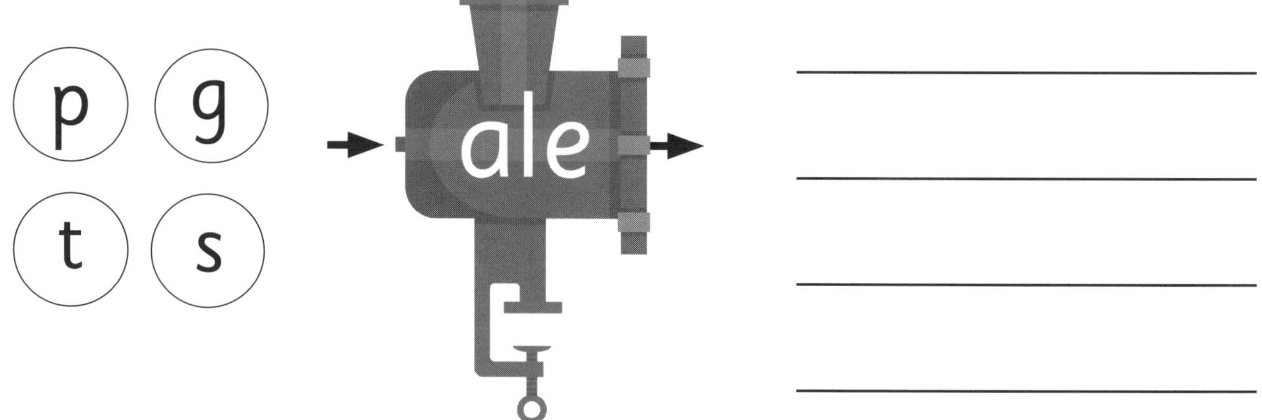

3 Colour the **long a** words.

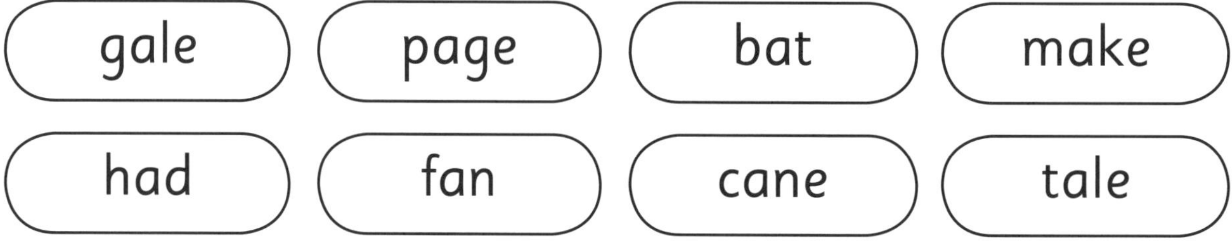

Name

Check

a-e

Lesson 95 • Worksheet 4

1 Complete the crossword. Use the picture clues to help you.

2 Say the name of each picture. Colour its beginning sound, then its end sound. Write the word.

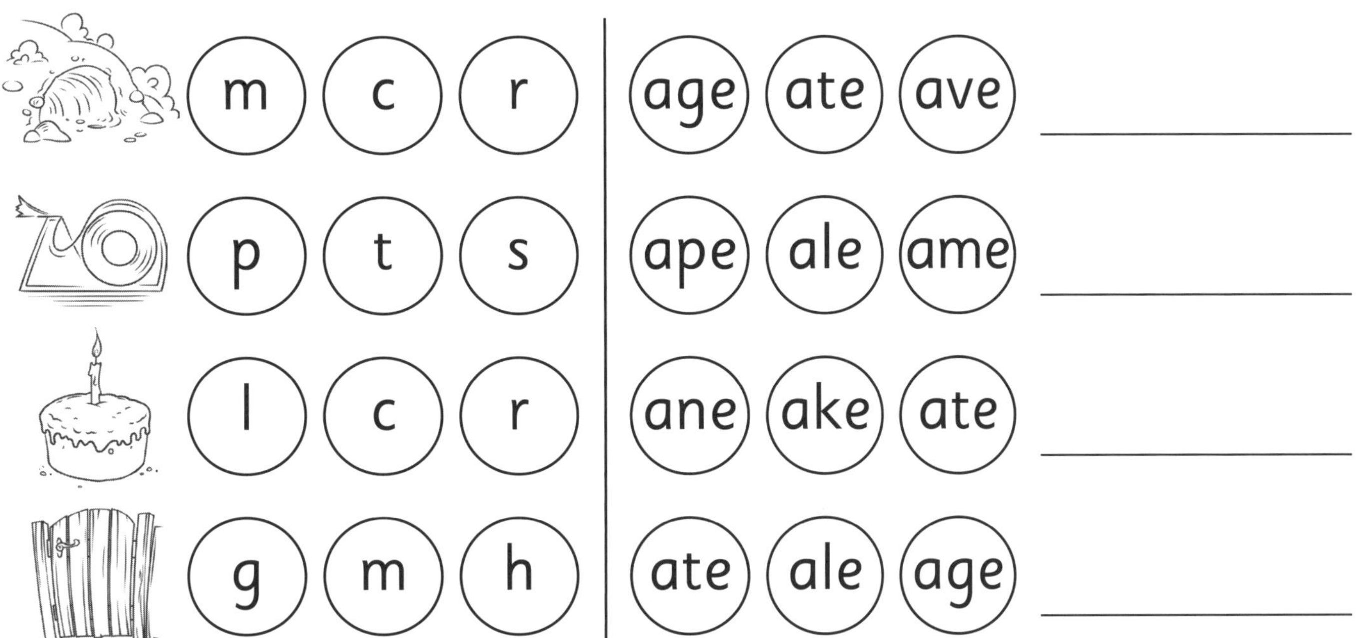

Lesson 96 the sound **ace**

Learning objectives

Children will:

- identify the rime ace.
- read and write ace words.
- revise other a-e word families.

Australian Curriculum Content Descriptions

Sound and letter knowledge

ACELA1439 listen to the sounds a student hears in the word, and write letters to represent those sounds; identify onset and rime in one-syllable spoken words

ACELA1457 replace sounds in spoken words; recognise words that start with a given sound, end with a given sound, have a given medial sound, rhyme with a given word

ACELA1458 say words with the same rime as a given word; recognise sound-letter matches including common vowel and consonant digraphs and consonant blends

ACELA1459 recognise that letters can have more than one sound; recognise sounds that can be produced by different letters

Expressing and developing ideas

ACELA1435 learn that word order in sentences is important for meaning

ACELA1438 build word families using onset and rime

ACELA1778 write one-syllable words containing known blends; know that regular one-syllable words are made up of letters and common letter clusters that correspond to the sounds heard, and how to use visual memory to write high-frequency words

Interpreting, analysing and evaluating

ACELY1659 combine knowledge of context, meaning, grammar and phonics to decode text; recognise most high-frequency sight words when reading text

Word families

ace, face, lace, race, space, place, trace

Vocabulary words

count, sky, clouds, night, switch, stars, above, higher, plane

Extra assistance

The *ice* and *ace* words combine two spelling rules – soft *c* and the split digraph. Point out to students that most of them were using the soft *c* rule without even realising it. They were focused on the split digraphs, but they knew to use a soft *c* with the *e*. Praise their use of the spelling and pronunciation rules they have learnt so far and give them opportunities to earn more praise with reading activities.

Classroom activities

Which Hat?

Place three hats on the floor with the labels *ace*, *ake* and *ate*. Discuss the sounds. Have a pile of objects or pictures of objects that end with *ace*, *ake* and *ate*. Each student chooses one and works out which hat it must go in. Discuss their choice with the class.

Bingo!

Give students a laminated board with ten squares on it. Ask them to write a word in each square from the list of *a-e* words (use whiteboard markers). Say words from the list. Students put a cross on that word on their board. First one to ten calls out 'bingo' and wins!

Reading Eggs Lesson sequence	**TEACH Content and skills**	**PRACTISE Children will:**	**APPLY**
Hear: *Animated Lesson*	Introduce the sound *ace* through words and the song *Sid's in Space.*	identify the *ace* sound. Make *ace* words.	**Worksheet 1** Word families
Write: *Rocket Launch, Write the Banner*	Identify sounds in a word and make the word. Recognise correct word order for a sentence.	select the correct onset and rime to make the word. Choose the correct words to make a sentence.	**Worksheet 2** Vocabulary
Find: *Word Family, Shooting Stars, Frog Logs*	Identify the correct onset letter to complete the word. Recognise a given word.	choose the correct initial letter to make the word. Find the given word in a group.	**Worksheet 3** Sight words
Vocabulary: *Today's Topic Words, Power Words*	Build vocabulary skills: Recognise key vocabulary.	match pictures to words.	**Worksheet 4** Check
Read: *Book*	Read aloud book.	listen, follow the reading and read along.	**Reading Eggs Story book** Space race

Related Reading Eggs Activities, Interactives, Songs and Books

Spelling Bank

Fish

Lesson 44

Focus sound words: bake, cake, late, mate, same, name, ate

High frequency sight words: came, made, make

Challenge: fireplace, surface

Reading Eggs Puzzle Park

What is it?

Transport

Arrows

Do You Know?

Driving Tests

Music Café

Sid's in Space

Reading Eggs Library Books

My Program Books

Reading Eggs Posters

Split Digraph a-e

During Reading

Teacher Toolkit

- Spelling Activities
- Grammar Lessons
- Comprehension Lessons
- Targeting Comprehension Interactively
- Targeting Text Interactively

Reading Eggs Apps

Eggy Sight words

Eggy Snap

Eggy Phonics 2

Critter Card

Baby face

ace

Lesson 96 • Worksheet 1

Name

Word families

1 Say the words. Join them to the correct critter.

2 Join the jigsaw pieces together. Write each word.

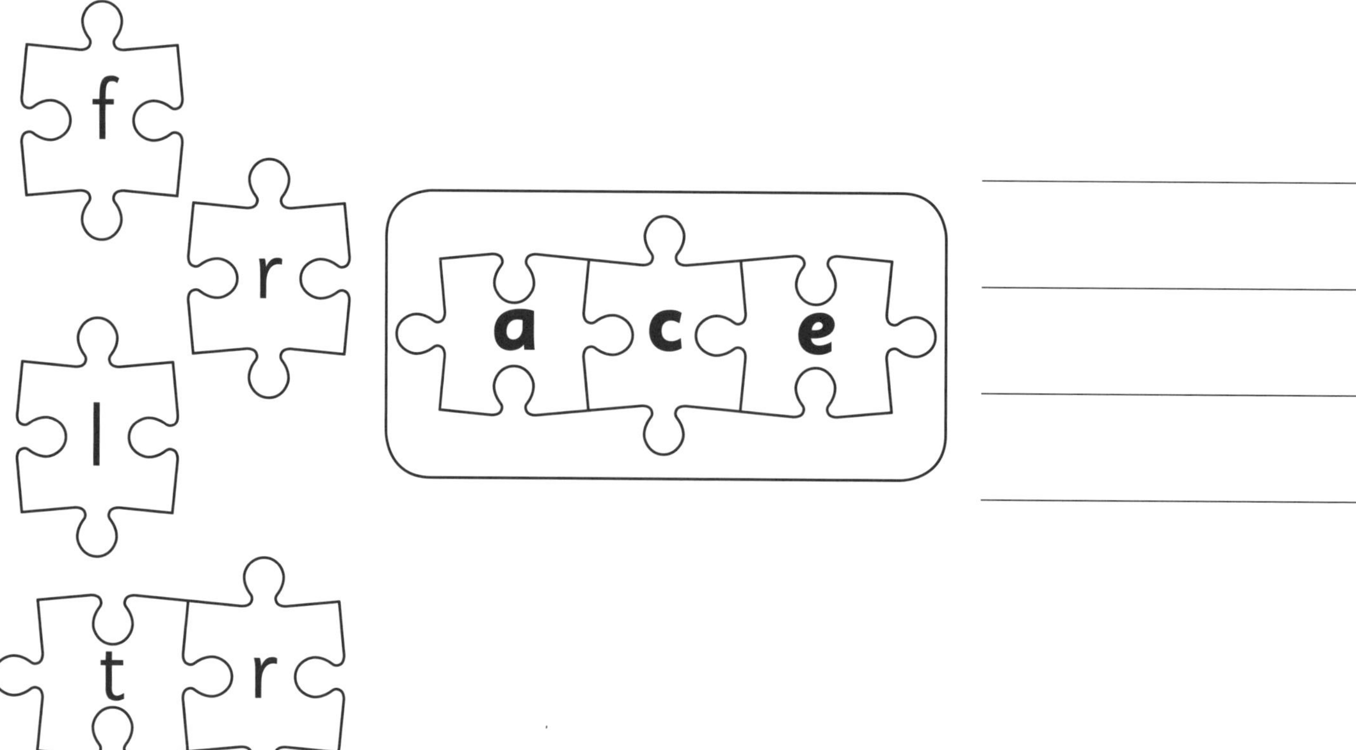

Name

Vocabulary

ace

Lesson 96 · Worksheet 2

1 Match each word to a picture.

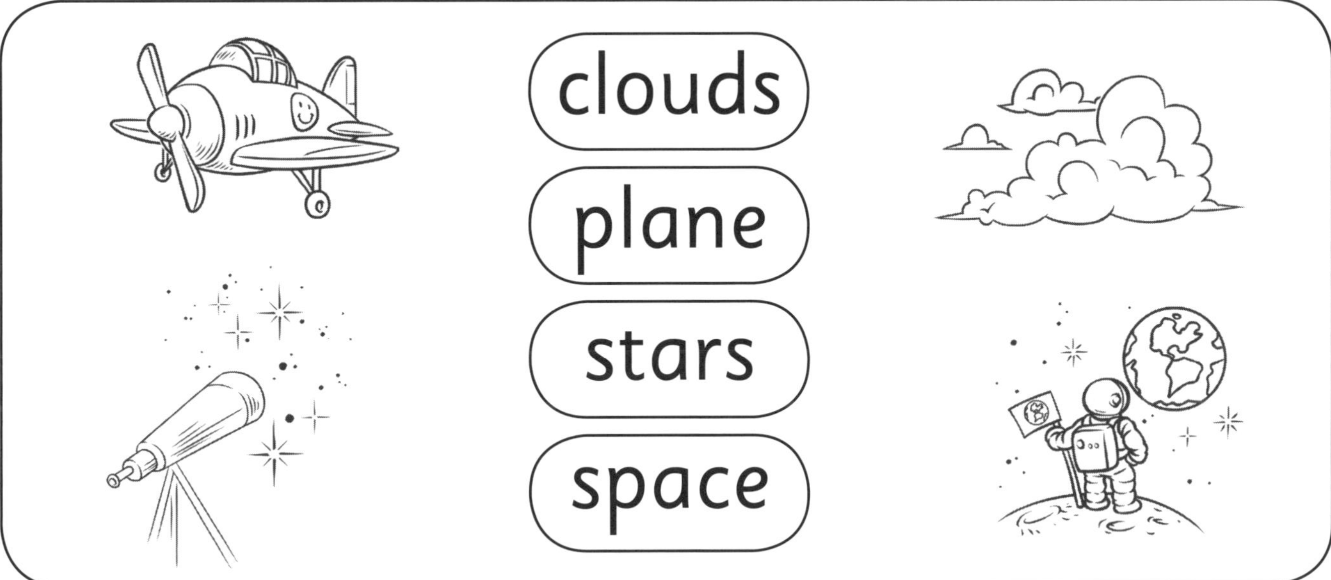

2 Draw a line under the correct sentence.

Baby face wants to go up in space.

Baby face wants to go under the zoo.

Baby face gets onto an apple.

Baby face gets onto a plane.

Baby face flies high above the clouds.

Baby face flies under the sea.

Sight words

Lesson 96 · Worksheet 3

Name

1 Trace and write the words.

above

higher

2 Draw.

a plane **above** the clouds

a **higher** hill

Name

Check

Lesson 96 • Worksheet 4

1 Draw a line of stars to make a word.
Write each word you make.

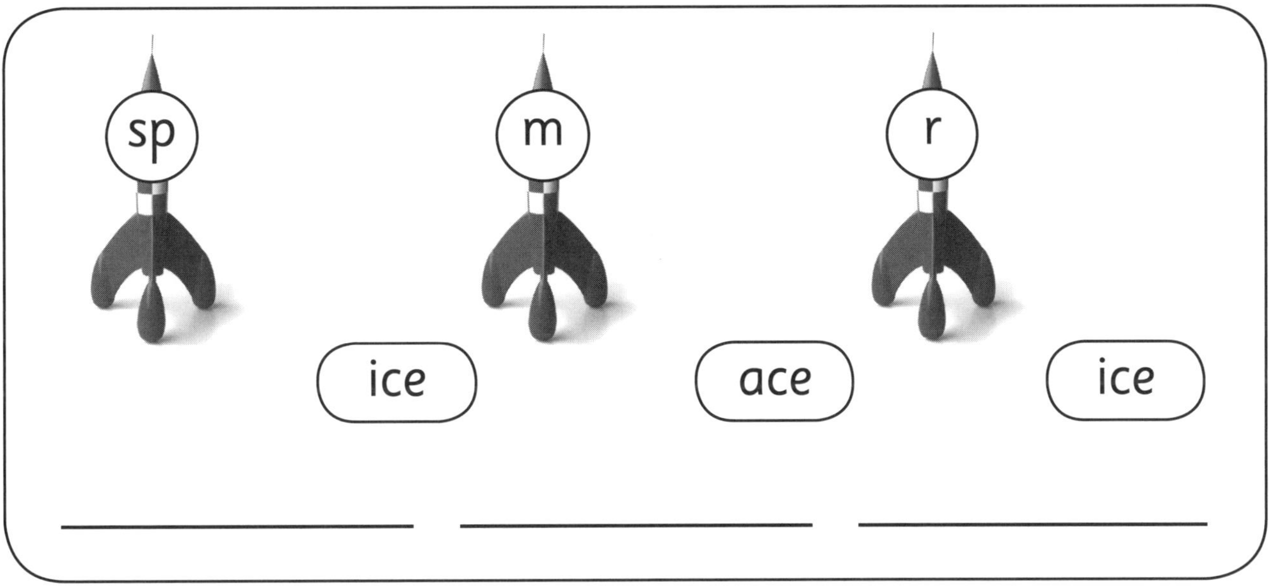

2 Colour the correct word. Cross out the wrong word.

The plane flies (above) (higher) the clouds.

Baby face sees (mice) (stars) in the sky.

3 Colour the **soft c** words.

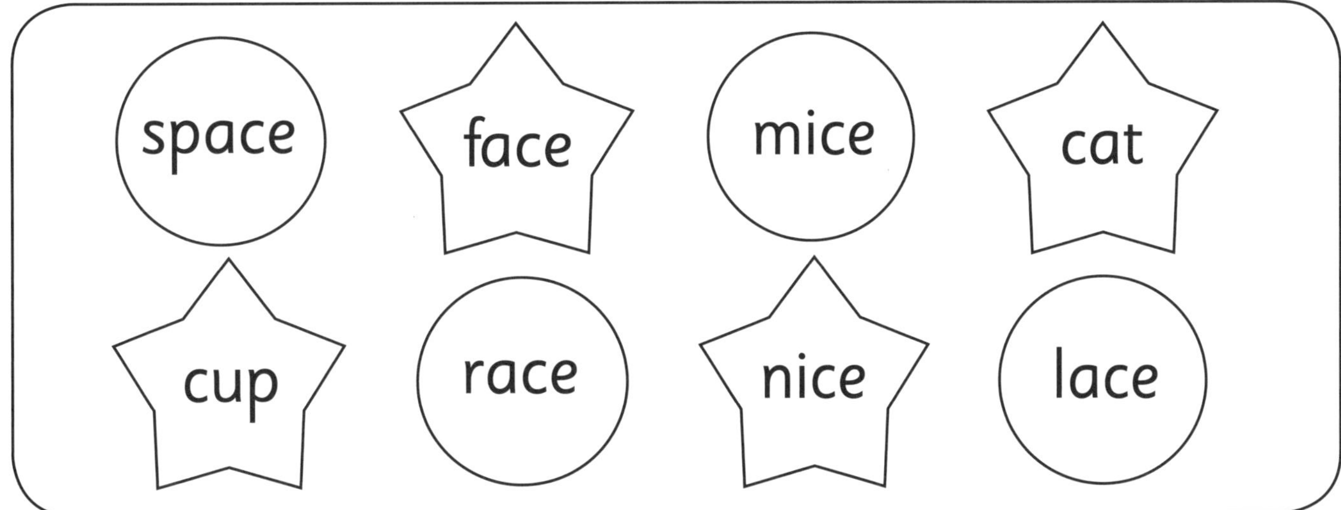

Lesson 97 the **vowels**

Learning objectives

Children will:

- identify the vowel letters.
- learn space theme words.
- read and write compound words.

Australian Curriculum Content Descriptions

Sound and letter knowledge

ACELA1458 recognise sound-letter matches including common vowel and consonant digraphs and consonant blends

ACELA1459 recognise that letters can have more than one sound; recognise sounds that can be produced by different letters

Expressing and developing ideas

ACELA1435 learn that word order in sentences is important for meaning

ACELA1455 build word families from common morphemes; use morphemes to read words

ACELA1758 recognise the most common sound made by each letter of the alphabet, including consonants and short vowel sounds

ACELA1778 know that regular one-syllable words are made up of letters and common letter clusters that correspond to the sounds heard, and how to use visual memory to write high-frequency words

Interpreting, analysing and evaluating

ACELY1659 combine knowledge of context, meaning, grammar and phonics to decode text; recognise most high-frequency sight words when reading text

Vocabulary words

spacesuit, music, photo, outside, astronaut, exercise, spacewalk, hours, check, straw, spaceship, space, shipwreck, sunflower

Extra assistance

There are many activities a class can do to reinforce the division of letters into vowels and consonants. Give them a sheet of words and ask them to circle the vowels and underline the consonants. Have them sort a bucket of magnetic letters. Ask them to find a word around the classroom with a specific number of vowels and/or consonants, eg find a word with 1 vowel and 3 consonants. Designate an area for vowels and an area for consonants, then say a letter and they have to move to the appropriate area.

Classroom activities

Memory Game

Write the word *astronaut* on the board. Sound it out with the class. Have students trace the word on someone's back or in the air with their finger. Rub out the word and write these words on the board: astonaut, astronut, atronut, astronot, astronaut. Ask them to identify which is correct, then discuss what is wrong with the other versions.

Vowel or Consonant?

Give students a card with the word vowel on one side and consonant on the other. Say a word and ask students to show you whether it began with a vowel or a consonant using their cards. Discuss the word and initial letter. Use clear, recognisable words such as *egg, bug, astronaut, space.*

Reading Eggs Lesson sequence	TEACH Content and skills	PRACTISE Children will:	APPLY
Hear: *Animated Lesson*	Introduce the idea of vowels and consonants.	identify the vowels amongst the consonants.	**Worksheet 1** Phonics
Write: *Bird Words*	Recognise correct word order for a sentence.	choose the correct words to make a sentence.	**Worksheet 2** Read and write
Find: *Dragon Fire, Pack the Shelves*	Recognise a given word. Identify the correct word to complete the sentence.	find the given word in a group. Choose the word which completes the sentence.	**Worksheet 3** Vocabulary
Vocabulary: *Today's Topic Words, Word Whiz, Make a Monster, Scrapbook*	Build vocabulary skills: Recognise key vocabulary. Identify the parts of a compound word.	match pictures to words. Tap on the word being said and put in a sentence. Read and follow instructions. Choose two words to make a compound word.	**Worksheet 4** Check
Read: *Book*	Read aloud book.	listen, follow the reading and read along.	**Reading Eggs nonfiction book** Life in Space

Related Reading Eggs Activities, Interactives, Songs and Books

Driving Tests

Spelling Bank

Reading Eggs Puzzle Park

Do it
Making Music
Transport
Do You Know?

Reading Eggs Posters

- Vowels and Consonants
- Compound Words

Reading Eggs Library Books

My Program Books

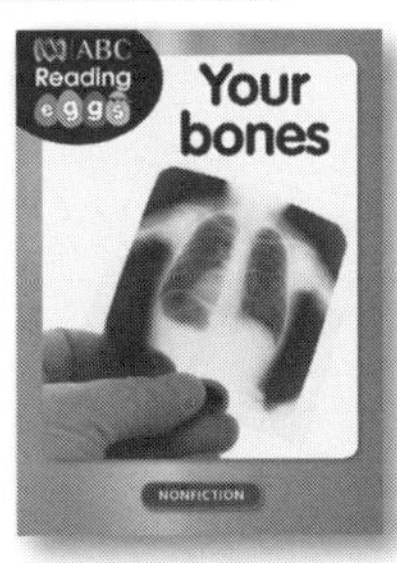

Teacher Toolkit

- Spelling Activities
- Grammar Lessons
- Comprehension Lessons
- Targeting Comprehension Interactively
- Targeting Text Interactively

Reading Eggs Apps

Eggy Sight words

Eggy Snap

Eggy Vocab

Critter Card

The vowel machine

Vowels

Lesson 97 • Worksheet 1

Name

Phonics

The letters **a, e, i, o, u** are called **vowels**.
The other letters are called **consonants**.

1 Colour the vowels **red**. Colour the consonants **blue**.

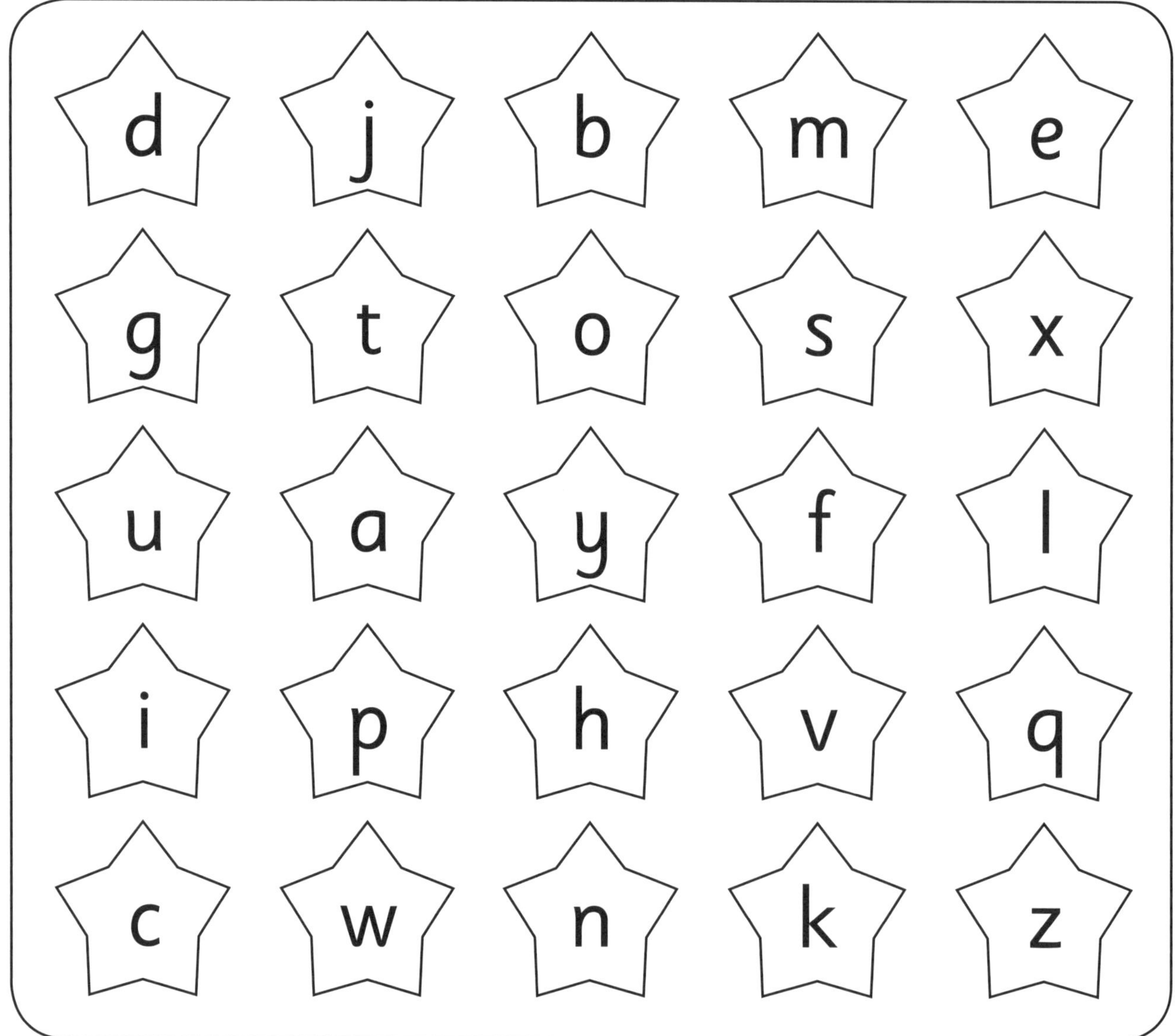

2 Complete.

I found ☆ consonants. I found ☆ vowels.

Name

Read and write

Lesson 97 · Worksheet 2

1 Join the right words to the word space to make compound words.

space ______________________ dog suit

space ______________________ walk tree

space ______________________ bee ship

2 Use the compound words above to complete the sentences.

An astronaut wears a ______________ .

A ______________ flies in space.

A ______________ is going outside the spaceship.

3 Read and draw.

The astronaut went on a spacewalk.

Vocabulary

Lesson 97 · Worksheet 3

Name

1 Match the action words to the pictures.

2 Join the astronaut to the things they need in space.

Name

Check

Vowels

1 Say each word. Write in the vowel.

a e i o u

p____n

b____d

m____p

h____t

m____g

t____n

2 Help Bunky boo get to school. Join up all the vowels.

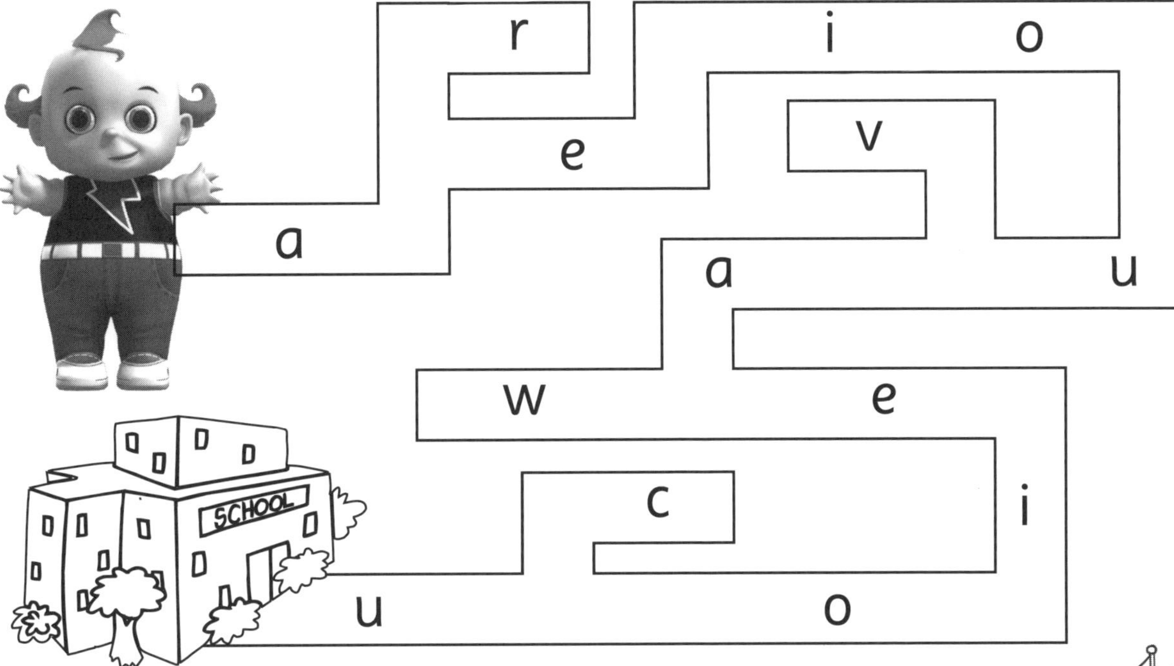

3 Unjumble the words. Write the sentence.

has This spacesuit. a astronaut

____

Lesson 98 the vowel sounds

Learning objectives

Children will:

- identify the long and short vowel sounds.
- read and write with craft theme words.
- learn the word eight.

Australian Curriculum Content Descriptions

Sound and letter knowledge

ACELA1439 identify and manipulate sounds (phonemes) in spoken words

ACELA1457 replace sounds in spoken words; recognise words that start with a given sound, end with a given sound, have a given medial sound, rhyme with a given word

ACELA1458 recognise sound-letter matches including common vowel and consonant digraphs and consonant blends

ACELA1459 recognise that letters can have more than one sound; recognise sounds that can be produced by different letters

Expressing and developing ideas

ACELA1435 learn that word order in sentences is important for meaning

ACELA1758 recognise the most common sound made by each letter of the alphabet, including consonants and short vowel sounds; know that spoken words are written down by listening to the sounds heard in the word and then writing letters to represent those sounds

ACELA1778 learn an increasing number of high-frequency sight words recognised in shared texts and in texts being read independently; know that regular one-syllable words are made up of letters and common letter clusters that correspond to the sounds heard, and how to use visual memory to write high-frequency words

Interpreting, analysing and evaluating

ACELY1659 combine knowledge of context, meaning, grammar and phonics to decode text; recognise most high-frequency sight words when reading text

Sight words

these, make, things, out

Word families

cap, cape, can, cane, pin, pine, pip, pipe, cub, cube, cut, cute, Sam, same

Vocabulary words

paper, glue, butterflies, pipe cleaners, spiders, eight, paint, snakes, dough, fish, stripes, puppet

Extra assistance

Many languages do not distinguish between long and short vowel sounds. Give students opportunities to practise pronunciation with pairs of words, eg *mad* and *made*, *din* and *dine*, or tongue twisters. Students also need to learn the spelling rules to know when to use long vowel sounds when reading aloud and also how to spell long vowel sounds in their writing. A handy booklet of vowel spelling rules could be made by students, who add to it each time they learn a new rule.

Classroom activities

Long or Short?

Place two boxes on the floor labelled Long and Short. Discuss the long and short vowel sounds with the class. Have a pile of flashcards and ask students one at a time to choose a card, read the word aloud and decide which box it should go in. Discuss their choice as a class.

Reading Eggs Lesson sequence	TEACH Content and skills	PRACTISE Children will:	APPLY
Hear: *Animated Lesson*	Introduce the long and short vowel sounds.	turn short vowel words into long vowel words.	**Worksheet 1** Phonics
Write: *Bird Words*	Recognise correct word order for a sentence.	choose the correct words to make a sentence.	**Worksheet 2** Read and write
Find: *Frog Logs, Shooting Stars*	Recognise a given word.	find the given word in a group.	**Worksheet 3** Vocabulary
Vocabulary: *Today's Topic Words, City Zoo, Rockpool*	Build vocabulary skills: Recognise key vocabulary.	match pictures to words. Read and follow instructions.	**Worksheet 4** Check
Read: *Book Ends, Book*	Read sentences using basic vocabulary. Read aloud book.	choose a word to finish the sentence. Listen, follow the reading and read along.	**Reading Eggs nonfiction book** Make a zoo

Classroom activities

Word Pairs

Give half the class a vowel on a card. Give the other half of the class a short word which is missing its vowel – have half CVC words (l_p) and half split digraph words (l_k_). Ask the children to find a partner to make a word and sit together. Ask each vowel person to write their word on the board. Have the pairs swap cards and play again – they must make a different word this time!

Related Reading Eggs Activities, Interactives, Songs and Books

Driving Tests

Spelling Bank

Reading Eggs Puzzle Park

- More Than One
- Animal Fun
- Baby Animals
- Animal Colours

Music Café

Long Vowels Rap

Reading Eggs Library Books

My Program Books

Reading Eggs Posters

- Vowels Sounds a
- Split Digraph a-e

Teacher Toolkit

- Spelling Activities
- Grammar Lessons
- Comprehension Lessons
- Targeting Comprehension Interactively
- Targeting Text Interactively

Reading Eggs Apps

Eggy Sight words

Eggy Phonics 1

Eggy Phonics 2

Eggy Vocab

Critter Card

Ayee I owe you

Vowel sounds

Lesson 98 • Worksheet 1

Name

Phonics

1 Circle the short vowel word in each row.

kite	bike	top	ride
mice	cake	rake	rat
bee	nine	hot	lime
cage	page	snake	pat

2 Write the words in the correct box.

hop take leg pie mate sun

short vowel

long vowel

Name

Read and write

Lesson 98 • Worksheet 2

1 Match each sentence to a picture.

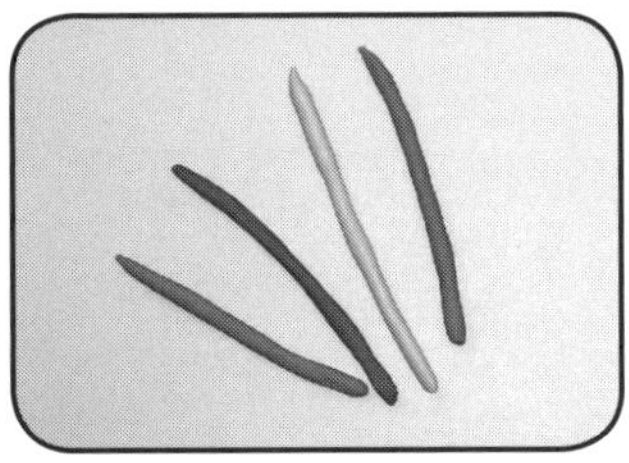

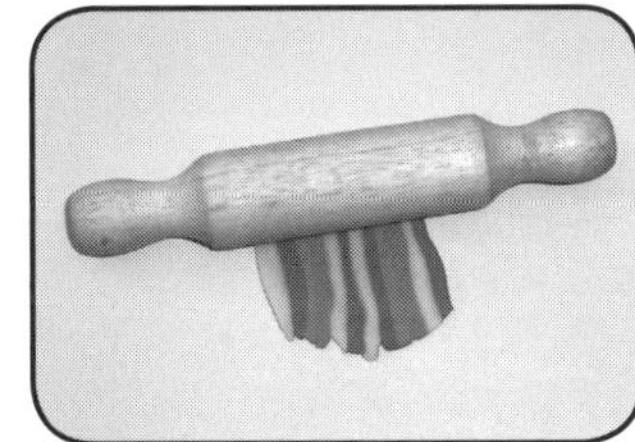

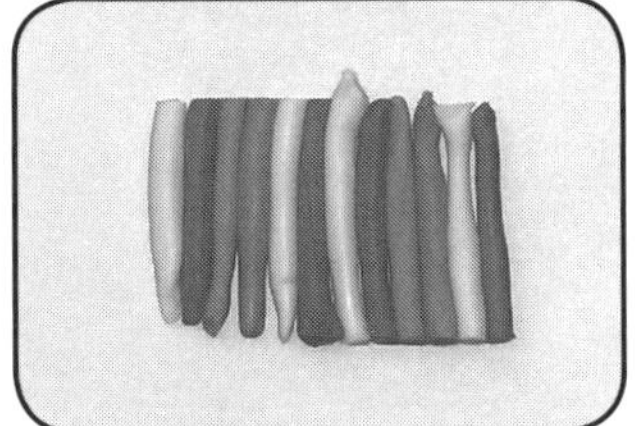

Flatten the play dough with the rolling pin.

Cut out some fish shapes.

Roll the play dough into sausage shapes.

Line up all the play dough sausages.

2 Complete the sentences.

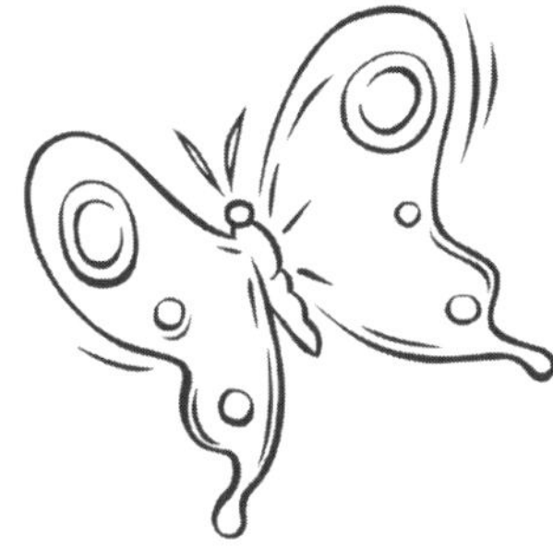

eight long wings

These butterflies have big ________.

These spiders have ________ legs.

These snakes are very ________.

Vocabulary

Lesson 98 · Worksheet 3

Name

1 Label each picture.

roll paint felt paper glue play dough

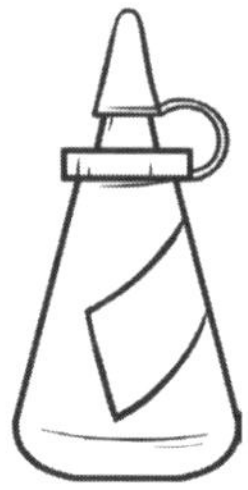

g

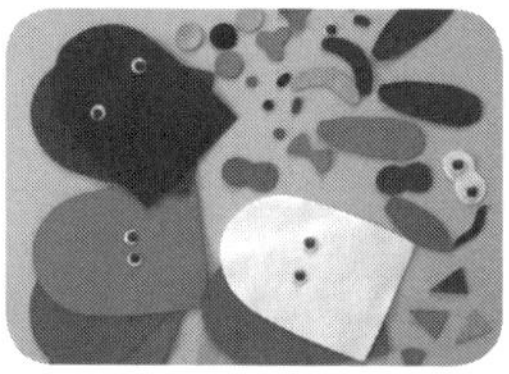

f

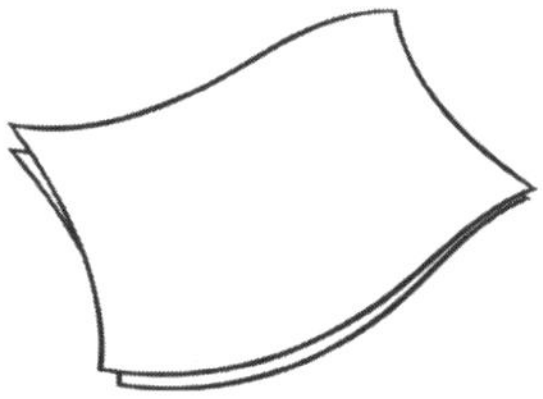

p

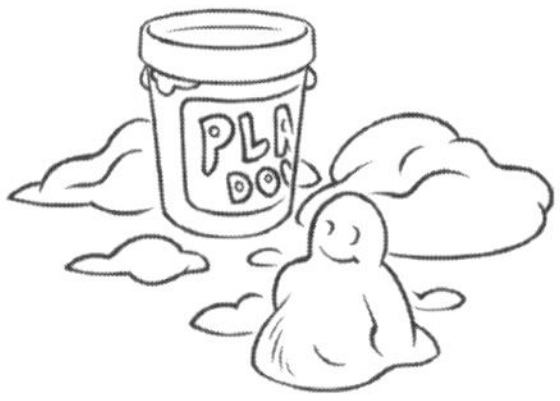

p

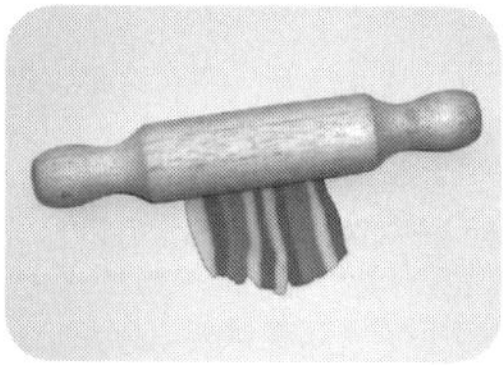

r

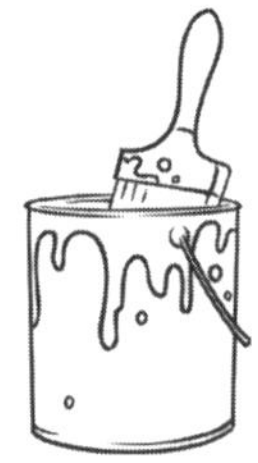

p

2 Trace and copy.

butterflies

cardboard

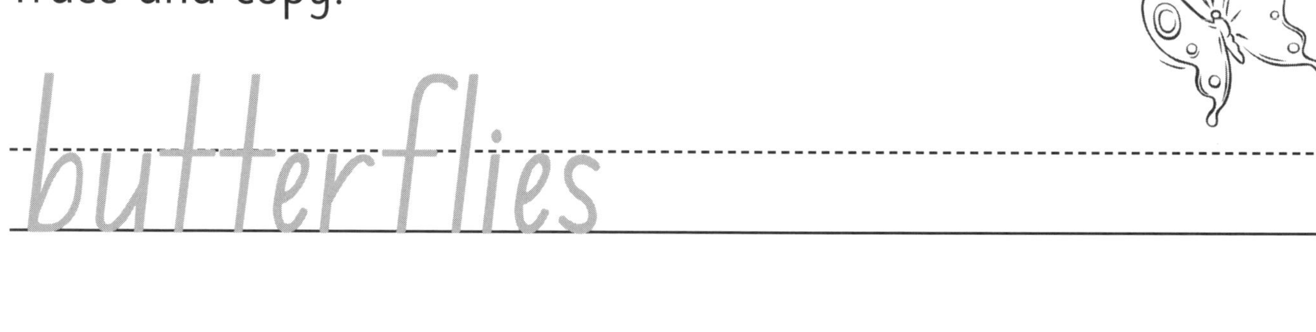

Name

Check

Lesson 98 • Worksheet 4

1 Colour **short vowel** words red, colour **long vowel** words yellow.

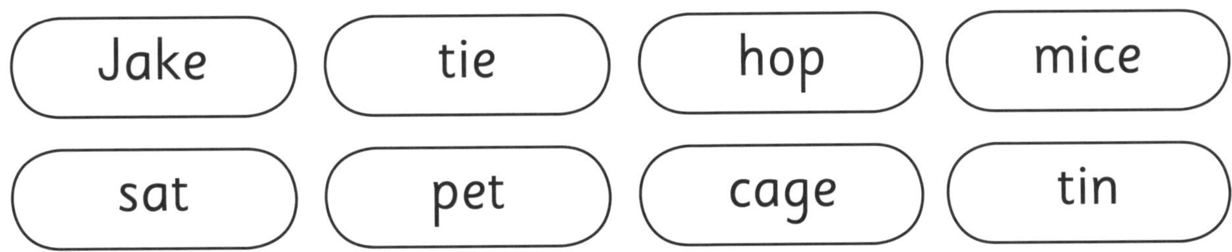

2 Unjumble the words. Write the sentence.

make can fish. You

____

3 Guess the word by its shape. Write each word in a box.

glue paper paint felt

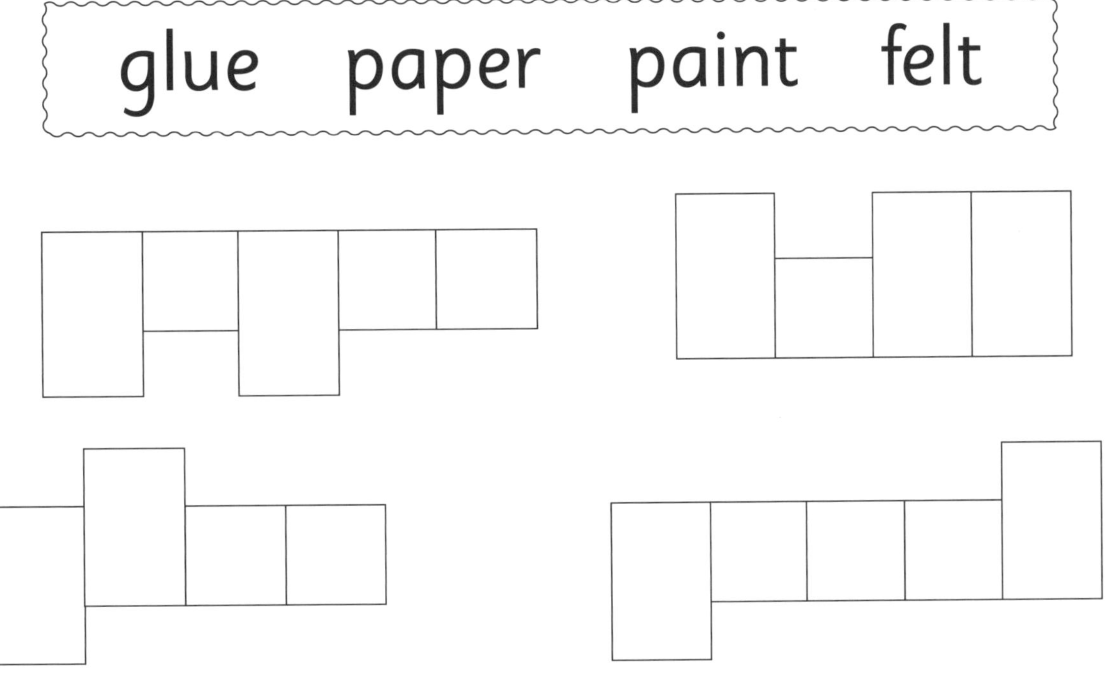

Lesson 99 the ending **y**

Learning objectives

Children will:

- review the sound ee.
- use the letter y as a word ending.
- read and write words that end with y.

Australian Curriculum Content Descriptions

Sound and letter knowledge

ACELA1439 identify and manipulate sounds (phonemes) in spoken words

ACELA1457 recognise words that start with a given sound, end with a given sound, have a given medial sound, rhyme with a given word

ACELA1458 recognise sound-letter matches including common vowel and consonant digraphs and consonant blends

ACELA1459 recognise that letters can have more than one sound; recognise sounds that can be produced by different letters

Expressing and developing ideas

ACELA1435 learn that word order in sentences is important for meaning

ACELA1455 build word families from common morphemes; use morphemes to read words

ACELA1758 know that spoken words are written down by listening to the sounds heard in the word and then writing letters to represent those sounds

ACELA1778 learn an increasing number of high-frequency sight words recognised in shared texts and in texts being read independently

Interpreting, analysing and evaluating

ACELY1659 combine knowledge of context, meaning, grammar and phonics to decode text; recognise most high-frequency sight words when reading text

Word families

sleepy, lucky, rusty, party, hairy, itchy, creepy, smelly, floppy, easy

Vocabulary words

escape, cage, giant, chest, circus, work

Extra assistance

The letter *y* is the only letter which can function both as a consonant and a vowel. Make a list of words where *y* is a consonant and a list of y as a vowel words. As a consonant it makes the /y/ sound as in *yellow*. As an ending, it makes the vowel /ee/ sound at the end of *lucky*. It can also make the /i/ sound as in *gym*. And it can complete a diphthong such as the /oi/ sound in *boy*. The rules for when *y* is a vowel are quite complex. This lesson just covers using y as an /ee/ ending to start with.

Classroom activities

Add a y

Put a list of words on the board – *hair, smell, sleep, itch, rust*. Take one word and rewrite it with a *y* on the end, eg *hair* and *hairy*. Discuss the meaning of the original word and then the second version. Put them both into sentences to show their meaning: He has hair on his chin. He has a hairy chin.

Now ask the students to do the same in their books with one of the other words. Share their sentences and discuss.

Reading Eggs Lesson sequence	TEACH Content and skills	PRACTISE Children will:	APPLY
Hear: *Animated Lesson*	Review the sound *ee*. Introduce the sound *y* on the end of a word.	add *y* to the end of words to make an *ee* sound.	**Worksheet 1** Phonics 1
Write: *Write the Banner*	Recognise correct word order for a sentence.	choose the correct words to make a sentence.	**Worksheet 2** Phonics 2
Find: *1, 2, 3, 4, Buzzy's Word Machine, Pack the Shelves*	Identify the order of a sequence of events. Identify word endings. Identify the correct word to complete the sentence.	put pictures in order to show a sequence of events. Match the word to its ending. Choose the word which completes the sentence.	**Worksheet 3** Vocabulary
Vocabulary: *Today's Topic Words, Define It*	Build vocabulary skills: Recognise key vocabulary. Identify words by their definitions.	match pictures to words. Choose the correct word to match the definition.	**Worksheet 4** Check
Read: *I Read You Read, Book*	Read sentences using basic vocabulary. Read aloud book.	listen, follow the reading and read along.	**Reading Eggs Story book** Can Vinny Escape?

Classroom activities

Bingo!

Give students a laminated board with ten squares on it. Ask them to write a word in each square from the list of words ending in *y* (use whiteboard markers). Say words from the list. Students put a cross on that word on their board. First one to ten calls out 'bingo' and wins!

Related Reading Eggs Activities, Interactives, Songs and Books

Driving Tests

Test 12

Letters and sounds: city, happy, puppy, celery, fly, party, sky, busy, giant, circus

Spelling Bank

Reading Eggs Puzzle Park

Describe it

What is it?

Do You Know?

Reading Eggs Posters

/ee/

Adjectives (i)

Reading Eggs Library Books

My Program Books

Teacher Toolkit

- Spelling Activities
- Grammar Lessons
- Comprehension Lessons
- Targeting Comprehension Interactively
- Targeting Text Interactively

Reading Eggs Apps

Eggy Sight words

Eggy Snap

Eggy Vocab

Critter Card

Airy fairy

Phonics 1

Name

Lesson 99 • Worksheet 1

1 Colour the words that end in the sound **ee**.

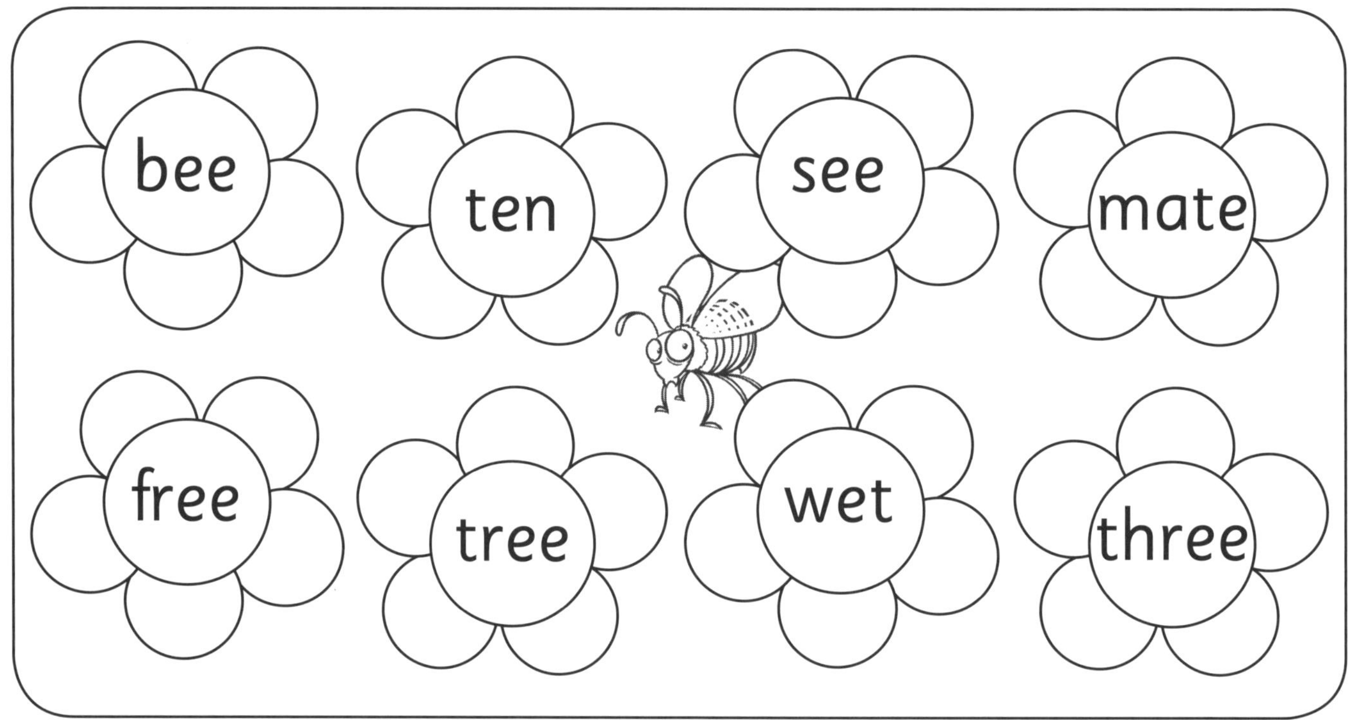

2 Use Zee Wee's **ee** to make words. Write each word. Read each word.

m_____t

k_____p

f_____t

b_____n

Name

Phonics 2

Lesson 99 · Worksheet 2

1 Colour the words that end in **y**.

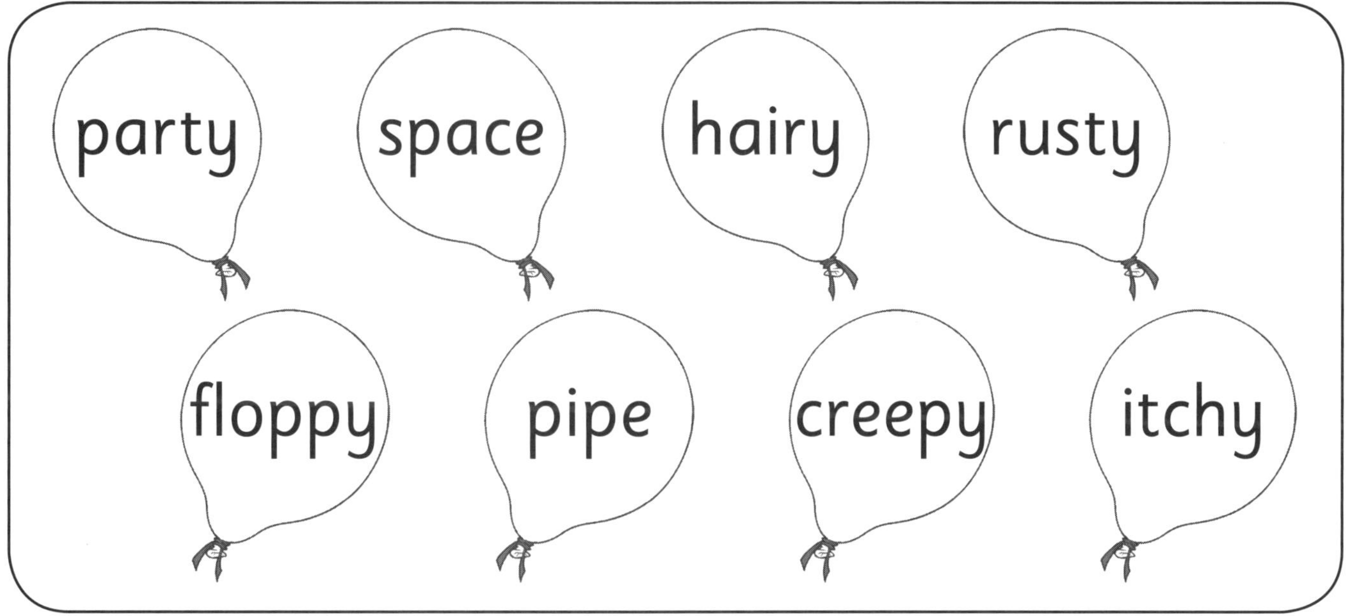

2 Use Airy fairy's **y** to make words. Write each word. Read each word.

bend____

rust____

flopp____

part____

Vocabulary

Lesson 99 · Worksheet 3

Name

1 Match each word to a picture.

2 Complete the sentences.

tank box chest

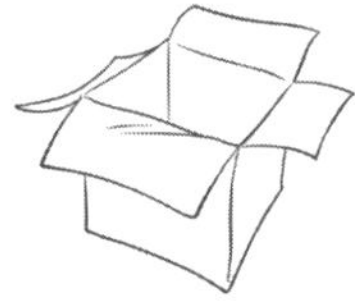 Vinny can escape from a ______________.

 Vinny can escape from a ______________.

 Vinny can escape from a ______________.

Name

Check

Lesson 99 · Worksheet 4

1 Join Vinny to the words that end in **y**.

2 Complete the crossword. Use the picture clues to help you.

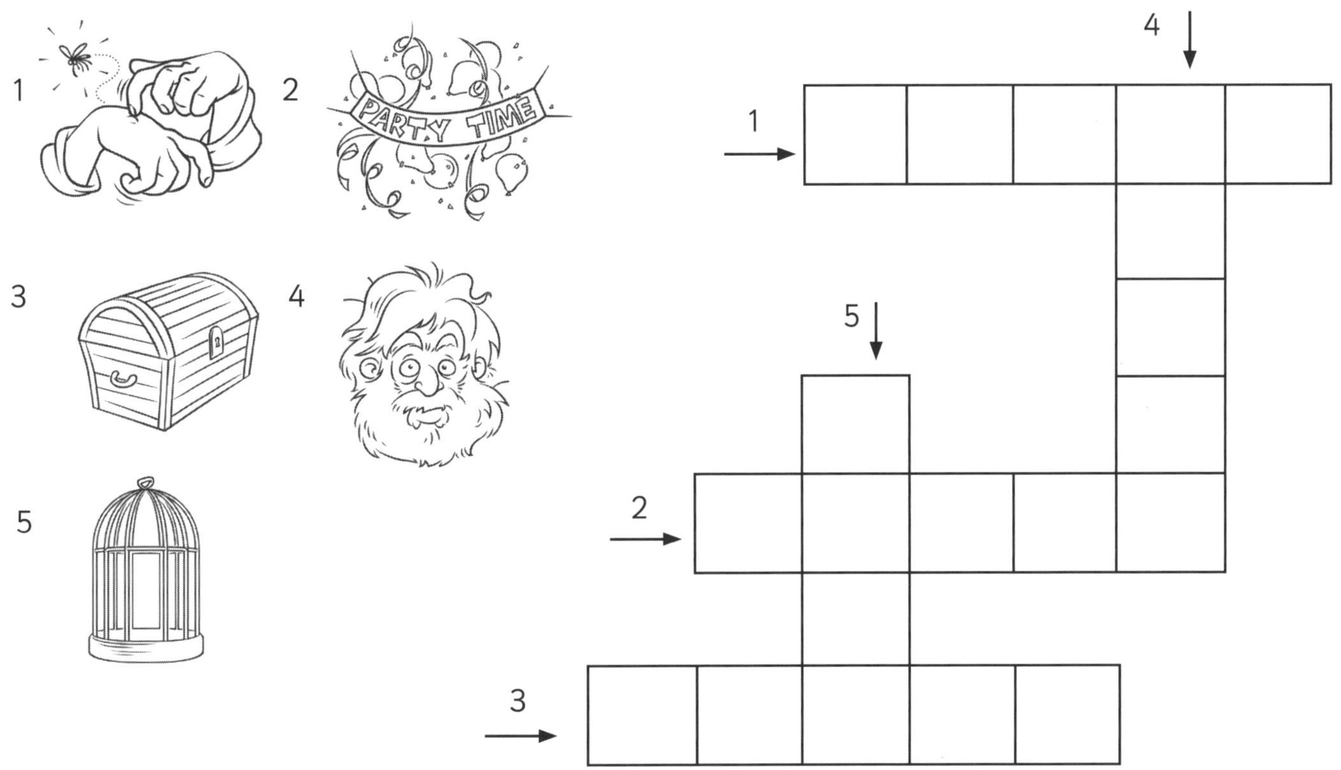

Lesson 100 Review

Learning objectives

Children will:

- review the sounds i-e, a-e and y on the end of a word.
- recognise sight words and theme words.

Australian Curriculum Content Descriptions

Sound and letter knowledge

ACELA1439 listen to the sounds a student hears in the word, and write letters to represent those sounds

ACELA1457 replace sounds in spoken words; recognise words that start with a given sound, end with a given sound, have a given medial sound, rhyme with a given word

ACELA1458 recognise sound-letter matches including common vowel and consonant digraphs and consonant blends

ACELA1459 recognise that letters can have more than one sound; recognise sounds that can be produced by different letters

Expressing and developing ideas

ACELA1438 build word families using onset and rime

ACELA1758 know that spoken words are written down by listening to the sounds heard in the word and then writing letters to represent those sounds

ACELA1778 write one-syllable words containing known blends; learn an increasing number of high-frequency sight words recognised in shared texts and in texts being read independently; know that regular one-syllable words are made up of letters and common letter clusters that correspond to the sounds heard, and how to use visual memory to write high-frequency words

Interpreting, analysing and evaluating

ACELY1659 combine knowledge of context, meaning, grammar and phonics to decode text

Word families

i-e, a-e, ending in y

Vocabulary words

night, day, in, out, up, down, awake, asleep, full, empty

Extra assistance

Students now know so many rimes that writing some rhyming lines of their own should be easy. Encourage them to write a series of lines that end with rhyming words. Suggest that they consult word family charts or put a list of rimes on the board to help them – short vowel endings (*an, et, id*, etc.), and the *ie, i-e* and *a-e* digraphs. Emphasise that the sentences should be related, for example:

There was this one time
I had to eat a lime.
I began to suck
but it tasted yuck.
I stopped then.
I did not eat ten!

Classroom activities

Find the Start

Give students a list of words with the first letter missing. Ask them to figure out which letter could be the starter for all the given words, for example:

_ell _ake _ent _ape _ash

Discuss the answers as a class. Was there more than one possible answer?

Reading Eggs Lesson sequence	TEACH Content and skills	PRACTISE Children will:	APPLY
Hear: *Animated Lesson*	Review word families, vocabulary and sight words.	identify words learnt in previous lessons.	**Worksheet 1** Phonics
Write: *Look, Listen and Spell*	Identify sounds in a word and write the word.	sound out a word and select letters to spell it correctly.	**Worksheet 2** Read and write
Find: *Rocket Launch*	Identify sounds in a word and make the word.	select the correct onset and rime to make the word.	**Worksheet 3** Vocabulary
Vocabulary: *Opposite Pairs, Words per Minute*	Build vocabulary skills: Identify words whose meanings are opposites. Recognise key vocabulary.	select pairs of cards which are opposites. Match pictures to words.	**Worksheet 4** Check
Read: *Book Ends, Bubble Popper, Book*	Read sentences using basic vocabulary. Read aloud book.	choose a word to finish the sentence. Read and follow instructions. Listen, follow the reading and read along.	**Reading Eggs book** Word families for soft c, soft g, ice, ake, ape, ane, ave, ame, ate

Classroom activities

Build a House

Put the class in two teams. Think of a vocabulary word. Put a series of lines on the board for how many letters are in the word. Each team takes turns guessing a letter. For every letter they get right, draw part of their house – 1 floor, 2 walls, 2 roof lines. When they get a letter right they get another guess. If they can guess the word before it is complete their house gets finished. Play again. See which team ends up with the most houses.

Related Reading Eggs Activities, Interactives, Songs and Books

Driving Tests

Test 4

Sight words: out, day, down, up

Spelling Bank

Reading Eggs Puzzle Park

Animal Fun

Colour Code

Opposites

Number Nuts

Reading Eggs Posters

- Alternate Sounds c
- Alternate Sounds g
- Split Digraph a-e

Reading Eggs Library Books

My Program Books

Teacher Toolkit

- Spelling Activities
- Grammar Lessons
- Comprehension Lessons
- Targeting Comprehension Interactively
- Targeting Text Interactively

Reading Eggs Apps

Eggy Sight words

Eggy Snap

Eggy Phonics 2

Eggy Vocab

Critter Card

Piece of cake

Review

Lesson 100 • Worksheet 1

Name

Phonics

Say the name of each picture. Write in the missing sound.

ice ch th sh ike ie

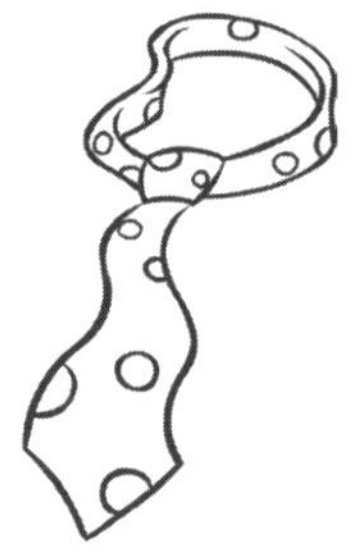

t__________

__________ips

__________ark

__________ree

m__________

bru__________

fi__________

__________eese

b__________

Name

Read and write

Review

Lesson 100 · Worksheet 2

1 Complete the sentences.

gelato plane ice

Icy mice love to skate on ______________.

Gemma giraffe likes to eat ______________.

Jet set is a very fast ______________.

2 Use the wheels to make words. Write the words.

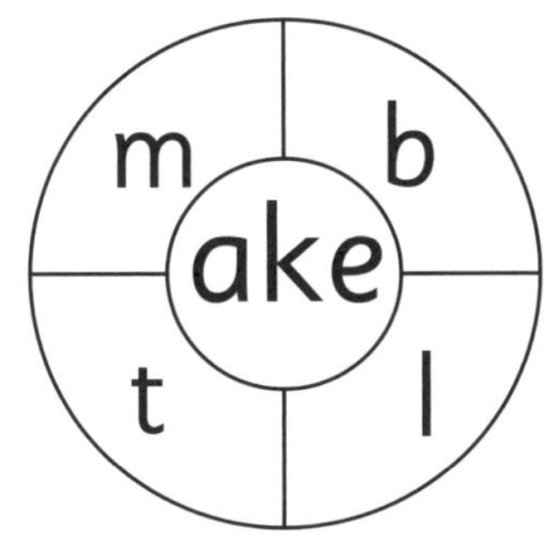

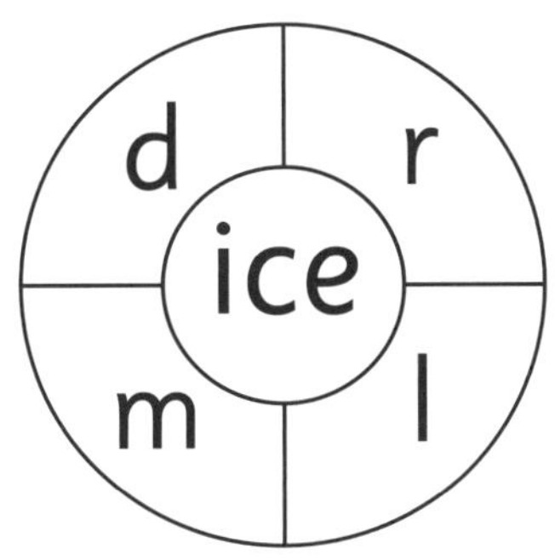

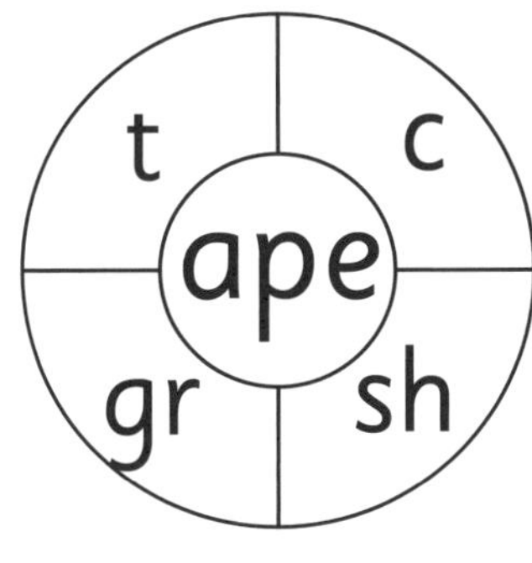

______________	______________	______________
______________	______________	______________
______________	______________	______________
______________	______________	______________

Review

Lesson 100 • Worksheet 3

Name

Vocabulary

1 Join each picture to a word.

2 Unjumble the words.

Name

Check

Review

Lesson 100 · Worksheet 4

1 Find the words.
Colour **city** = red, **cage** = orange, **lake** = blue, **gate** = green.

l	a	k	e	c	i	t	y
c	a	g	e	g	a	t	e
c	i	t	y	l	a	k	e
g	a	t	e	c	a	g	e

2 Write each word.

____

____

3 Complete the sentences.

giraffe   mice   chips

Charlie likes to eat fish and _____________.

Gemma _____________ has very long legs.

The _____________ can smell the cheese.

Lesson 101 the sound **oo** (short)

Learning objectives

Children will:

- identify the short oo sound, as in book.
- read and write short oo words.

Australian Curriculum Content Descriptions

Sound and letter knowledge

ACELA1457 recognise words that start with a given sound, end with a given sound, have a given medial sound, rhyme with a given word

ACELA1458 recognise sound-letter matches including common vowel and consonant digraphs and consonant blends

Expressing and developing ideas

ACELA1435 learn that word order in sentences is important for meaning

ACELA1438 build word families using onset and rime

ACELA1455 build word families from common morphemes; use morphemes to read words

ACELA1778 write one-syllable words containing known blends; know that regular one-syllable words are made up of letters and common letter clusters that correspond to the sounds heard, and how to use visual memory to write high-frequency words

Interpreting, analysing and evaluating

ACELY1659 combine knowledge of context, meaning, grammar and phonics to decode text

Word families

took, cook, book, look, good, wood, wool, foot, soot, woof

Vocabulary words

cakes, lemon, banana, icing, cream, strawberry, chocolate, delicious, excited

Extra assistance

Students have already been introduced to the vowel digraph *ee*, as in *bee*, where the double letter takes the long sound of the vowel. Students may expect *oo* to also make the long sound of the letter - *oe* as in *toe*. However, this lesson introduces the short *oo* sound, as in *book*. Give students lots of examples of the pronunciation of *oo* words to solidify the sound.

Classroom activities

Word Wheel

Give each student two circles of cardboard, one larger than the other, joined through the centre with a split pin. On the visible edge of the larger circle write the consonant letters *b, c, g, h, l, n, r, t, w*. On the smaller circle write the rimes *ook* and *ood* so they will match up with the outer letters and make words. Have students turn the circles and write out the words they make.

Make Your Own Sentences

Write this sentence on the board: I like to bake __. Brainstorm a list of things that can be baked. For a more advanced group, brainstorm a list of describing words to use with them. Ask students to write the sentence starter and fill in their own ending, then illustrate.

Reading Eggs Lesson sequence	**TEACH Content and skills**	**PRACTISE Children will:**	**APPLY**
Hear: *Animated Lesson*	Introduce the short *oo* sound.	identify the short *oo* sound, sort *oo* words, write *oo* words.	**Worksheet 1** Phonics
Write: *Extra Word, Pack the Shelves*	Recognise correct word order for a sentence. Identify the correct word to complete the sentence.	put the words in order and cross out the extra words. Choose the word which completes the sentence.	**Worksheet 2** Read and write
Find: *Word Family, What's Missing?, Driving Trucks, Buzzy's Word Machine, Snowman*	Identify the correct sound to complete the word. Recognise a given word. Identify word endings.	choose the correct sound to make the word. Find the given word in a group. Match the word to its ending.	**Worksheet 3** Vocabulary
Vocabulary: *Today's Topic Words*	Build vocabulary skills: Recognise key vocabulary.	match pictures to words.	**Worksheet 4** Check
Read: *Q & A, Book*	Comprehend the meaning of a text. Read aloud book.	read the text and answer the questions. Listen, follow the reading and read along.	**Reading Eggs Story book** Soot's Cook Book

Related Reading Eggs Activities, Interactives, Songs and Books

Spelling Bank

Dogs

Lesson 28

Focus sound words: book, cook, took, look, hook, pool, cool

Challenge: school, shook

Reading Eggs Puzzle Park

More Than One

Describe it

Do You Know?

What is it?

Driving Tests

Reading Eggs Posters

Story Elements

Reading Eggs Library Books

My Program Books

Teacher Toolkit

- Spelling Activities
- Grammar Lessons
- Comprehension Lessons
- Targeting Comprehension Interactively
- Targeting Text Interactively

Reading Eggs Apps

Eggy Snap

Eggy Vocab

Critter Card

Soot the cook

Short oo

Lesson 101 • Worksheet 1

Name

Phonics

1 Colour the **oo** words.

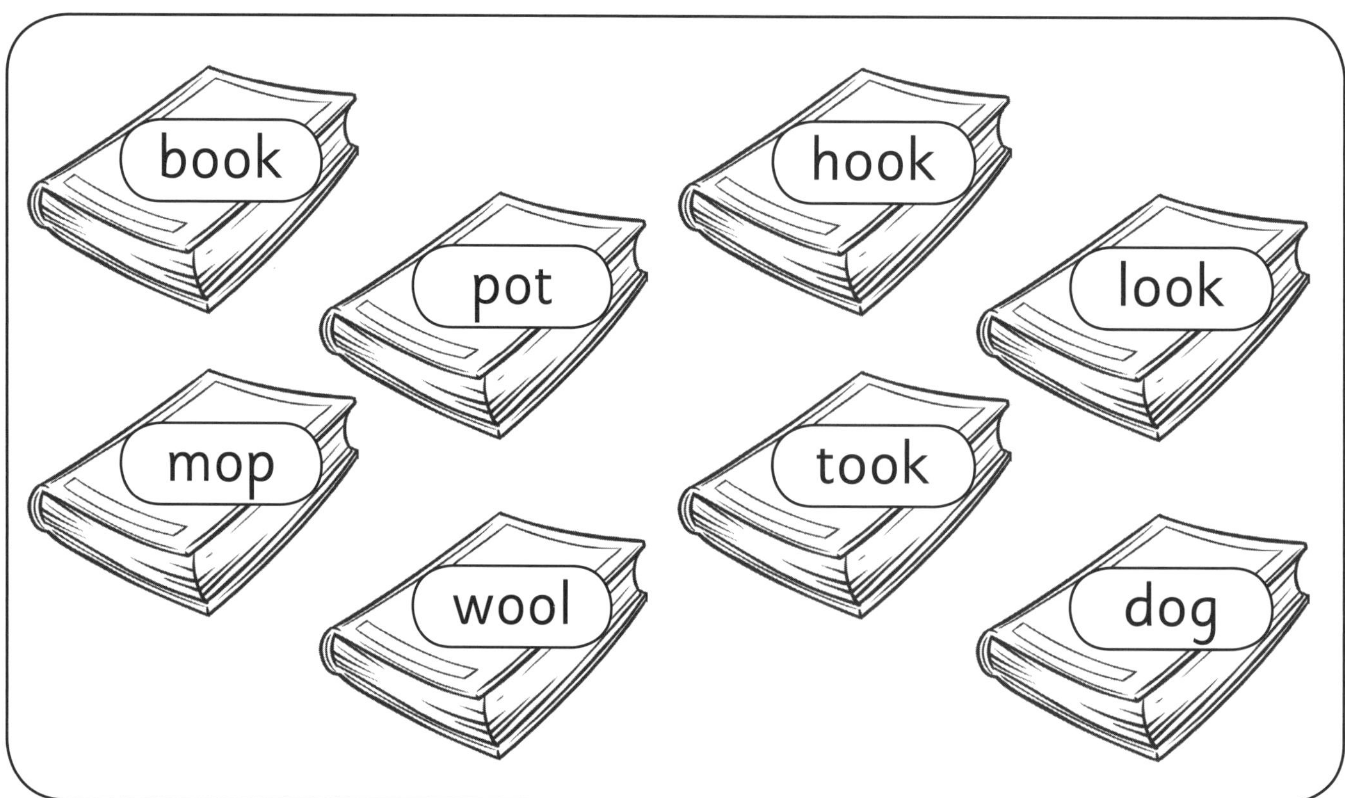

2 Use Soot the cook's **oo** to make words. Write each word. Read each word.

c____k

b____k

t____k

f____t

l____k

w____l

Name

Read and write

Short oo

Lesson 101 • Worksheet 2

1 Read the clue. Write the word.

You get me from a sheep. I am w__________.	I am brown and taste very sweet. I am ch__________.
I can bake cakes. I am Soot the c__________.	I am a yellow fruit. I am a b__________.

2 Draw a cake for Soot's cook book.

What is your cake called? ____________________

Vocabulary

Name

Lesson 101 · Worksheet 3

1 Join each word to a picture.

2 Complete each sentence.

strawberry cook cake

Soot the ____________ loves cake.

Jake baked a chocolate ____________.

Gemma giraffe made a ____________ gelato cake.

Name

Check

Short oo

Lesson 101 · Worksheet 4

1 Join Soot to the **oo** words.

took

hot

Soot

book

cook

mop

drop

look

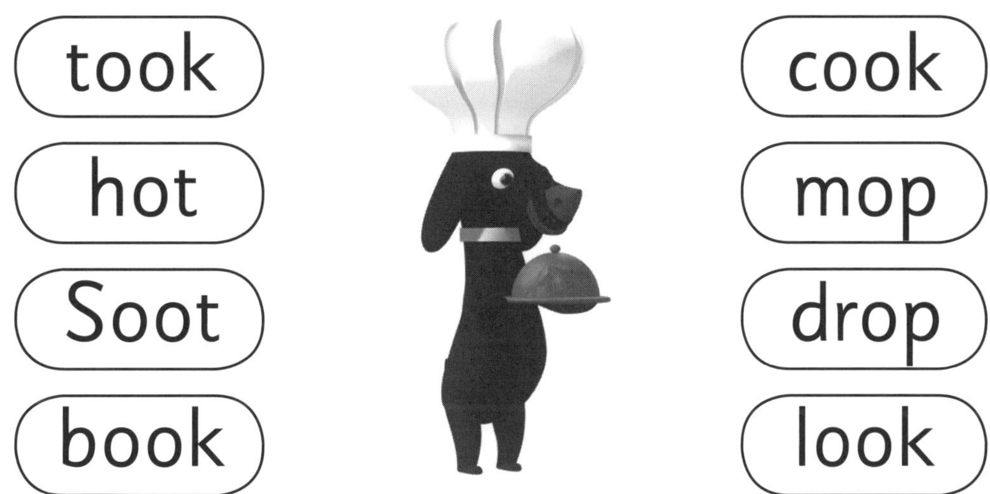

2 Label the pictures in Soot's cook book.

banana cake gelato

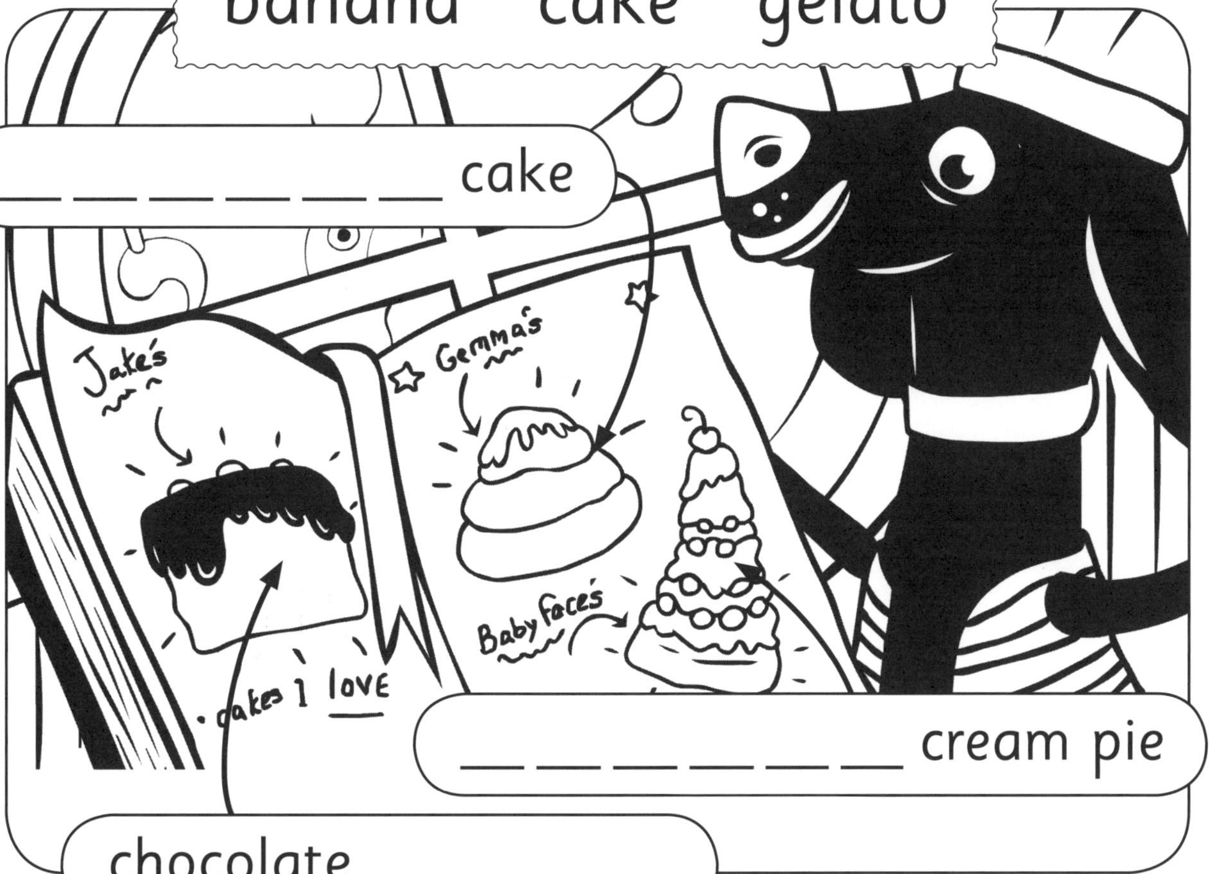

__________ cake

__________ cream pie

chocolate ______

Lesson 102 the sound **oo** (long)

Learning objectives

Children will:

- identify the long oo sound, as in soon.
- read and write long oo words.

Australian Curriculum Content Descriptions

Sound and letter knowledge

ACELA1457 replace sounds in spoken words; recognise words that start with a given sound, end with a given sound, have a given medial sound, rhyme with a given word

ACELA1458 recognise sound-letter matches including common vowel and consonant digraphs and consonant blends

ACELA1459 recognise that letters can have more than one sound; recognise sounds that can be produced by different letters

Expressing and developing ideas

ACELA1435 learn that word order in sentences is important for meaning

ACELA1438 build word families using onset and rime

ACELA1778 write one-syllable words containing known blends; know that regular one-syllable words are made up of letters and common letter clusters that correspond to the sounds heard, and how to use visual memory to write high-frequency words

Interpreting, analysing and evaluating

ACELY1659 combine knowledge of context, meaning, grammar and phonics to decode text; recognise most high-frequency sight words when reading text

Sight words

here, said, took, who

Word families

food, roof, loop, cool, room, pool, fool, tool, spoon, baboon, cockatoo, raccoon, kangaroo, moon, noon, hoop, coop, school, cocoon, zoo, moose, hoot, tooth, goose, noodles, broom, poodle, boo, too, goo, zoom, troop

Vocabulary words

cookbook, cupcake, butterfly, raincoat

Extra assistance

The vowel digraph *oo* has two sounds – a short *oo* sound as in look and a long *oo* as in *moon*. There is no clear rule to apply here for pronunciation, unfortunately these words just need to be learned. Play lots of games with *oo* word flashcards where the pronunciation is important. In the game Go Fish the students must ask for the cards, so if pronunciation is incorrect, they can be corrected.

Classroom activities

Mix and Match

Put the consonant letters of the alphabet on the board in magnetic letters. Write the sound *oo* on the board. Each student comes to the board and makes a word using *oo* and some of the other letters. Discuss their word with the class and write it in one of two lists – short *oo* and long *oo*.

Reading Eggs Lesson sequence	**TEACH Content and skills**	**PRACTISE Children will:**	**APPLY**
Hear: *Animated Lesson*	Introduce the long *oo* sound.	identify the long *oo* sound, recognise long *oo* words, write long *oo* words.	**Worksheet 1** Phonics
Write: *Rocket Launch, Extra Word, Write the Banner*	Identify sounds in a word and make the word. Recognise correct word order for a sentence.	select the correct onset and rime to make a word. Put words in order and cross out extra words.	**Worksheet 2** Read and write
Find: *Shooting Stars*	Recognise a given word.	find the given word in a group.	**Worksheet 3** Vocabulary
Vocabulary: *Today's Topic Words, Scrapbook, Define It, City Zoo*	Build vocabulary skills: Recognise key vocabulary. Identify the parts of a compound word. Identify words by their definitions.	match pictures to words. Choose two words to make a compound word. Choose the correct word to match the definition.	**Worksheet 4** Check
Read: *Q & A, Book*	Comprehend the meaning of a text. Read aloud book.	read the text and answer the questions. Listen, follow the reading and read along.	**Reading Eggs Story book** A Cook at the Zoo

Classroom activities

Mind the Gap!

Show the children the following sentences:

It is _____ at the zoo. This is _____ goo. The cook is cool with her _______.
Provide flashcards with the missing words written on them, and ask children to read each sentence and work out what the missing word could be. They can then select the correct flashcard and correctly position it. Discuss with the class.

Related Reading Eggs Activities, Interactives, Songs and Books

Spelling Bank

Dogs

Lesson 29

Focus sound words: boot, hoot, loot, root, foot, room, zoom

High frequency sight words: here

Challenge: broom, shoot

Reading Eggs Puzzle Park

Animal Fun

Baby Animals

Do You Know?

What is it?

Driving Tests

Reading Eggs Posters

Compound Words

Reading Eggs Library Books

My Program Books

Teacher Toolkit

- Spelling Activities
- Grammar Lessons
- Comprehension Lessons
- Targeting Comprehension Interactively
- Targeting Text Interactively

Reading Eggs Apps

Eggy Sight words

Eggy Snap

Eggy Vocab

Critter Card

Boots the kangaroo

Lesson 102 • Worksheet 1

Name

Phonics

1 Colour the **oo** words.

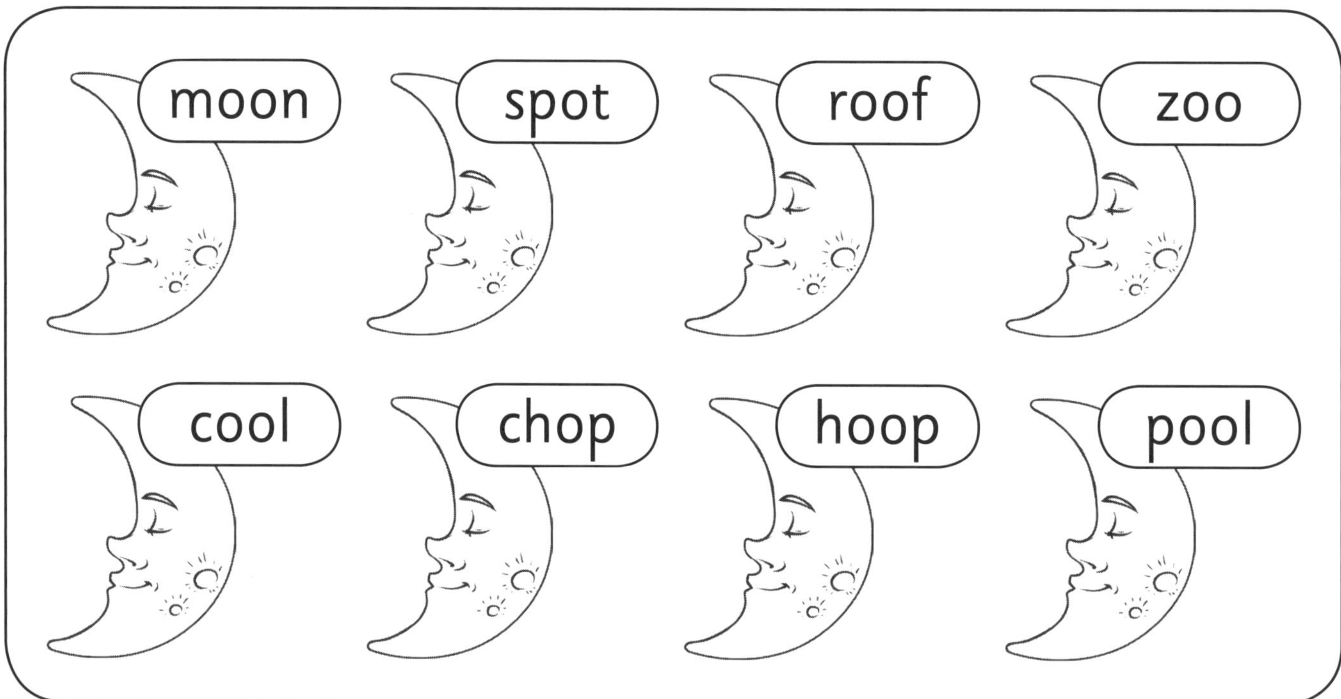

2 Use Bunky boo's **oo** to make words. Write each word. Read each word.

z_____m

n_____n

m_____n

sp_____n

h_____p

Name

Read and write

Long oo

Lesson 102 · Worksheet 2

1 Read the clue. Write the word.

Lots of animals live here. It is a z__________.	This word means the same as midday. n__________
You use me to eat your soup. I am a s__________.	A hammer, a saw and a drill are all t__________.

2 Write the words in the correct order.

kangaroos. can three I see

____

____

Lesson 102 • Worksheet 3

Name

Vocabulary

1 Join each word to a picture.

2 Colour the correct word. Cross out the wrong word.

A [cockatoo] [baboon] is a big, white bird.

A [raccoon] [kangaroo] can jump very far.

You can eat gelato with a [tools] [spoon].

Name

Check

Long oo

Lesson 102 · Worksheet 4

1 Write the **oo** words in the zoo.

2 Circle the word that rhymes with the picture.

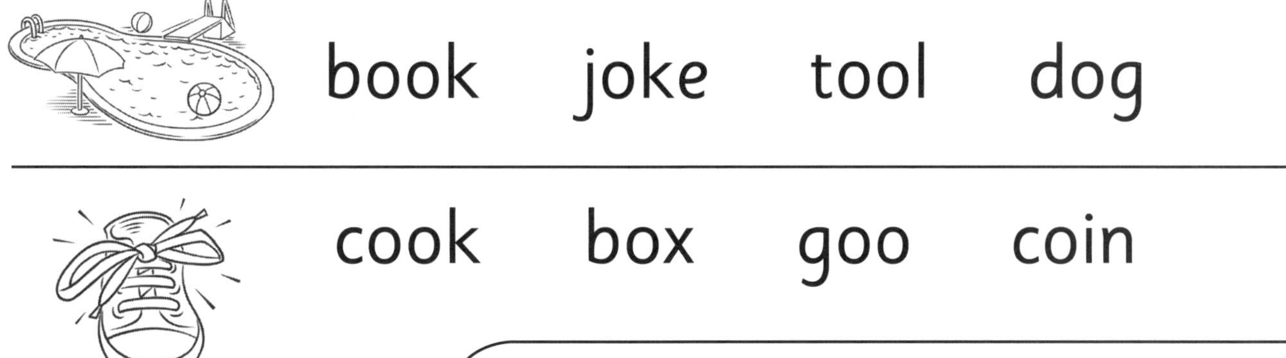

3 Draw a baboon at the zoo eating goo with a spoon!

Lesson 103 the sound **ole**

Learning objectives

Children will:

- identify the rime ole.
- read and write words ending with ole.

Australian Curriculum Content Descriptions

Sound and letter knowledge

ACELA1439 identify onset and rime in one-syllable spoken words

ACELA1457 replace sounds in spoken words; recognise words that start with a given sound, end with a given sound, have a given medial sound, rhyme with a given word

ACELA1458 recognise sound-letter matches including common vowel and consonant digraphs and consonant blends

ACELA1459 recognise that letters can have more than one sound; recognise sounds that can be produced by different letters

Expressing and developing ideas

ACELA1435 learn that word order in sentences is important for meaning

ACELA1438 build word families using onset and rime

ACELA1455 using morphemes to read words

ACELA1778 write one-syllable words containing known blends; know that regular one-syllable words are made up of letters and common letter clusters that correspond to the sounds heard, and how to use visual memory to write high-frequency words

Interpreting, analysing and evaluating

ACELY1659 combine knowledge of context, meaning, grammar and phonics to decode text

Word families

mole, sole, hole, pole, stole, joke, poke, woke, stone, cone, phone, bone, home, tone

Vocabulary words

ground, scary, own, dark, ringing, thinking, hopped, stopped, rabbit, wombat, bear, kangaroo, snake

Extra assistance

The long *o* sound is made with the split digraph *o-e*. This is two letters functioning as a single unit to make one sound. It is not an *o* and a silent or magic *e*. The *e* makes the *o* say its name, as in *hole*, not *hot*. This is a different sound to the *oo* sounds previously introduced. Be sure to give students time to practise their pronunciation of the long *o* sound and compare it with the other sounds made with the letter *o*. Use sets of words to contrast *lot, look, loom, lone*.

Classroom activities

Which Hat?

Place three hats on the floor with the labels *o, oo* and *o-e*. Discuss the sounds. Have a pile of objects or pictures of objects that use the sounds *o, oo* and *o-e*. Each student chooses one and works out which hat it must go in. Discuss their choice with the class.

Reading Eggs Lesson sequence	**TEACH Content and skills**	**PRACTISE Children will:**	**APPLY**
Hear: *Animated Lesson*	Introduce the sound *o-e* through *ole* words and the song *Moe the Mole lives in a hole.*	identify the *ole* sound. Make *ole* words.	**Worksheet 1** Word families 1
Write: *Pack the Shelves, Bird Words*	Identify the correct word to complete the sentence. Recognise correct word order for a sentence.	choose the correct words to make the sentences.	**Worksheet 2** Vocabulary
Find: *Word Family, Dragon Fire, Snowman, Buzzy's Word Machine, Bowling*	Identify the correct onset letter to complete the word. Recognise a given word. Select word endings. Identify the rime in the word.	choose the correct initial letter to make the word. Find the given word in a group. Match the word to its ending.	**Worksheet 3** Word families 2
Vocabulary: *City Zoo*	Build vocabulary skills: Recognise key vocabulary.	match pictures to words.	**Worksheet 4** Check
Read: *Book Ends, Book*	Read sentences using basic vocabulary. Read aloud book.	choose a word to finish the sentence. Listen, follow the reading and read along.	**Reading Eggs Story book** A Deep Dark Hole

Classroom activities

Memory Game

Write the word *stone* on the board. Sound it out with the class and discuss the *st* sound and the use of the letter *o*. Have students trace the word on someone's back or in the air with their finger. Rub out the word and write these words on the board: ston, stoon, stone, sone, soon. Ask them to identify which is correct, then discuss what is wrong with the other versions.

Related Reading Eggs Activities, Interactives, Songs and Books

Spelling Bank

Fish

Lesson 46

Focus sound words: hole, pole, bone, cone

Challenge: whole, phone

Driving Tests

Reading Eggs Puzzle Park

Animal Fun

Describe it

Do You Know?

What is it?

Music Café

Moe the Mole lives in a hole

Reading Eggs Posters

Split Digraph o-e

- Suffixes -ing
- Suffixes -ed

Reading Eggs Library Books

My Program Books

Teacher Toolkit

- Spelling Activities
- Grammar Lessons
- Comprehension Lessons
- Targeting Comprehension Interactively
- Targeting Text Interactively

Reading Eggs Apps

Eggy Sight words

Eggy Snap

Eggy Phonics 2

Critter Card

Moe the mole

ole

Lesson 103 · Worksheet 1

Name

Word families 1

1 Trace.

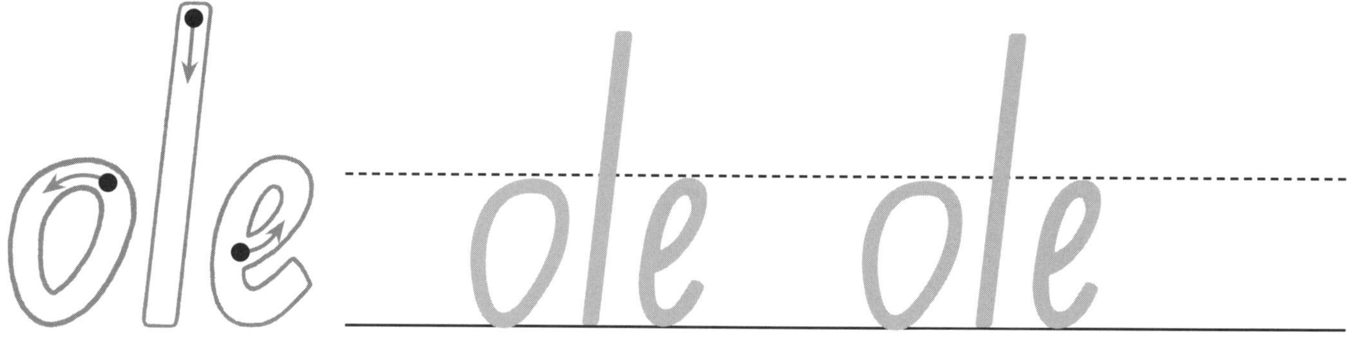

2 Complete the words. Use Moe the mole's letters.

_____ole

_____ole

_____ole

_____ole

3 Label each picture.

hole mole pole

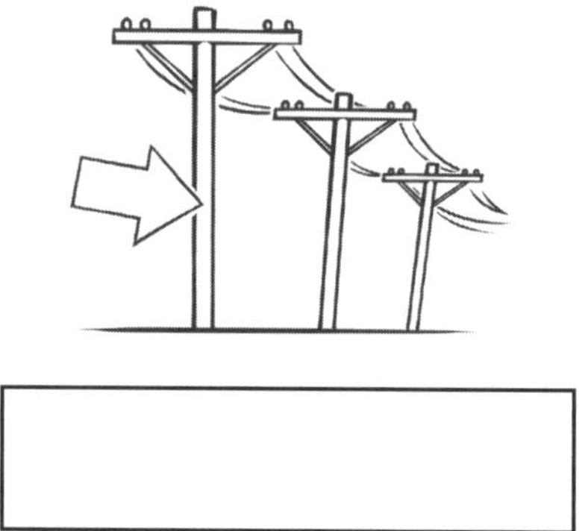

Name

Vocabulary

Lesson 103 • Worksheet 2

1 Join each word to a picture.

2 Read the clue. Write the word.

I like to dig holes. I am Moe the m__________.	I have a long body and no legs. I am a s__________.
I have fur and very sharp claws. I am a b__________.	I have large ears. I love to eat carrots. I am a __________.

Word families 2

Lesson 103 · Worksheet 3

Name

1 Use the word wheels to make words. Write the words.

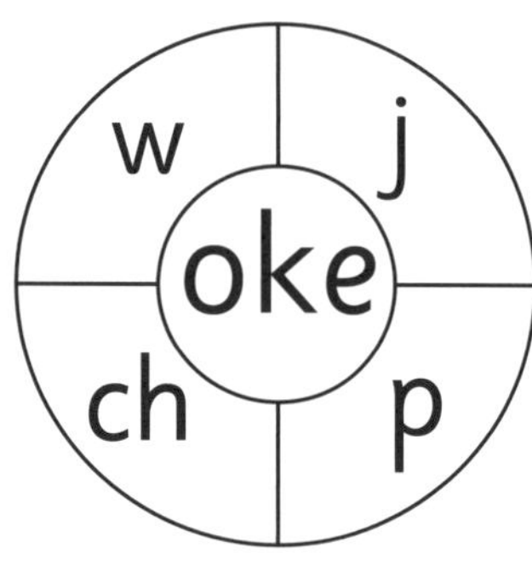

st
c
one
b
ph

2 Colour **oke** words red. Colour **one** words green.

bone phone joke

poke cone

woke stone choke

Name

Check

Lesson 103 • Worksheet 4

1 Circle the rhyming word in each row.

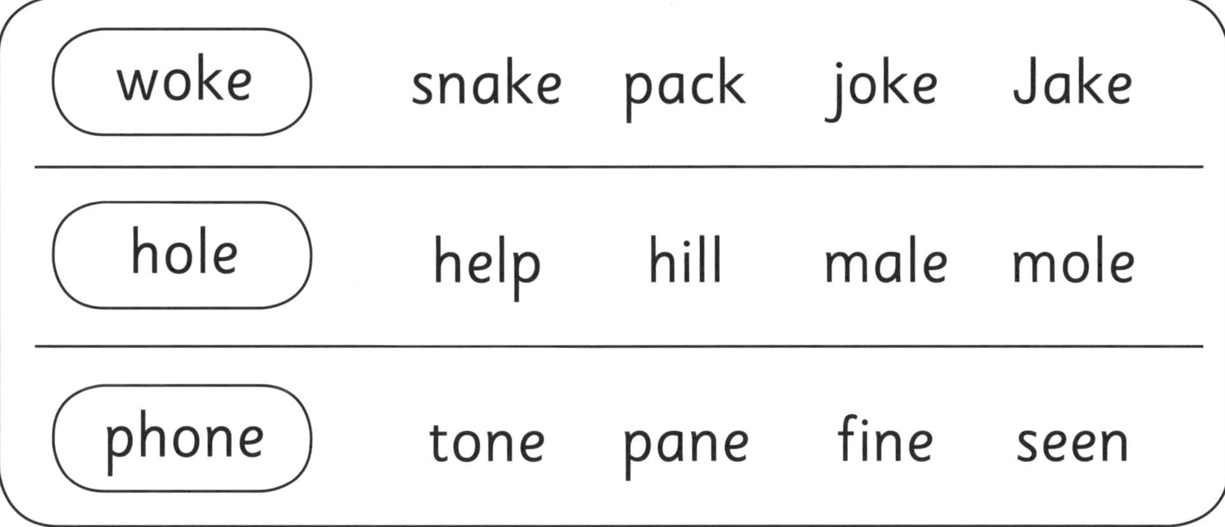

2 Complete the sentences.

home woke phone

Moe lost his ______________ down a hole.

We will see if anyone is ______________ .

"Hello, hello, who is this? You ______________ me up."

3 Colour the word if it makes a **long o** sound.

woke	cow	mole	home
hole	clown	phone	tone

Lesson 104 the sound **o-e**

Learning objectives

Children will:

- identify the rimes that can be made with o-e.
- read and write o-e words.
- make compound words.

Australian Curriculum Content Descriptions

Sound and letter knowledge

ACELA1457 replace sounds in spoken words; recognise words that start with a given sound, end with a given sound, have a given medial sound, rhyme with a given word

ACELA1458 recognise sound-letter matches including common vowel and consonant digraphs and consonant blends

ACELA1459 recognise that letters can have more than one sound; recognise sounds that can be produced by different letters

Expressing and developing ideas

ACELA1435 learn that word order in sentences is important for meaning

ACELA1438 build word families using onset and rime

ACELA1455 build word families from common morphemes; use morphemes to read words

ACELA1778 write one-syllable words containing known blends; learn an increasing number of high-frequency sight words recognised in shared texts and in texts being read independently; know that regular one-syllable words are made up of letters and common letter clusters that correspond to the sounds heard, and how to use visual memory to write high-frequency words

Word families

nose, hose, rose, note, vote, joke, smoke, rode, code, goat, boat, float, coat

Vocabulary words

pond, ribbons, stripes, flagpole, seaweed, tadpole, wavy, around, together, through, behind, tangled, molehill, underwater, bigger, swimming, getting, puffing

Extra assistance

When making a word family list for the split digraph *o-e*, students will identify words with the long *o* sound which have a different spelling – *boat, flow* or *toe* for example. It is important to explain why these words don't fit into the *o-e* list while still praising the student for finding the correct long *o* sound. As the alternate spelling will be taught later, put these words in a list to be brought out then.

Classroom activities

For Starters

Put the rime *ose* on the board in magnetic letters. Put all the letters of the alphabet around it. Students take turns to make *ose* words by simply changing the initial phoneme. For a challenge get students to use a blend.

Change the rime to *oke*, then *ode*, then *ote* and repeat the activity.

Reading Eggs Lesson sequence	**TEACH Content and skills**	**PRACTISE Children will:**	**APPLY**
Hear: *Animated Lesson*	Review the sound *o-e* with a variety of consonants.	identify the letters that make the long *o* sound. Make *o-e* words.	**Worksheet 1** Word families
Write: *Write the Banner*	Recognise correct word order for a sentence.	choose the correct words to make a sentence.	**Worksheet 2** Read and draw
Find: *Word Family, Dragon Fire, Squirter, Snowman, Buzzy's Word Machine*	Identify the correct onset letter to complete the word. Recognise a given word. Identify word endings.	choose the correct initial letter to make the word. Find the given word in a group. Match the word to its ending.	**Worksheet 3** Vocabulary
Vocabulary: *Today's Topic Words, Scrapbook*	Build vocabulary skills: Recognise key vocabulary. Identify the parts of a compound word.	match pictures to words. Choose two words to make a compound word.	**Worksheet 4** Check
Read: *Q & A, Book*	Comprehend the meaning of a text. Read aloud book.	read the text and answer the questions. Listen, follow the reading and read along.	**Reading Eggs Story book** The Pond Cup

Classroom activities

Run to it!

This is best done in a hall or on the playground. Label four corners or areas with signs saying *ose, oke, ote* and *ode*. The students stand in the middle and when the teacher calls out a word containing one of these sounds, they must run to the matching corner. Try harder words, with more than one syllable, for example *decode, remote, awoke, suppose*.

Related Reading Eggs Activities, Interactives, Songs and Books

Driving Tests

Test 11

Sight words: under, those

Letters and sounds: race, wave, cone, phone, dome, Rome, weed, hose, rose, woke, broke

Reading Eggs Puzzle Park

Baby Animals

Opposites

Do it

What is it?

Spelling Bank

Reading Eggs Posters

Split Digrapgh o-e

Suffixes -er and -est

Reading Eggs Library Books

My Program Books

Teacher Toolkit

- Spelling Activities
- Grammar Lessons
- Comprehension Lessons
- Targeting Comprehension Interactively
- Targeting Text Interactively

Reading Eggs Apps

Eggy Snap

Eggy Phonics 2

Critter Card

Coal the tadpole

o-e

Lesson 104 • Worksheet 1

Name

Word families

1 Say the word for each picture. Complete the word families.

r ose ______ sm oke ______

n ______ j ______

h ______ p ______

cl ______ w ______

2 Complete the words using the letters on the fridge.

______ ote ______ ode

______ ote ______ ode

Name

Read and draw

Lesson 104 · Worksheet 2

Draw a picture for each sentence.

Coal the tadpole lives in a pond.	
Tony the tadpole has green spots. He gets tangled in seaweed.	
The tadpoles race under the bubbly foam and over the blue stones.	

Vocabulary

Name

Lesson 104 • Worksheet 3

1 Join each word to a picture.

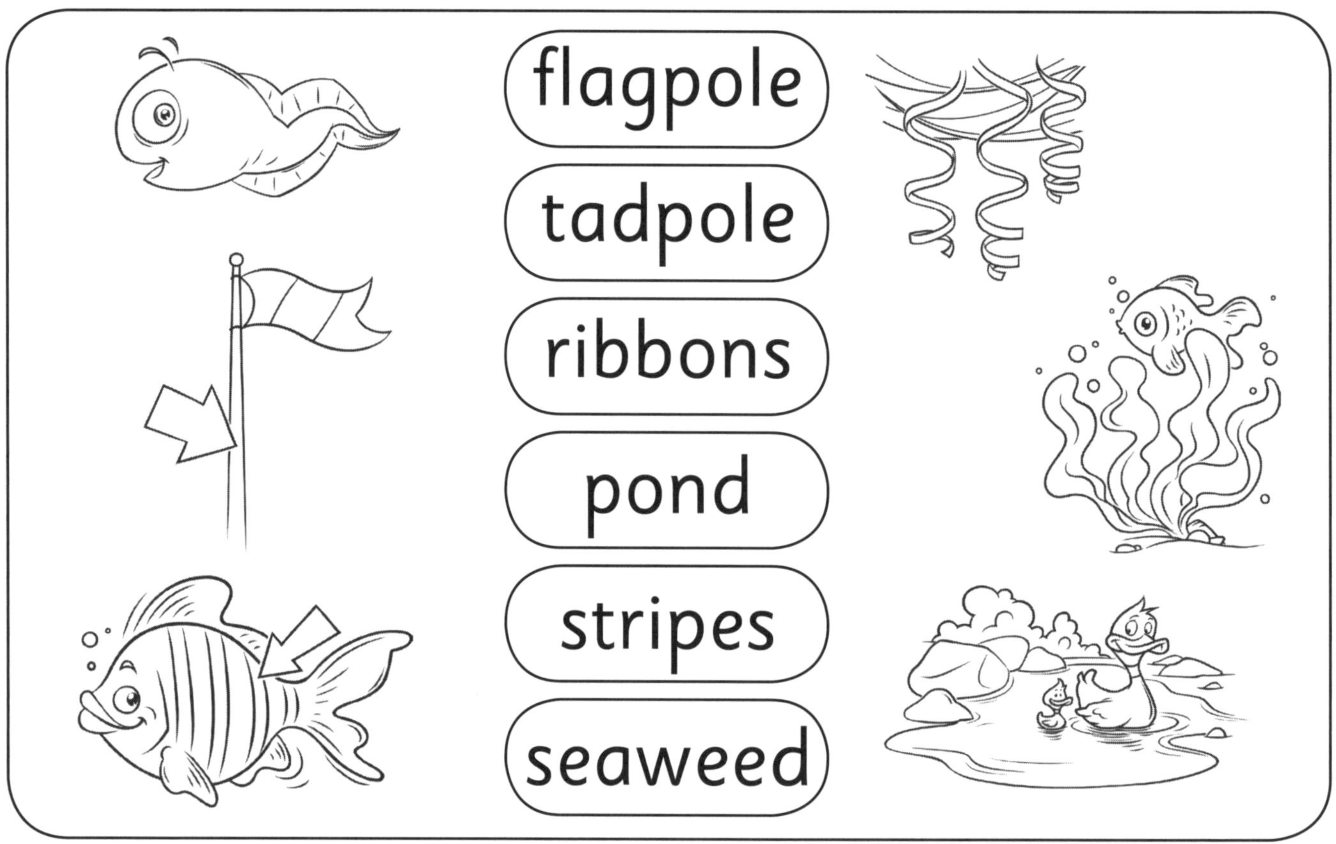

2 Colour the correct word. Cross out the wrong word.

Coal the tadpole lives in a [stripes] [pond].

Every year, the [ribbons] [tadpoles] have a race around the pond.

Poor Tony got stuck in some [seaweed] [flagpole].

Name

Check

Lesson 104 • Worksheet 4

1 Colour the tadpoles if they have a **long o** sound.

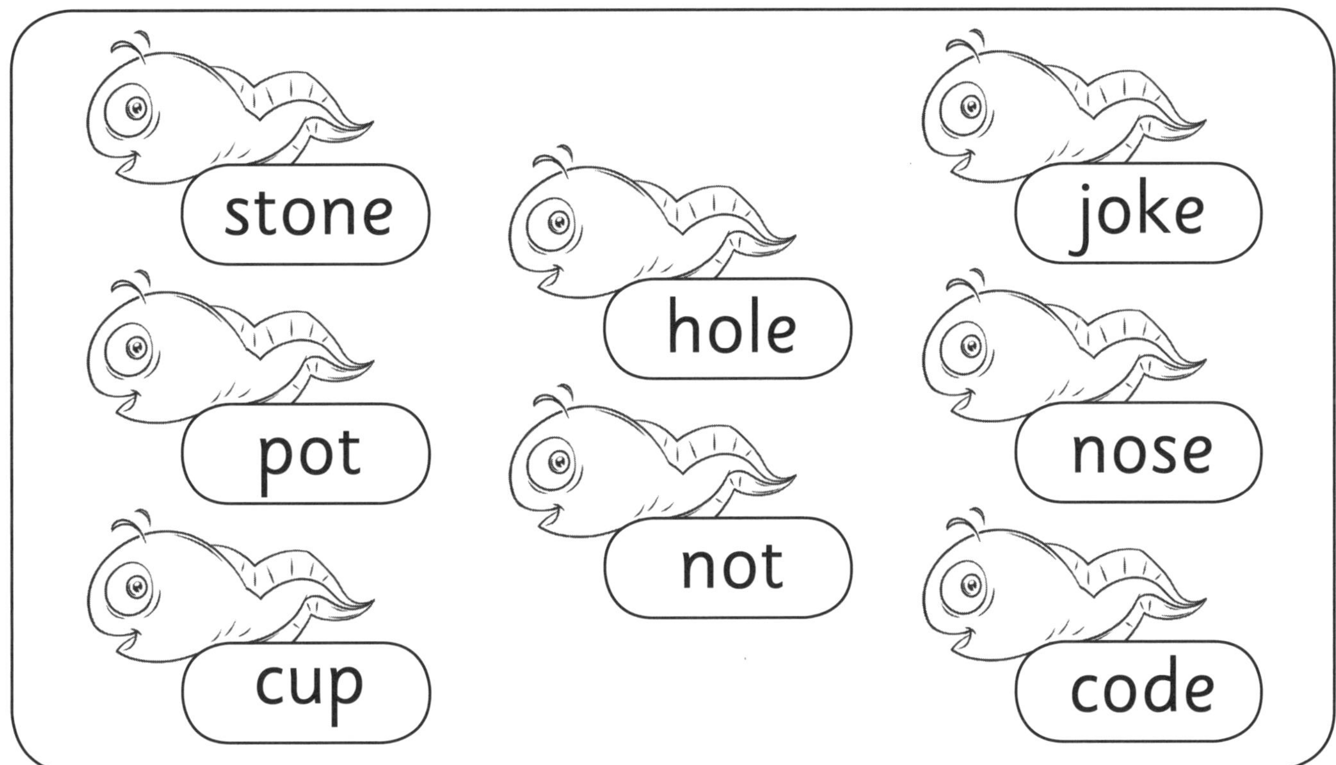

2 Label the pictures.

n________

j________

st________

h________

c________

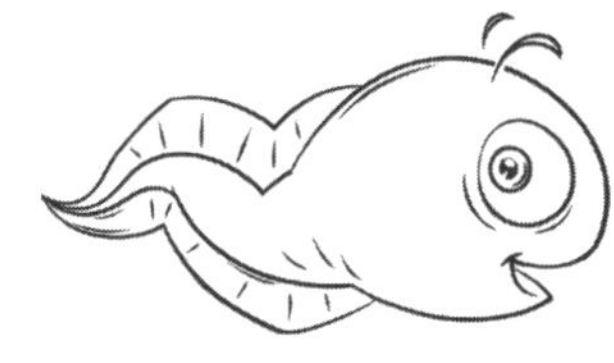

tad________

Lesson 105 blends

Learning objectives

Children will:
- identify blends.
- read and write words with blends.

Australian Curriculum Content Descriptions

Sound and letter knowledge

ACELA1439 identify onset and rime in one-syllable spoken words

ACELA1457 replace sounds in spoken words; recognise words that start with a given sound, end with a given sound, have a given medial sound, rhyme with a given word

ACELA1458 recognise sound-letter matches including common vowel and consonant digraphs and consonant blends

Expressing and developing ideas

ACELA1435 learn that word order in sentences is important for meaning

ACELA1438 build word families using onset and rime

ACELA1455 using morphemes to read words

ACELA1778 write one-syllable words containing known blends; learn an increasing number of high-frequency sight words recognised in shared texts and in texts being read independently; know that regular one-syllable words are made up of letters and common letter clusters that correspond to the sounds heard, and how to use visual memory to write high-frequency words

Interpreting, analysing and evaluating

ACELY1659 combine knowledge of context, meaning, grammar and phonics to decode text; recognise most high-frequency sight words when reading text

Word families

plane, smoke, brush, frog, whale, scarf, crash, flash, trash, grub, slam, pram, tram, clam, swam, crab, plug, grab, slug, friends

Extra assistance

Many students with an Asian language background will confuse *r* and *l* blends as they are not common in their home language. They need to practise their pronunciation. Choral response, where groups of students recite the same words, are an effective tool to build familiarity with difficult sounds. Have the students repeat words after you or try some tongue twisters such as these:

How can a clam cram in a clean cream can?
Green glass globes glow greenly.

Classroom activities

Word Pairs

Give half the class a consonant blend on a card. Give the other half of the class a word ending on a card. Ask the children to find a partner to make a word and sit together. Ask each blend person to write their word on the board. Have the pairs swap cards and play again – they must make a different word this time!

Reading Eggs Lesson sequence	**TEACH Content and skills**	**PRACTISE Children will:**	**APPLY**
Hear: *Animated Lesson*	Introduce blends at the beginnings of words with the song *Frankie the Frog's swingin' club.*	make words by combining blends and word endings. Identify blends.	**Worksheet 1** Initial sounds 1
Write: *Rocket Launch, Extra Word, Bird Words*	Identify sounds in a word and make the word. Recognise correct word order for a sentence.	select the correct onset and rime to make the word. Put the words in order and cross out the extra words.	**Worksheet 2** Read and write
Find: *Word Family, Frog Logs*	Identify the correct onset letter to complete the word. Recognise a given word.	choose the correct initial letter to make the word. Find the given word in a group.	**Worksheet 3** Initial sounds 2
Vocabulary: *Word Dominoes, Words per Minute*	Build vocabulary skills: Recognise key vocabulary.	match pictures to words.	**Worksheet 4** Check
Read: *Book Ends, Q & A, Book*	Read sentences using basic vocabulary. Comprehend the meaning of a text. Read aloud book.	choose a word to finish the sentence. Read the text and answer the questions. Listen, follow the reading and read along.	**Reading Eggs Story book** Clem the Clam

Classroom activities

Bingo!

Give students a laminated board with ten squares on it. Ask them to write a word in each square from a list of words with initial blends (use whiteboard markers). Say words from the list. Students put a cross on that word on their board. First one to ten calls out 'bingo' and wins!

Related Reading Eggs Activities, Interactives, Songs and Books

Spelling Bank

Cats

Lesson 22

Focus sound words: plan, plot, plop, plum, plus, plug, plant

High frequency sight words: play

Challenge: pluck, plump

Driving Tests

Reading Eggs Puzzle Park

Animal Fun

Transport

Making Music

Music Café

Frankie the Frog's swingin' club

Reading Eggs Posters

The wh Sound

Spelling Strategies

Reading Eggs Library Books

My Program Books

Teacher Toolkit

- Spelling Activities
- Grammar Lessons
- Comprehension Lessons
- Targeting Comprehension Interactively
- Targeting Text Interactively

Reading Eggs Apps

Eggy Sight words

Eggy Snap

Eggy Phonics 3

Critter Card

Bree the bear

Blends

Lesson 105 • Worksheet 1

Name

Initial sounds 1

1 Join Clem to the **cl words**.

2 Write the word above the correct rock.

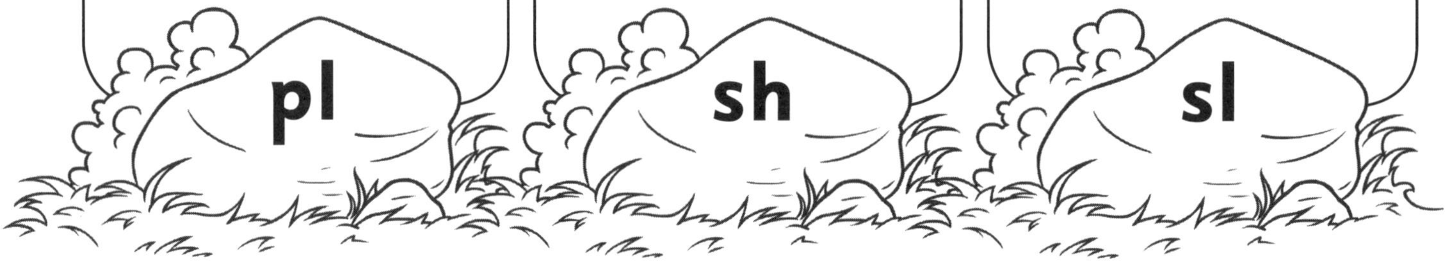

pl **sh** **sl**

shell slam slips plug play shut

Name

Read and write

Blends

Lesson 105 • Worksheet 2

1 Complete the sentences.

slams clam fly

Clem is a ____________.

"I want to ____________ like a bird."

Clem's shell ____________ shut.

2 Write the words in the correct order.

Clem to A tried the eat bird clam.

____

____

3 Draw.

A fish tries to eat Clem the clam.

Blends

Name

Initial sounds 2

Lesson 105 • Worksheet 3

1 Say the name of each picture. Write the beginning sound.

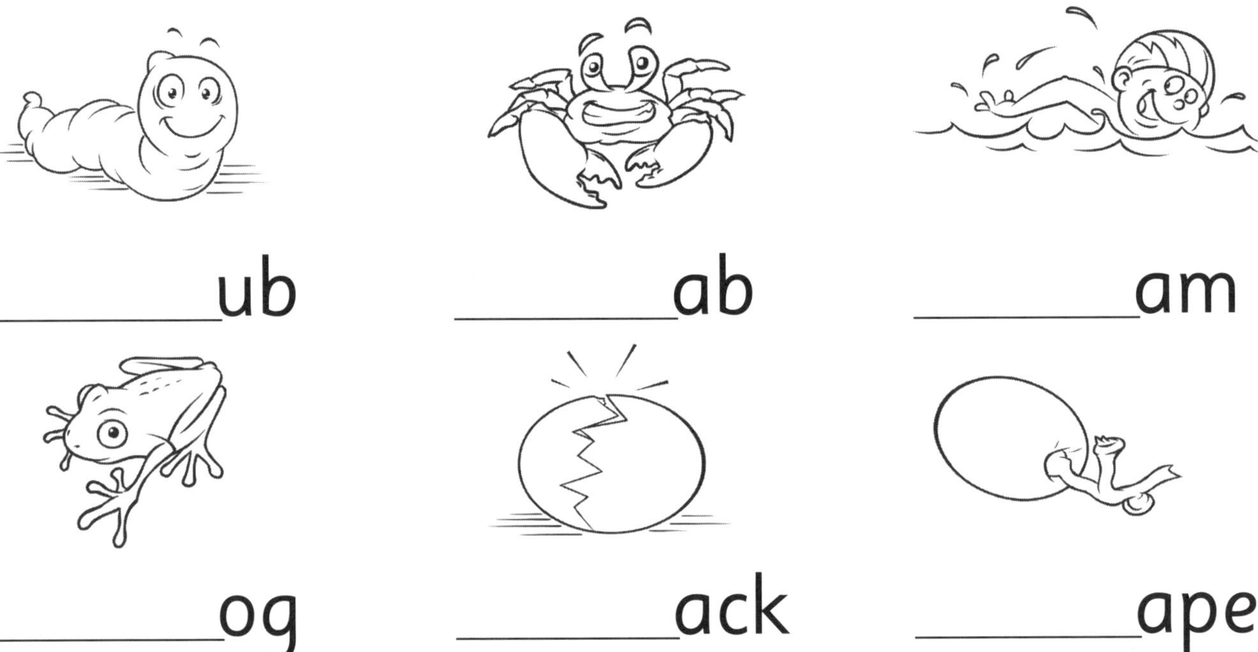

2 Join the jigsaw pieces together. Write each word.

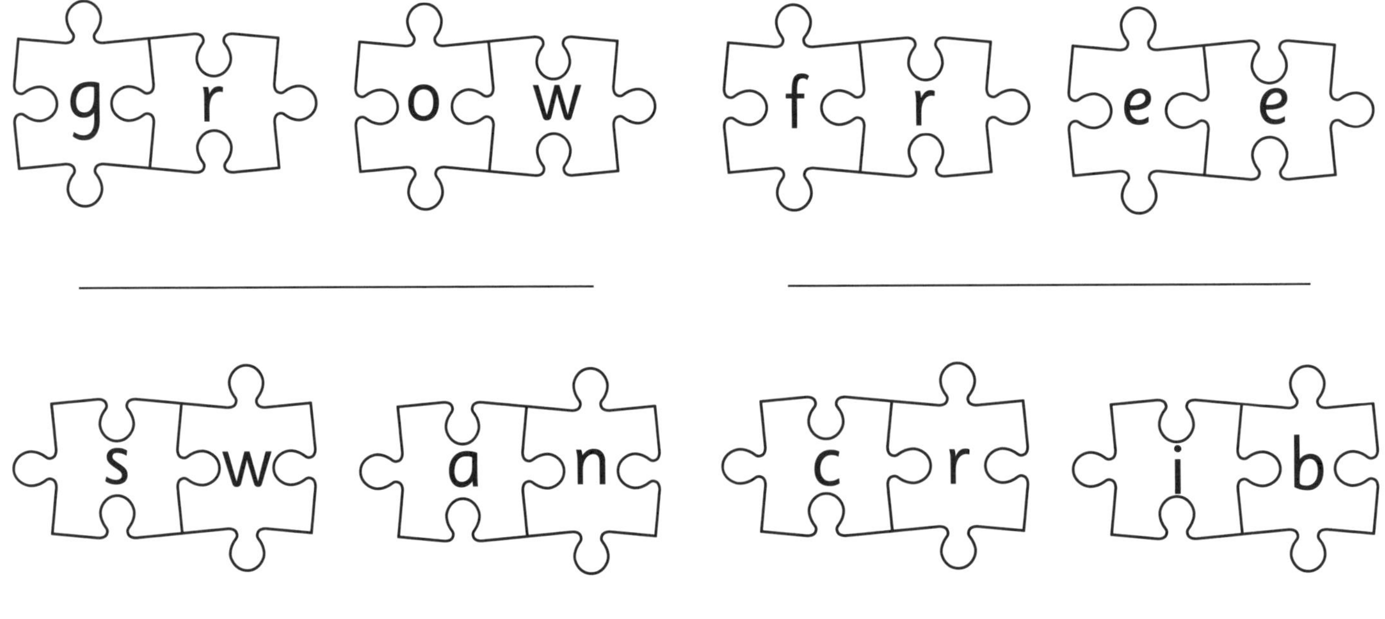

Name

Check

Blends

Lesson 105 · Worksheet 4

1 Complete the crossword.
Use the picture clues to help you.

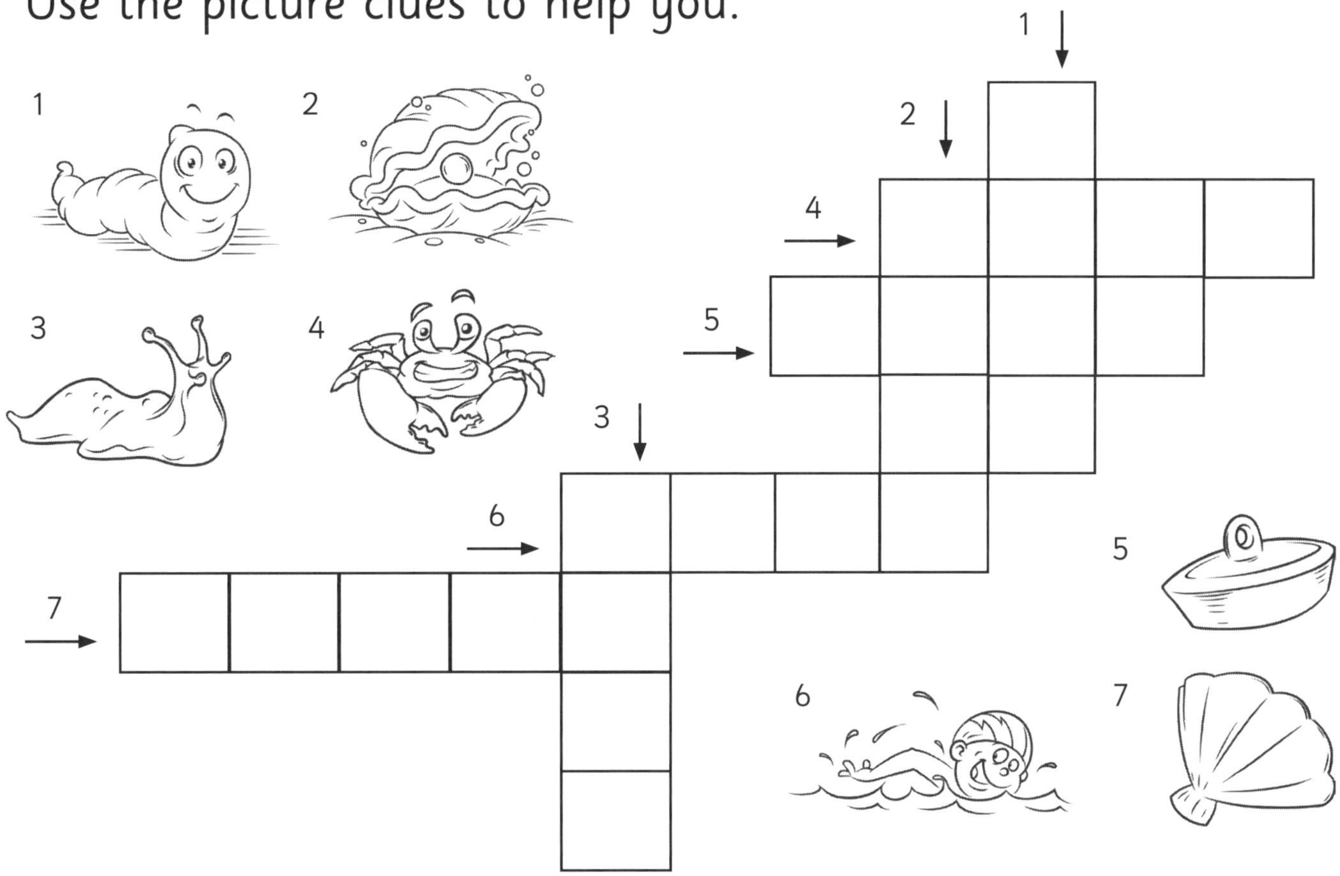

2 Guess the word by its shape. Write each word in a box.

frog slam Clem shell

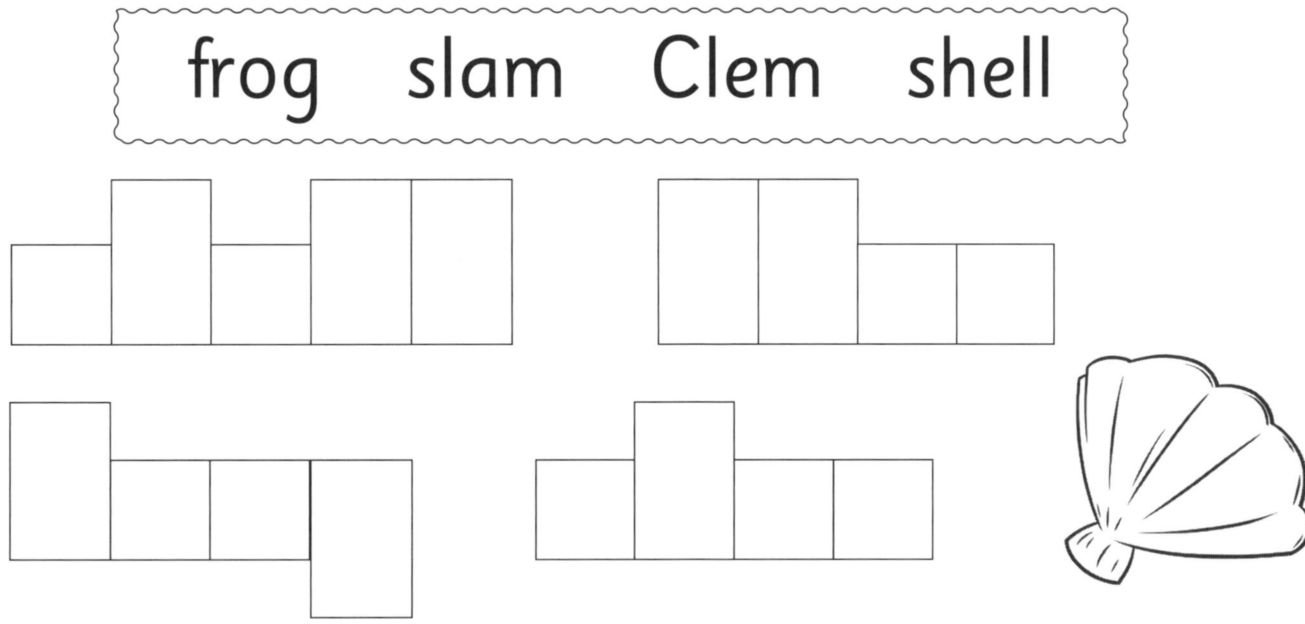

Lesson 106 blends

Learning objectives

Children will:

- identify more blends.
- read and write words with blends.

Australian Curriculum Content Descriptions

Sound and letter knowledge

ACELA1439 identify onset and rime in one-syllable spoken words

ACELA1457 replace sounds in spoken words; recognise words that start with a given sound, end with a given sound, have a given medial sound, rhyme with a given word

ACELA1458 recognise sound-letter matches including common vowel and consonant digraphs and consonant blends

ACELA1459 recognise that letters can have more than one sound; recognise sounds that can be produced by different letters

Expressing and developing ideas

ACELA1435 learn that word order in sentences is important for meaning

ACELA1438 build word families using onset and rime

ACELA1778 write one-syllable words containing known blends; learn an increasing number of high-frequency sight words recognised in shared texts and in texts being read independently; know that regular one-syllable words are made up of letters and common letter clusters that correspond to the sounds heard, and how to use visual memory to write high-frequency words

Interpreting, analysing and evaluating

ACELY1659 combine knowledge of context, meaning, grammar and phonics to decode text

Word families

crab, snail, spider, clam, frog, fly, flamingo, tree, grub, green, brick, trunk, grin, blue, crash

Vocabulary words

lunch, hungry, happy, boat, mole, whale

Extra assistance

When students are learning to pronounce blends, they can develop a habit of adding a vowel sound between the consonants, for example, *froze* becomes 'fer-rose', or *blue* becomes 'buh-loo'. Sometimes teachers may find that they are also doing this when sounding out words, eg 'tuh-r-ee'. All blend pronunciations should be sounded out together – *tr-ee, bl-ue, fr-oze*.

Classroom activities

Memory Game

Write the word *hungry* on the board. Sound it out with the class and discuss the blend in the middle – *gr* – and the *y* on the end. Have students trace the word on someone's back or in the air with their finger. Rub out the word and write these words on the board: hungree, hungrie, hungry, hungy, hugry. Ask them to identify which is correct, then discuss what is wrong with the other versions.

Reading Eggs Lesson sequence	TEACH Content and skills	PRACTISE Children will:	APPLY
Hear: *Animated Lesson*	Introduce more blends for the beginnings of words.	make words by combining blends and word endings.	**Worksheet 1** Initial sounds 1
Write: *Look, Listen and Spell, Pelican Spelling, Write the Banner*	Identify sounds in a word and write the word. Recognise correct word order for a sentence.	select letters to spell a word correctly. Choose the correct words to make a sentence.	**Worksheet 2** Read and write
Find: *Squirter, What's Missing?, Pack the Shelves*	Recognise a given word. Identify the missing sound in a word. Identify the correct word to complete the sentence.	find the given word in a group. Choose the correct letter to make the word. Choose the word which completes the sentence.	**Worksheet 3** Initial sounds 2
Vocabulary: *Bingo Stars, Power Words, Bubble Popper*	Build vocabulary skills: Recognise key vocabulary. Read sentences using basic vocabulary.	tap on the word being said. Match pictures to words. Read and follow instructions.	**Worksheet 4** Check
Read: *Book*	Read aloud book.	listen, follow the reading and read along.	**Reading Eggs Story book** Fred the Frog

Classroom activities

Say it Right!

Have a set of pictures of things which start with a blend. Hold up a picture and say the word incorrectly, using the wrong blend, eg *drog* for *frog*. Students need to call out the right word.

Related Reading Eggs Activities, Interactives, Songs and Books

Spelling Bank

Elephants

Lesson 39

Focus sound words: grab, grin, grub, frill, frog, fresh, from

High frequency sight words: green, grow

Challenge: grandmother, friend

Reading Eggs Puzzle Park

Animal Fun

Animal Colours

Baby Animals

What is it?

Driving Tests

Reading Eggs Posters

The wh Sound

Vowel and Consonant sounds

Reading Eggs Library Books

My Program Books

Teacher Toolkit

- Spelling Activities
- Grammar Lessons
- Comprehension Lessons
- Targeting Comprehension Interactively
- Targeting Text Interactively

Reading Eggs Apps

Eggy Vocab

Eggy Snap

Eggy Phonics 3

Critter Card

Frankie the frog

Blends

Lesson 106 • Worksheet 1

Name

Initial sounds 1

1 Say the word for each picture. Complete the beginning sounds.

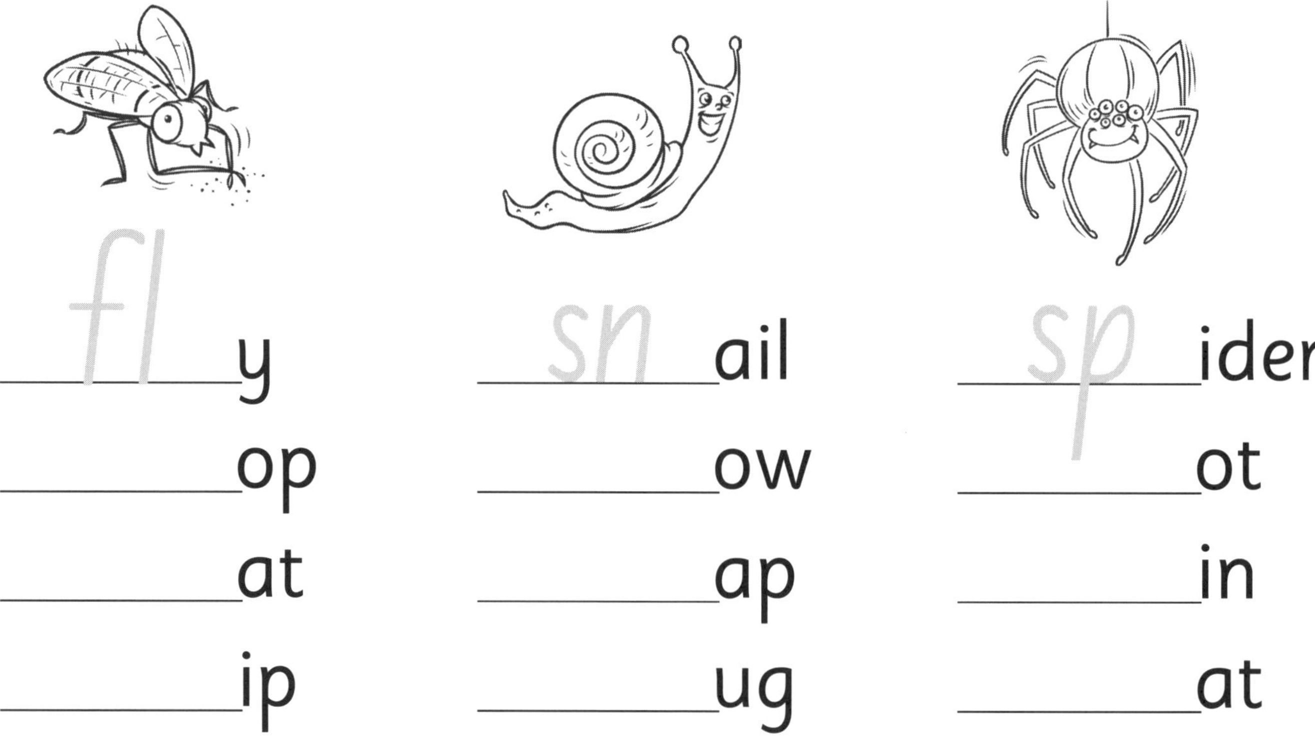

2 Write the words in the correct flag.

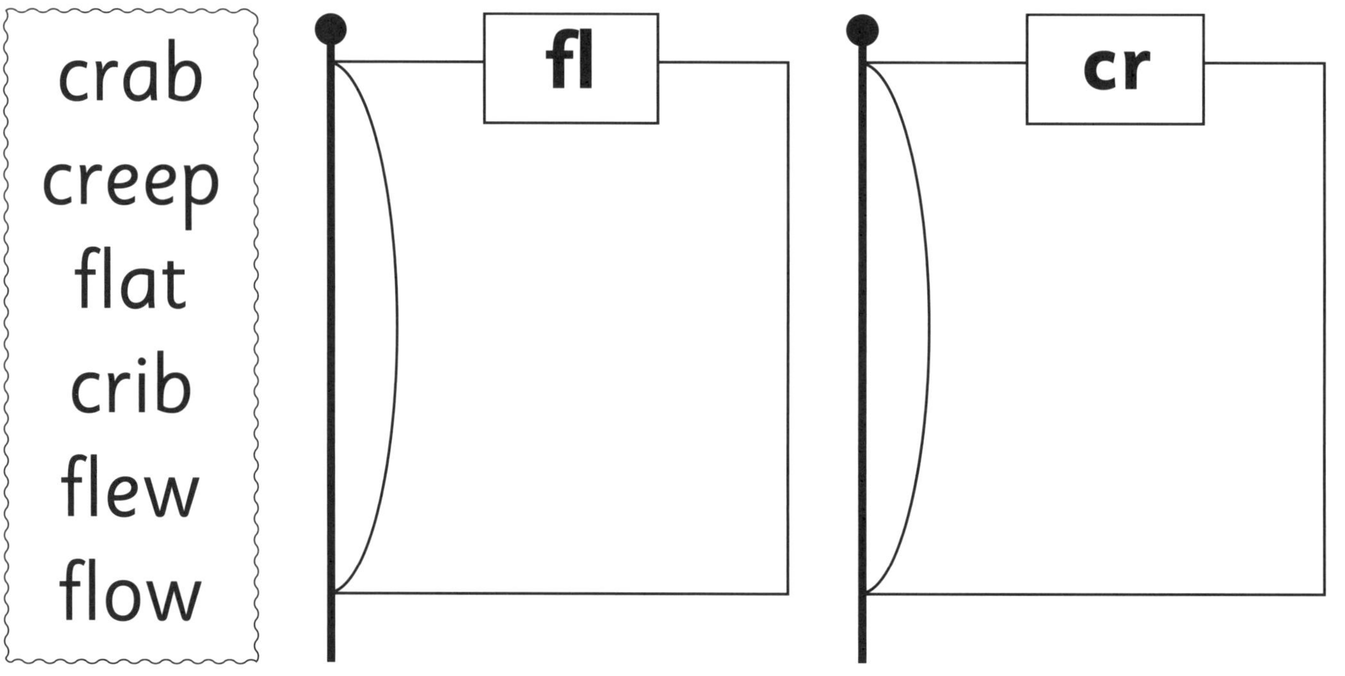

Name

Blends

Lesson 106 • Worksheet 2

Read and write

1 Complete the sentences.

fr gr cr

Fred is a big, ______een tree ______og.

Fred likes to ______unch on ______ubs.

He is a happy ______og!

2 Draw.

a grotty grub grinning

a green tree frog creeping up a tree trunk

3 Circle the odd one out.

flap press flat flan flag

Blends

Lesson 106 · Worksheet 3

Name

Initial sounds 2

1 Say the word for each picture. Complete the beginning sounds.

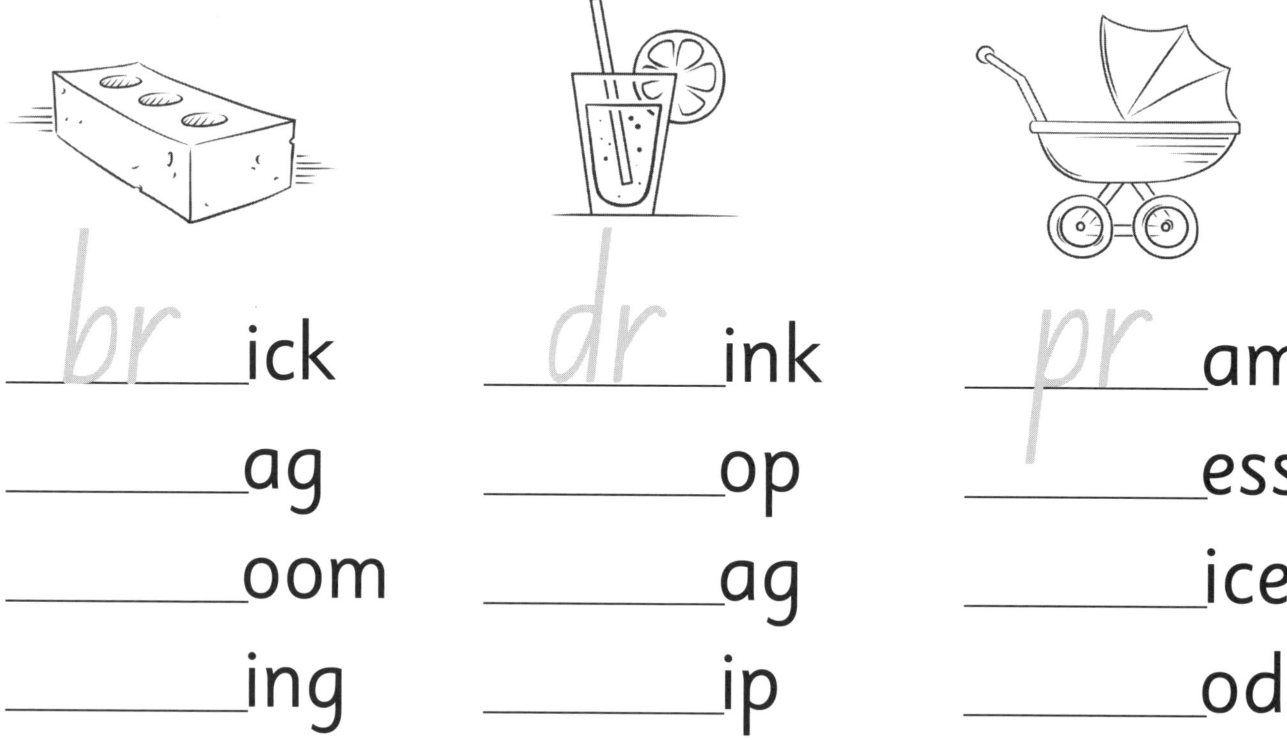

2 Write the words on the correct brick.

green
grub
tree
grab
trap
trip

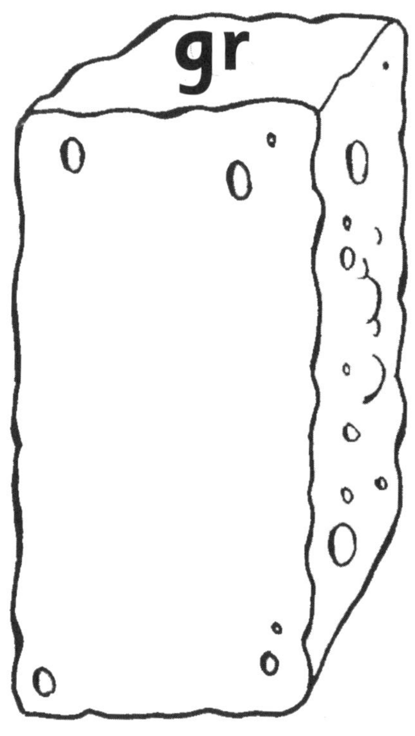

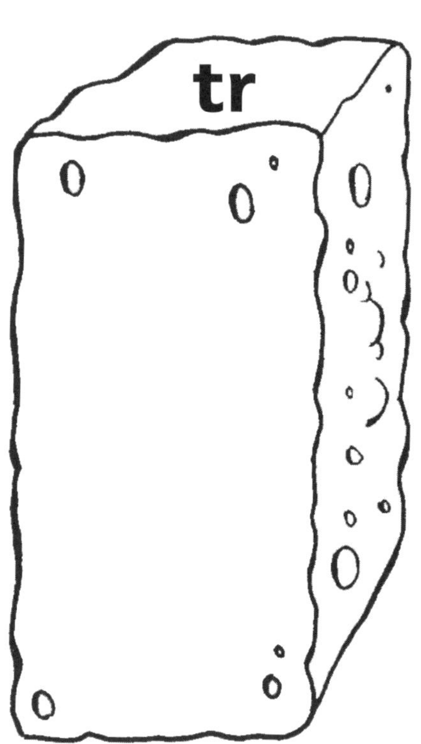

Name

Blends

Lesson 106 · Worksheet 4

Check

1 Power words. Join the letters to make a word.

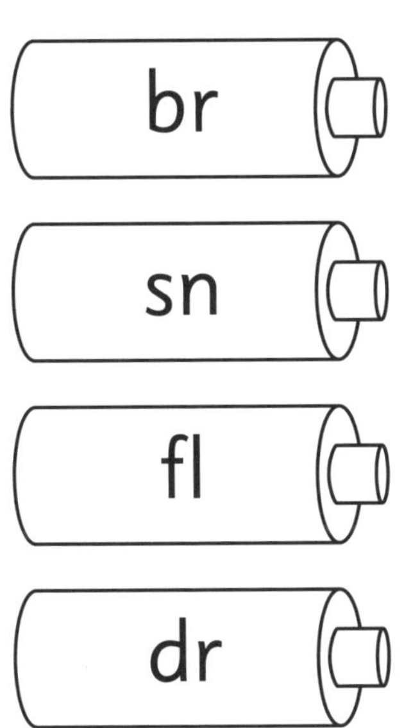

2 Colour the correct word. Cross out the wrong word.

I like to [drink] [snap] pink milk.

There are lots of [stones] [stars] in the sky.

He used a [crow] [broom] to sweep the floor.

3 Guess the word by its shape.

spot prop trot

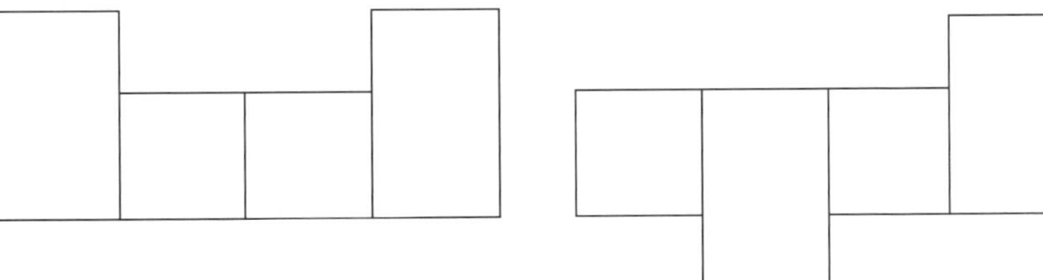

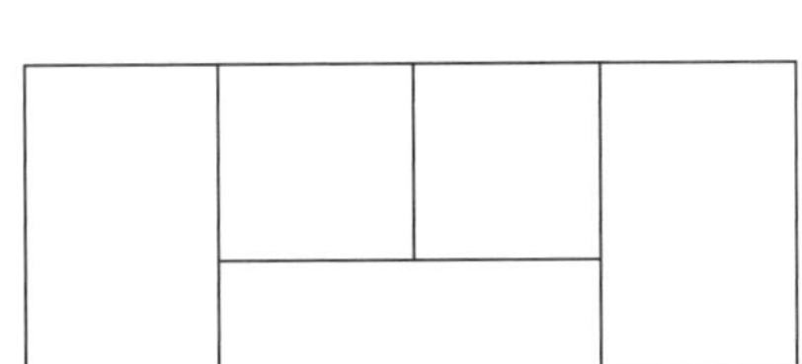

Lesson 107 the sound **ea**

Learning objectives

Children will:

- recognise that the digraph ea makes the sound /ee/.
- read and write ea words.
- identify words which have opposite meanings.

Australian Curriculum Content Descriptions

Sound and letter knowledge

ACELA1457 replace sounds in spoken words; recognise words that start with a given sound, end with a given sound, have a given medial sound, rhyme with a given word

ACELA1458 recognise sound-letter matches including common vowel and consonant digraphs and consonant blends

ACELA1459 recognise that letters can have more than one sound; recognise sounds that can be produced by different letters

Expressing and developing ideas

ACELA1435 learn that word order in sentences is important for meaning

ACELA1438 build word families using onset and rime

ACELA1455 build word families from common morphemes; using morphemes to read words

ACELA1778 write one-syllable words containing known blends; know that regular one-syllable words are made up of letters and common letter clusters that correspond to the sounds heard, and how to use visual memory to write high-frequency words

Interpreting, analysing and evaluating

ACELY1659 combine knowledge of context, meaning, grammar and phonics to decode text; recognise most high-frequency sight words when reading text

Sight words

down, up

Word families

leaf, seal, meal, heal, real, squeal, eat, meat, seat, heat, neat, treat, east, feast, beast, yeast, least, team, dream, steam, beam, cream, scream, peach, beach, pea, sea, clean, mean, leave, peace, squeak

Vocabulary words

sleep, waves, blue, pink, green, sitting, eating, looking, lovely, asleep, awake, clean, dirty, full, empty, dark, light

Extra assistance

The use of *ea* to make the */ee/* sound can be confusing for students. There is no rule for when to use one or the other, so students just have to learn these words. Here is a rhyme to help students remember how to pronounce words with a vowel digraph:

When two vowels go walking,
the first one does the talking.

This means that generally a vowel digraph uses the long sound of the first letter – *ee* in *beat*, *ay* in *pain*, *oo* in *blue*, eye in *pie*, *oh* in *boat*.

Classroom activities

Word Wheel

Give each student two circles of cardboard, one larger than the other, joined through the centre with a split pin. On the visible edge of the larger circle write the consonant letters *b, h, m, p, s, t* and the blend *st*. On the smaller circle write the rimes *eal*, *eat*, *east*, *ean*, *eam*, *each*, so they will match up with the outer letters and make words. Have students turn the circles and write out the words they make.

Reading Eggs Lesson sequence	TEACH Content and skills	PRACTISE Children will:	APPLY
Hear: *Animated Lesson*	Recognise that *ea* and *ee* both make the sound */ee/* with the song *Driving too fast.*	identify the digraphs *ea* and *ee* in isolation and in words. Make *ea* words.	**Worksheet 1** Phonics 1
Write: *Extra Word, Write the Banner*	Recognise correct word order for a sentence.	put the words in order and cross out the extra words.	**Worksheet 2** Vocabulary
Find: *Snowman, Buzzy's Word Machine*	Recognise a given word. Identify word endings.	find the given word in a group. Match the word to its ending.	**Worksheet 3** Phonics 2
Vocabulary: *Today's Topic Words, Power Words, Opposite Pairs, City Zoo, Make a Monster*	Build vocabulary skills: Recognise key vocabulary. Identify words with opposite meanings.	match pictures to words. Select pairs of cards which are opposites. Read and follow instructions.	**Worksheet 4** Check
Read: *Book*	Read aloud book.	listen, follow the reading and read along.	**Reading Eggs Story book** A Green Pea

Classroom activities

Find the Letter

Give each student three cards with the sounds *ea, oo* and *ie*. Say a word and ask students to listen to the vowel sound. They should hold up the card which makes that sound. Use clear, recognisable words such as: *beat, boot, pie.*

Related Reading Eggs Activities, Interactives, Songs and Books

Driving Tests

Test 13

Sight words: read

Letters and sounds: dream

Content words: teaspoon

Spelling Bank

Reading Eggs Puzzle Park

Colour Code

Do it

Opposites

Do You Know?

Music Café

Driving too fast

Reading Eggs Posters

The ea Sound

Reading Eggs Library Books

My Program Books

Teacher Toolkit

- Spelling Activities
- Grammar Lessons
- Comprehension Lessons
- Targeting Comprehension Interactively
- Targeting Text Interactively

Reading Eggs Apps

Eggy Snap

Eggy Phonics 3

Eggy Vocab

Critter Card

Beaky squeak

ea

Lesson 107 • Worksheet 1

Name

Phonics 1

1 Use the little green pea's **ea** to make words. Write each word. Read each word.

2 Colour the leaf if it has the letters **ea**.

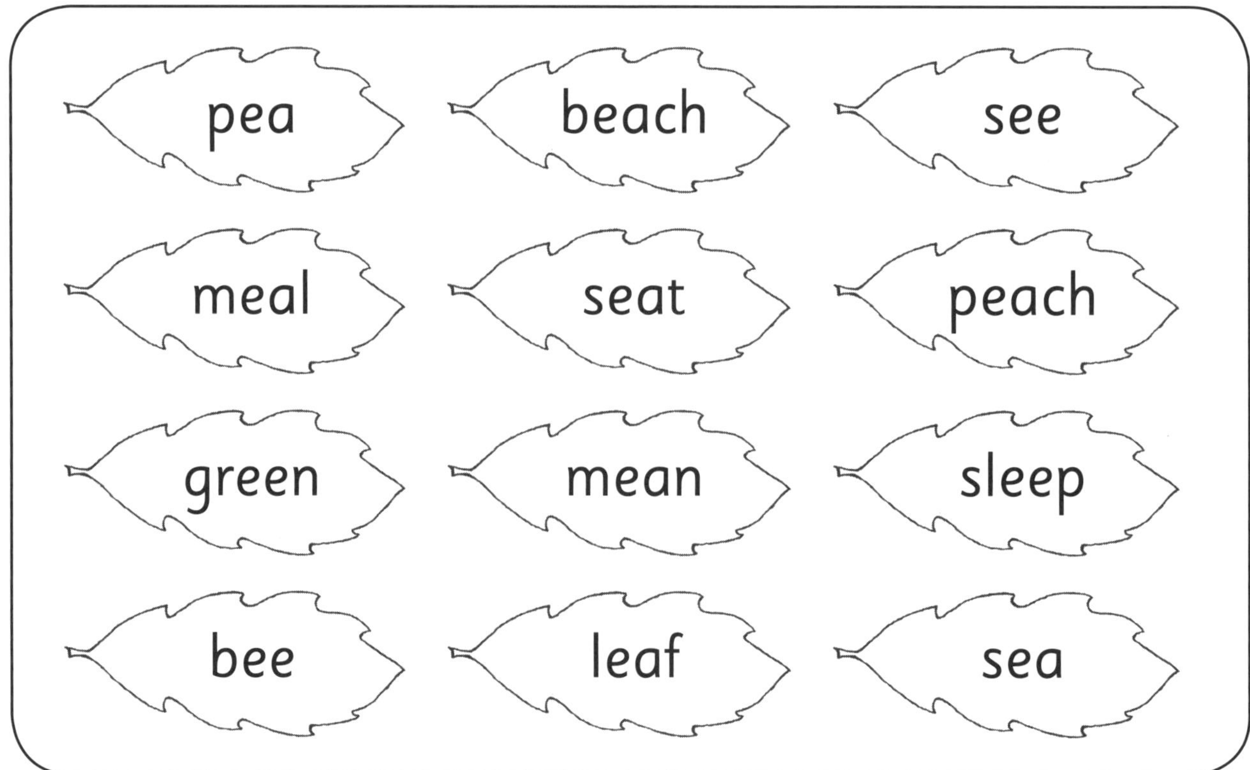

Name

Vocabulary

1 Join each word to a picture.

2 Read the clue. Write the word.

I am small, round and green. You can eat me. I am a p__________.	I am a big, scary monster. I am a b__________.
I am next to the sea. I have sand. I am a b__________.	I am green. I grow on trees. I am a l__________.

ea

Lesson 107 · Worksheet 3

Name

Phonics 2

1 Complete the labels.

ee ea

gr_______n

_______ts

sw_______t

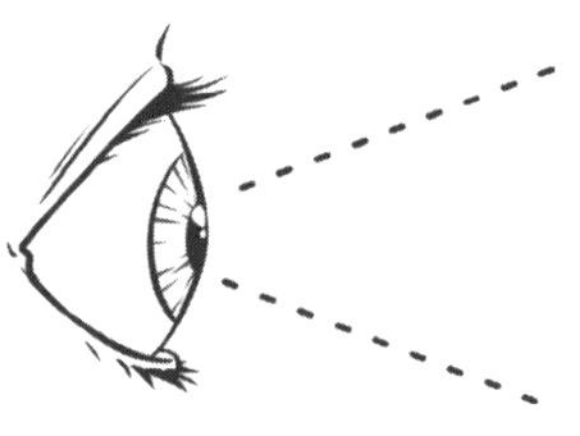

s_______s

dr_______m

m_______n

2 Complete the sentences.

ea ee e

W____ can s_________
Zee the b_________.
H____ is on a
gr_________n l_________f.

Name

Check

ea

Lesson 107 • Worksheet 4

1 Guess the word by its shape. Write each letter in a box.

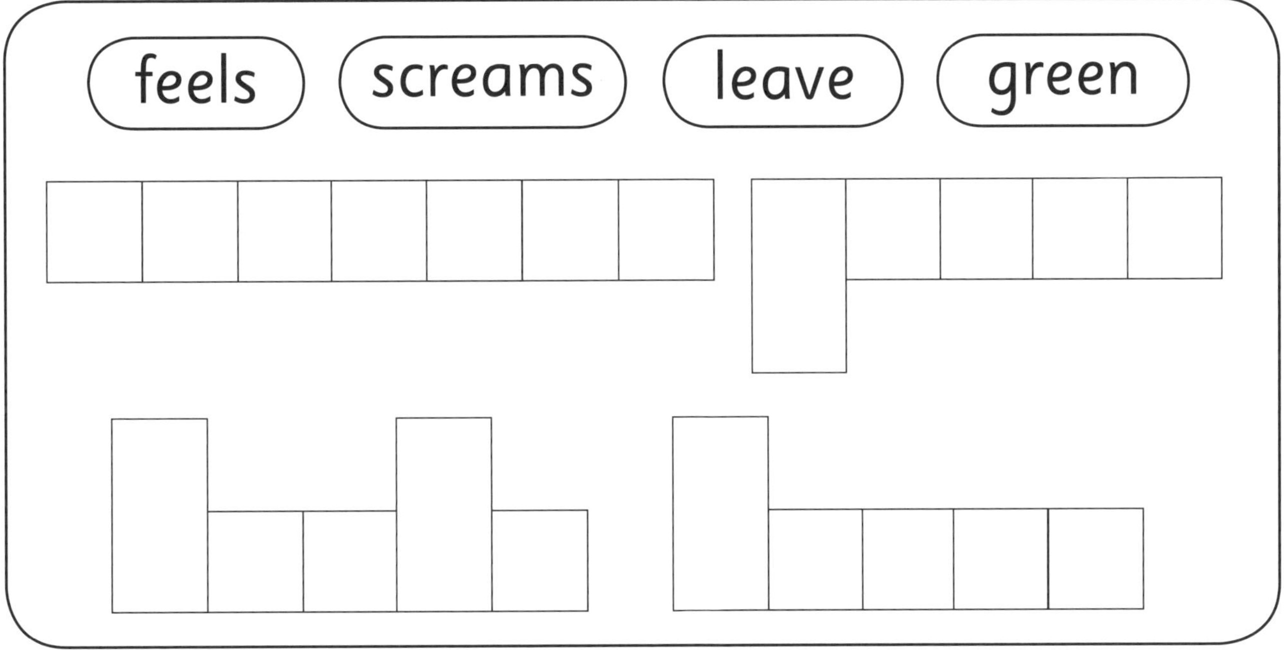

2 Colour the correct word. Cross out the wrong word.

The little green [pea] [bee] is very [meat] [sweet].

She is [meeting] [eating] a [beach] [peach].

The [mean] [meal] seal [seats] [eats] the pea.

3 Colour the **long e** words.

meet sea been

fell met heat

Lesson 108 the sound **u-e**

Learning objectives

Children will:

- identify the rimes that can be made with u-e.
- read and write u-e words.

Australian Curriculum Content Descriptions

Sound and letter knowledge

ACELA1457 replace sounds in spoken words; recognise words that start with a given sound, end with a given sound, have a given medial sound, rhyme with a given word

ACELA1458 recognise sound-letter matches including common vowel and consonant digraphs and consonant blends

ACELA1459 recognise that letters can have more than one sound; recognise sounds that can be produced by different letters

Expressing and developing ideas

ACELA1435 learn that word order in sentences is important for meaning

ACELA1438 build word families using onset and rime

ACELA1778 write one-syllable words containing known blends; learn an increasing number of high-frequency sight words recognised in shared texts and in texts being read independently; know that regular one-syllable words are made up of letters and common letter clusters that correspond to the sounds heard, and how to use visual memory to write high-frequency words

Interpreting, analysing and evaluating

ACELY1659 combine knowledge of context, meaning, grammar and phonics to decode text; recognise most high-frequency sight words when reading text

Word families

duke, use, fuse, tube, cute, tune, cube, June, mute, flute, dune, blue

Vocabulary words

worried, perfect

Extra assistance

The *u-e* digraph can be pronounced as *yoo* as well as occasionally the long *oo* sound. There is no clear rule, although you generally hear the *oo* sound after a blend. The *yoo* sound occurs in *duke*, *tube* and *fuse*. The *oo* sound can be heard in *dude, truce* and *flute*. Be aware of pronunciations which are incorrect in students who speak another language, for example, *tube* should be *t-yoo-b* rather than *toob*. Give students plenty of oral practice.

Classroom activities

Find the Start

Give students a list of words with the first letter missing. Ask them to figure out which letter could be the starter for all the given words, for example:

_ute _ube _lue _ure

Discuss the answers as a class. Was there more than one possible answer?

Reading Eggs Lesson sequence	TEACH Content and skills	PRACTISE Children will:	APPLY
Hear: *Animated Lesson*	Introduce the sound *u-e* with a variety of consonants.	identify the letters that make the *long u* sound. Make *u-e* words.	**Worksheet 1** Word families 1
Write: *Rocket Launch, Bird Words*	Identify sounds in a word and make the word. Recognise correct word order for a sentence.	select the correct onset and rime to make the word. Choose the correct words to make a sentence.	**Worksheet 2** Read and write
Find: *Driving Trucks, What's Missing?, Frog Logs*	Recognise a given word. Identify the missing sound in a word.	find the given word in a group. Choose the correct letter to make the word.	**Worksheet 3** Word families 2
Vocabulary: *Today's Topic Words, Words per Minute*	Build vocabulary skills: Recognise key vocabulary.	match pictures to words.	**Worksheet 4** Check
Read: *Book Ends, Q & A, Book*	Read sentences using basic vocabulary. Comprehend the meaning of a text. Read aloud book.	choose a word to finish the sentence. Read the text and answer the questions. Listen, follow the reading and read along.	**Reading Eggs Story book** Duke Plays the Flute

Classroom activities

Long or Short?

Place two boxes on the floor labelled Long and Short. Discuss the long and short vowel sounds with the class. Have a pile of flashcards and ask students one at a time to choose a card, read the word aloud and decide which box it should go in. Discuss their choice as a class.

Related Reading Eggs Activities, Interactives, Songs and Books

Spelling Bank

Fish

Lesson 47

Focus sound words: tube, cube, cute, flute, June, tune, use

Challenge: excuse, refuse

Reading Eggs Puzzle Park

What is it?

Animal Fun

Colour Code

Driving Tests

Reading Eggs Posters

The u-e Sound

Good Readers

Reading Eggs Library Books

My Program Books

Teacher Toolkit

- Spelling Activities
- Grammar Lessons
- Comprehension Lessons
- Targeting Comprehension Interactively
- Targeting Text Interactively

Reading Eggs Apps

Eggy Snap

Eggy Phonics 2

Critter Card

Duke the June bug

u-e

Lesson 108 • Worksheet 1

Name

Word families 1

1 Trace and write.

2 Use the letters on the fridge to complete the words.

3 Write the word on the correct tube.

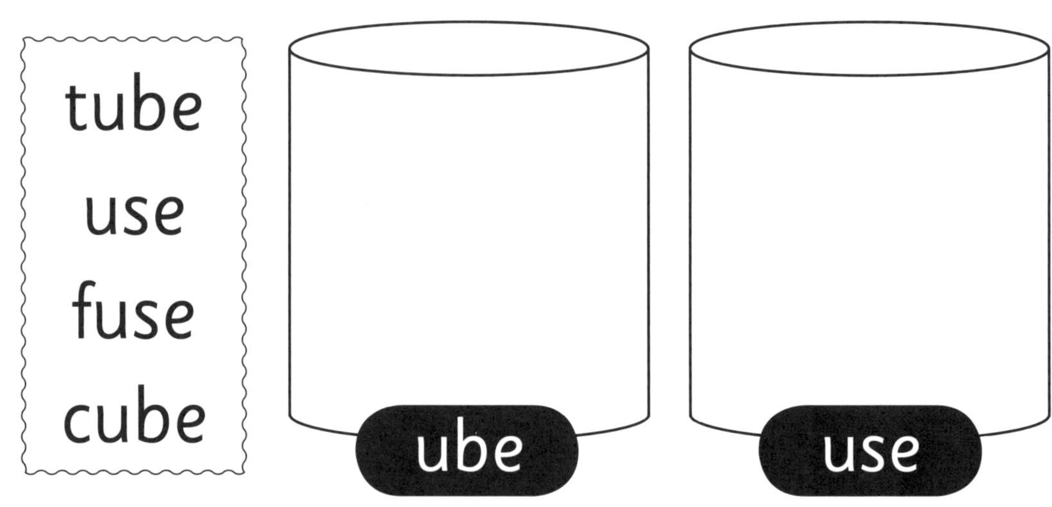

Name

Read and write

1 Circle the word that rhymes with the picture.

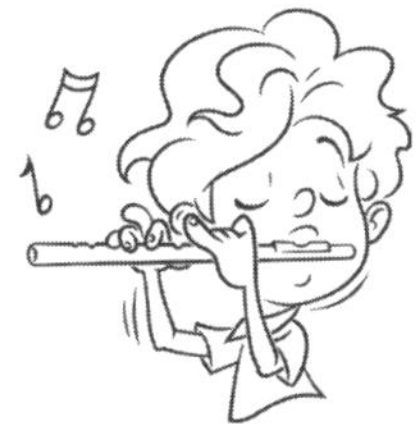	pet	cute	shop	bug
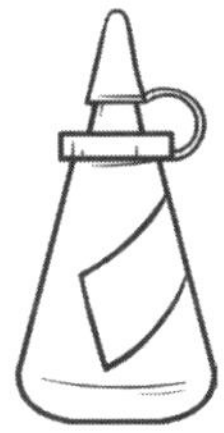	look	bird	blue	wing
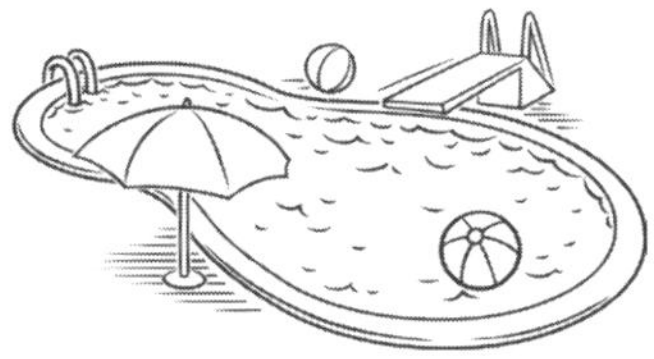	dog	spike	cake	rule
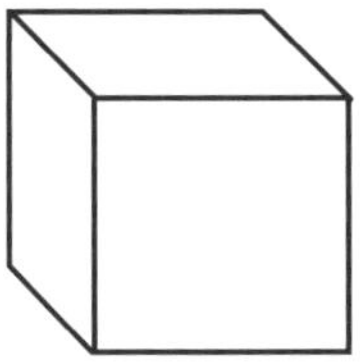	tube	fun	mice	store

2 Complete the sentences.

use cute tune

Look at that __________ little puppy!

She can play a __________ on her flute.

You can __________ my pencils.

u-e

Lesson 108 · Worksheet 3

Name

Word families 2

1 Use Duke the June bug's **une** to make new words. Write each word. Read each word.

2 Join each sound to the **ute** machine. Write each word you make.

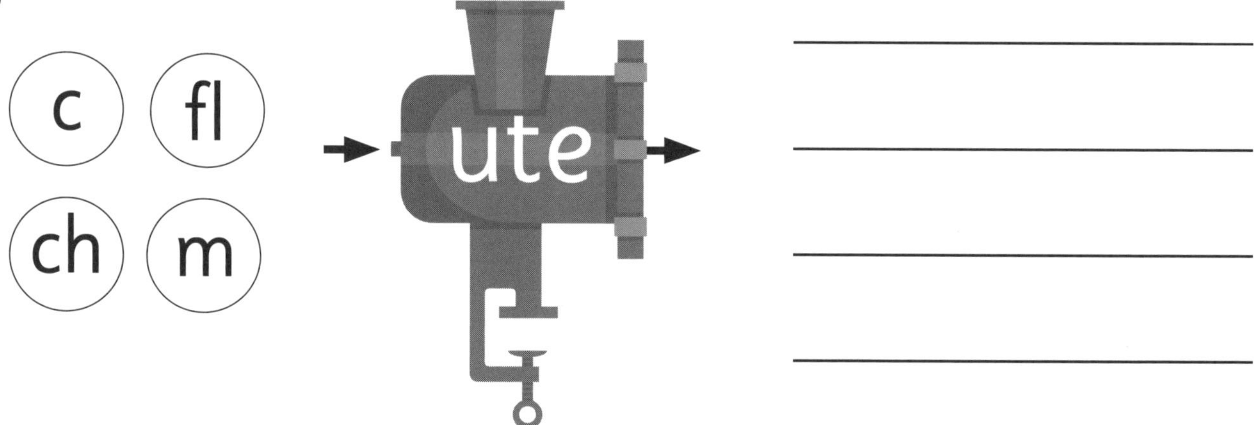

3 Write the word in the correct box.

flute dune
mute tune

ute

Name

Check

u-e

Lesson 108 • Worksheet 4

1 Join the word to Duke if it makes a **long u** sound.

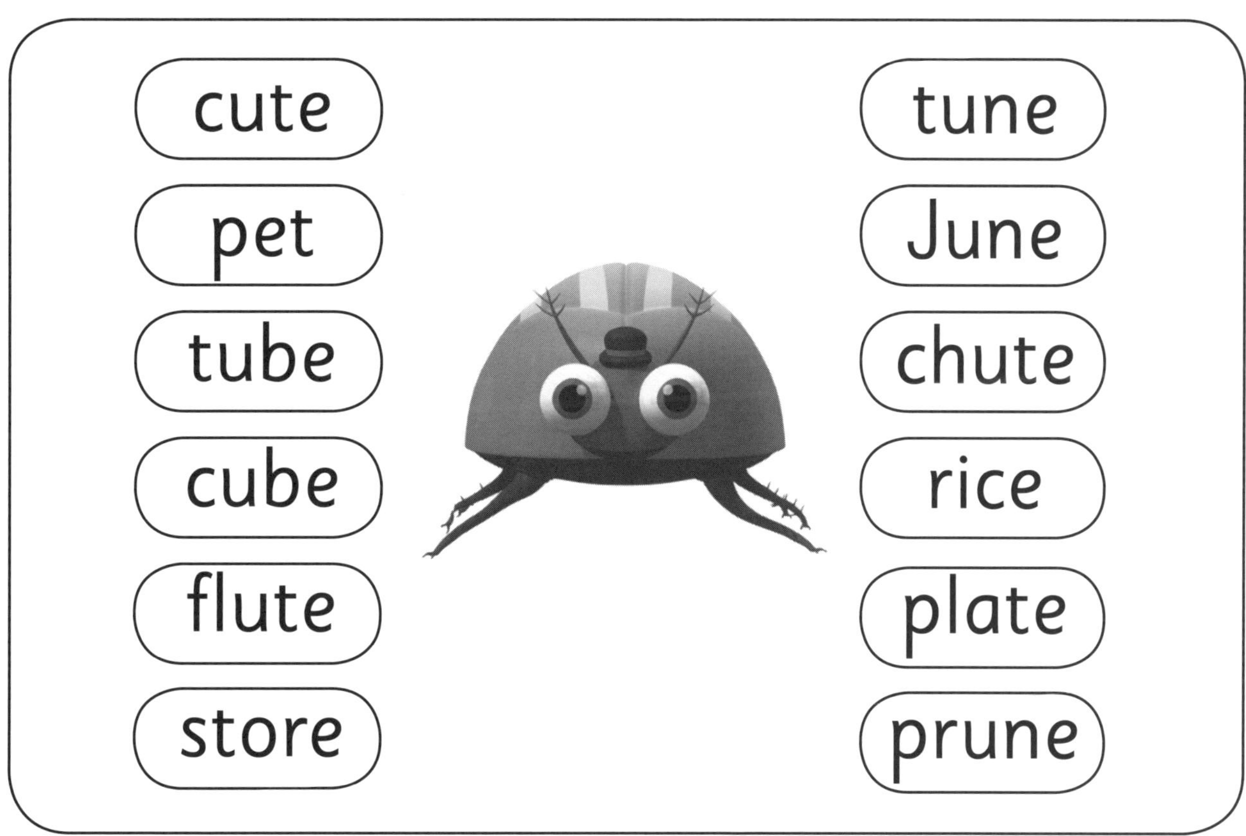

2 Complete the sentences.

cube flute cute

Duke liked to play the __________.

The Icy mice jumped onto a __________.

The __________ little Catty cakes had big ears.

Lesson 109 the sound **er**

Learning objectives

Children will:

- identify the word ending er.
- read and write words that end with er.
- add er to name occupations.

Australian Curriculum Content Descriptions

Sound and letter knowledge

ACELA1457 recognise words that start with a given sound, end with a given sound, have a given medial sound, rhyme with a given word

ACELA1459 recognise that letters can have more than one sound; recognise sounds that can be produced by different letters

Expressing and developing ideas

ACELA1435 learn that word order in sentences is important for meaning

ACELA1455 build word families from common morphemes; use morphemes to read words

ACELA1778 learn an increasing number of high-frequency sight words recognised in shared texts and in texts being read independently; know that regular one-syllable words are made up of letters and common letter clusters that correspond to the sounds heard, and how to use visual memory to write high-frequency words

Interpreting, analysing and evaluating

ACELY1659 combine knowledge of context, meaning, grammar and phonics to decode text; recognise most high-frequency sight words when reading text

Sight words

anything, everything

Word families

mother, badger, her, sister, father, brother, farmer, painter, gardener, banker, builder, printer, teacher, plumber, cleaner, helper, bigger, better, water, super

Vocabulary words

leaky, clean, build, house, room, sink, plant, green, hot, cold, garden, drip

Extra assistance

Students have a variety of word endings to learn in English – *ed, ing, s*, and so on. Each word ending changes the meaning or usage of the word. The ending *er* can change an object or place or activity into the name of an occupation – *paint* becomes *painter*, *farm* becomes *farmer*, *clean* becomes *cleaner*. It can also change an adjective into a comparative – *big* and *bigger*. Remind students that a comparative is comparing two things, for example: Today is hotter than yesterday.

Classroom activities

Using er

Put a list of words on the board and ask students if you can put *er* at the end of each word. Use singular and plural nouns, verbs and adjectives, a few of which do not work with *er*. Ask one pupil at a time to choose a word which works, write it on the board and give its meaning. See if the class can explain why some words work and some don't.

Reading Eggs Lesson sequence	TEACH Content and skills	PRACTISE Children will:	APPLY
Hear: *Animated Lesson*	Introduce the sound *er* and its use at the end of a word.	identify the *er* sound in words. Add *er* to the ends of words.	**Worksheet 1** Ending sound
Write: *Write the Banner*	Recognise correct word order for a sentence.	choose the correct words to make a sentence.	**Worksheet 2** Read and write
Find: *Dragon Fire, Buzzy's Word Machine, Frog Logs, Hairy Heads, Pack the Shelves*	Recognise a given word. Identify word endings. Select the correct word to complete the sentence.	find the given word in a group. Match the word to its ending. Choose the word which completes the sentence.	**Worksheet 3** Vocabulary
Vocabulary: *Today's Topic Words, Power Words*	Build vocabulary skills: Recognise key vocabulary.	match pictures to words.	**Worksheet 4** Check
Read: *Q & A, Book*	Comprehend the meaning of a text. Read aloud book.	read the text and answer the questions. Listen, follow the reading and read along.	**Reading Eggs Story book** Bigger Better Baxter

Classroom activities

Comparisons

Write this sentence on the board: An elephant is bigger than a mouse.

Discuss the concept of comparing things based on one attribute and the use of adjectives with *er* on the end to write comparisons. Brainstorm a list of comparatives and ask each student to write a comparison of their own.

Related Reading Eggs Activities, Interactives, Songs and Books

Driving Tests

Test 8

Sight words: after, other

Letters and sounds: sink, hot

Content words: sister, grandmother, brother, mother, daughter, father, grandfather, granddaughter

Reading Eggs Puzzle Park

Describe it

Name it

Do it

Do You Know?

Spelling Bank

Reading Eggs Posters

Suffixes -er and -est

Reading Eggs Library Books

My Program Books

Teacher Toolkit

- Spelling Activities
- Grammar Lessons
- Comprehension Lessons
- Targeting Comprehension Interactively
- Targeting Text Interactively

Reading Eggs Apps

Eggy Sight words

Eggy Phonics 3

Critter Card

Baxter the badger

er

Name

Ending sound

Lesson 109 • Worksheet 1

1 Use Baxter the badger's **er** to make new words. Write each word. Read each word.

2 Colour the words that end in **er**.

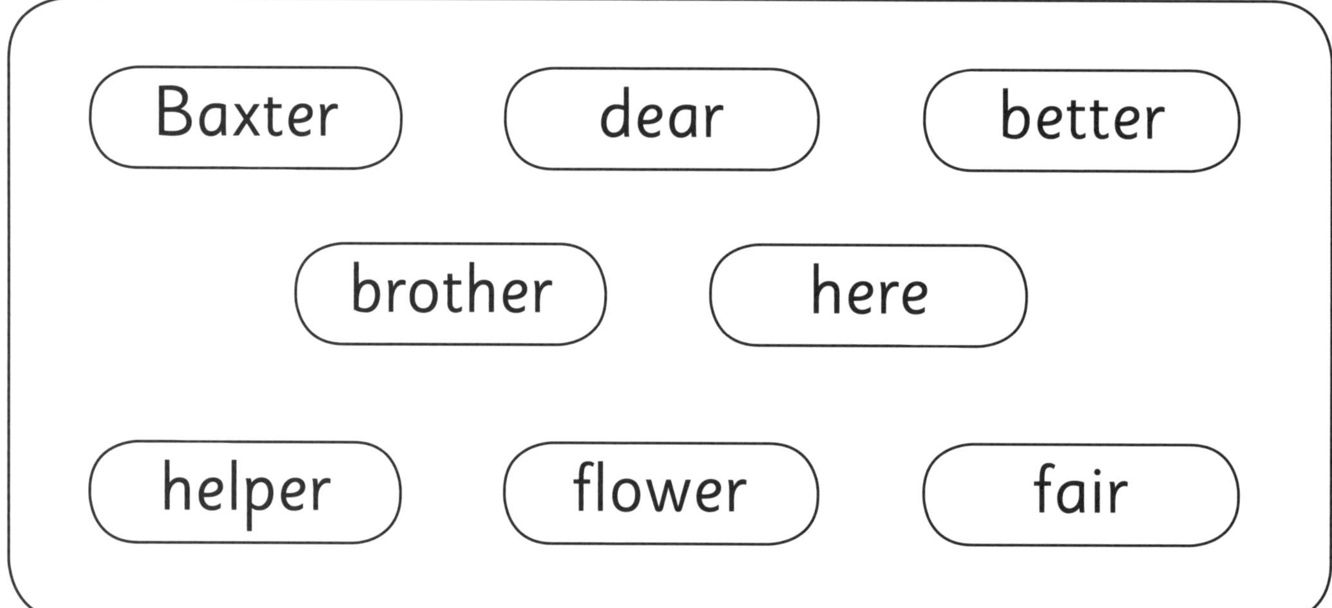

Name

er

Read and write

Lesson 109 · Worksheet 2

1 Complete the sentences.

better badger plumber

Baxter the ____________ can fix the leaky tap.

"Today I will be a ____________," he said.

Baxter put a bigger and ____________ tap on the sink.

2 Write a sentence using Baxter's word.

er

Name

Vocabulary

Lesson 109 • Worksheet 3

1 Join each word to a picture.

2 Read the clue. Write the word.

I fix broken pipes. I am a p______________.	I look after plants. I am a g______________.
This word is the opposite to **hotter**. c______________	This word is the opposite to **sister**. b______________

Name

Check

er

Lesson 109 • Worksheet 4

1 Join Baxter to the **er** words.

2 Guess the word by its shape. Write each word in a box.

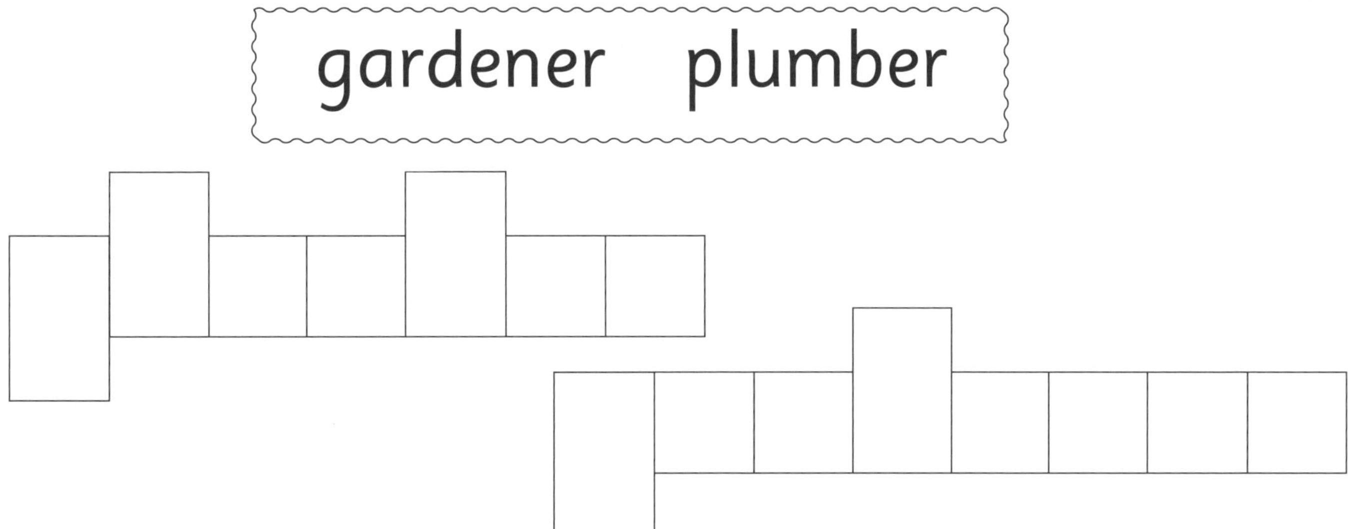

3 Write the words in the correct order.

Baxter be Today will builder. a

Lesson 110 blends

Learning objectives

Children will:

- review using initial blends.
- recognise and use adjectives.

Australian Curriculum Content Descriptions

Sound and letter knowledge

ACELA1457 recognise words that start with a given sound, end with a given sound, have a given medial sound, rhyme with a given word

ACELA1458 recognise sound-letter matches including common vowel and consonant digraphs and consonant blends

ACELA1459 recognise that letters can have more than one sound; recognise sounds that can be produced by different letters

Expressing and developing ideas

ACELA1435 learn that word order in sentences is important for meaning

ACELA1455 build word families from common morphemes (for example play, plays)

ACELA1778 write one-syllable words containing known blends; know that regular one-syllable words are made up of letters and common letter clusters that correspond to the sounds heard, and how to use visual memory to write high-frequency words

Interpreting, analysing and evaluating

ACELY1659 combine knowledge of context, meaning, grammar and phonics to decode text; recognise most high-frequency sight words when reading text

Word families

dress, train, smile, clock, plug, flower, brick, cloud, ground, drank, plum, tree, trunk, drink, sky

Vocabulary words

pretty, soft, hard, crunchy, squishy, strong, weak, flat, glossy, small, big, little, cold, hot, wet, dry, happy, sad, tall, short, plump, sweet, white, grey, brown, green, blue, wept, leaves, rain

Extra assistance

A good way to explain adjectives to younger students is that they are the words that tell us how something looks, sounds, smells, tastes and feels to touch. They are also words that tell us how something makes us feel. Make a list of adjectives to go on the wall for the class to refer to when writing. Under each of the five senses, brainstorm some basic describing words and then add some more interesting ones.

Classroom activities

Bingo!

Give students a laminated board with ten squares on it. Ask them to write a word in each square from a list of adjectives (use whiteboard markers). Say words from the list. Students put a cross on that word on their board. First one to ten calls out 'bingo' and wins!

Reading Eggs Lesson sequence	TEACH Content and skills	PRACTISE Children will:	APPLY
Hear: *Animated Lesson*	Review blends for the beginnings of words.	make words by combining blends and word endings.	**Worksheet 1** Phonics
Write: *Bird Words*	Recognise correct word order for a sentence.	choose the correct words to make a sentence.	**Worksheet 2** Reading
Find: *Shooting Stars*	Recognise a given word.	find the given word in a group.	**Worksheet 3** Vocabulary
Vocabulary: *Today's Topic Words, Word Whiz, Opposite Pairs, Bubble Popper, Words per Minute*	Build vocabulary skills: Recognise key vocabulary. Identify words with opposite meanings.	match pictures to words. Tap on the word being said and put in a sentence. Select pairs of cards which are opposites. Read and follow instructions.	**Worksheet 4** Check
Read: *Book Ends, Q & A, Book*	Read sentences using basic vocabulary. Comprehend the meaning of a text. Read aloud book.	choose a word to finish the sentence. Read the text and answer the questions. Listen, follow the reading and read along.	**Reading Eggs Story book** The Plum Tree

Classroom activities

Word Pairs

Give half the class a blend on a card. Give the other half of the class a word ending on a card. Ask the children to find a partner to make a word and sit together. Ask each blend person to write their word on the board. Have the pairs swap cards and play again – they must make a different word this time. (Make sure each blend matches with at least 2 endings and vice versa.)

Related Reading Eggs Activities, Interactives, Songs and Books

Spelling Bank

Elephants

Lesson 40

Focus sound words: drag, dress, drop, trap, trip, trot

Challenge: dragonfly, traffic

Reading Eggs Puzzle Park

Describe it

Sense it

Colour Code

Teddy Bear

Driving Tests

Reading Eggs Posters

Adjectives

Description

Reading Eggs Library Books

My Program Books

Teacher Toolkit

- Spelling Activities
- Grammar Lessons
- Comprehension Lessons
- Targeting Comprehension Interactively
- Targeting Text Interactively

Reading Eggs Apps

Eggy Phonics 3

Eggy Vocab

Critter Card

Bill the buffalo

Blends

Lesson 110 · Worksheet 1

Name

Phonics

1 Colour the plum if the word begins with **pl**.

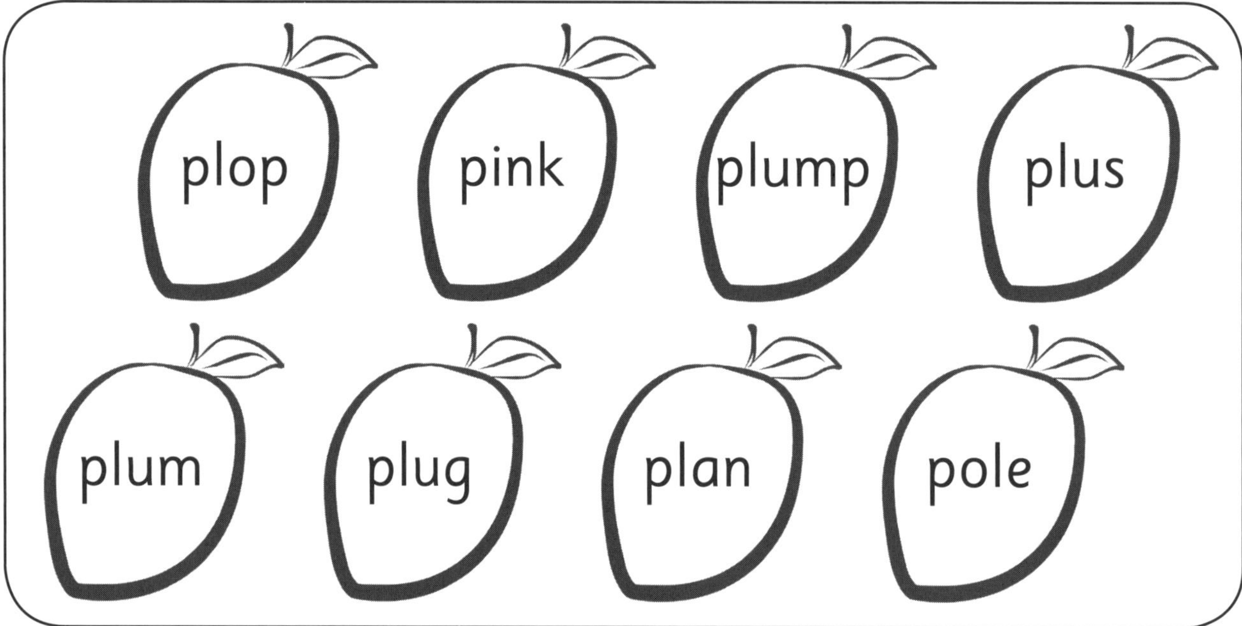

2 Complete the labels. fl dr

Name

Reading

Blends

Lesson 110 • Worksheet 2

1 Read the text.

Flossy was a plum tree. Flossy's trunk was brown and strong. Her flowers were white and pretty. Flossy's leaves were green and glossy.

Underline the correct answer.

2 What was Flossy?

- a plum
- a leaf
- a plum tree
- a flower

3 What colour was Flossy's trunk?

- white
- plum
- green
- brown

4 What were glossy?

- Flossy's flowers
- Flossy's leaves
- Flossy's plums
- Flossy's branches

Blends

Lesson 110 • Worksheet 3

Name

Vocabulary

1 Join each word to a picture.

2 Complete the sentences.

strong crunchy pretty

The rabbit ate a __________ carrot.

A __________ flower grew in the ground.

Flossy the plum tree had a big,

__________ trunk.

Name

Check

Blends

Lesson 110 • Worksheet 4

Join the blends to the endings to make the words.

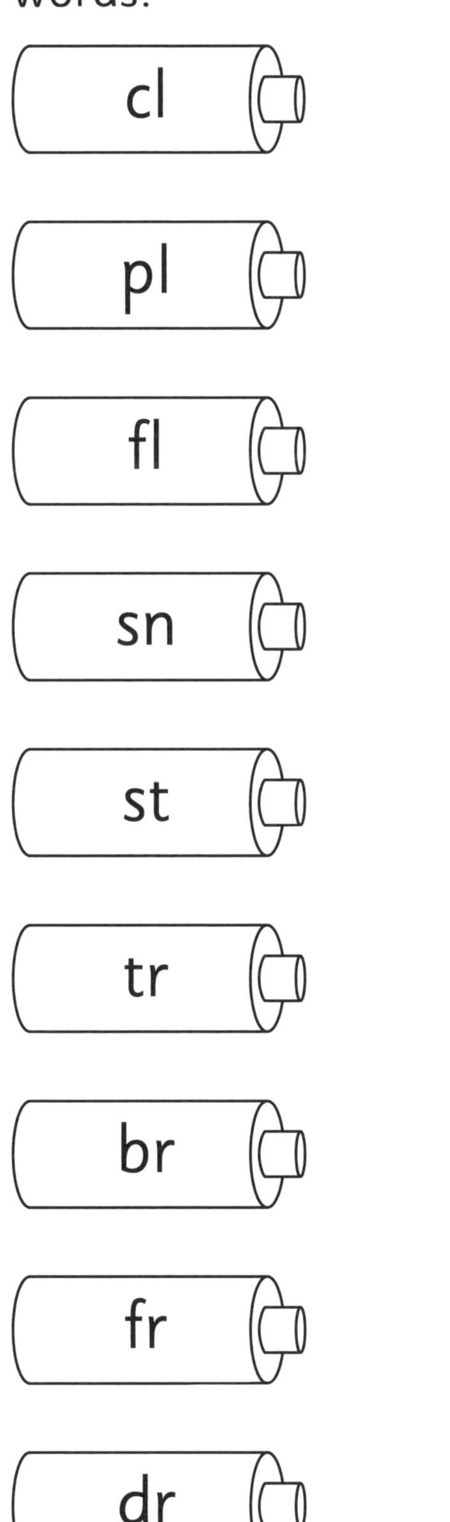

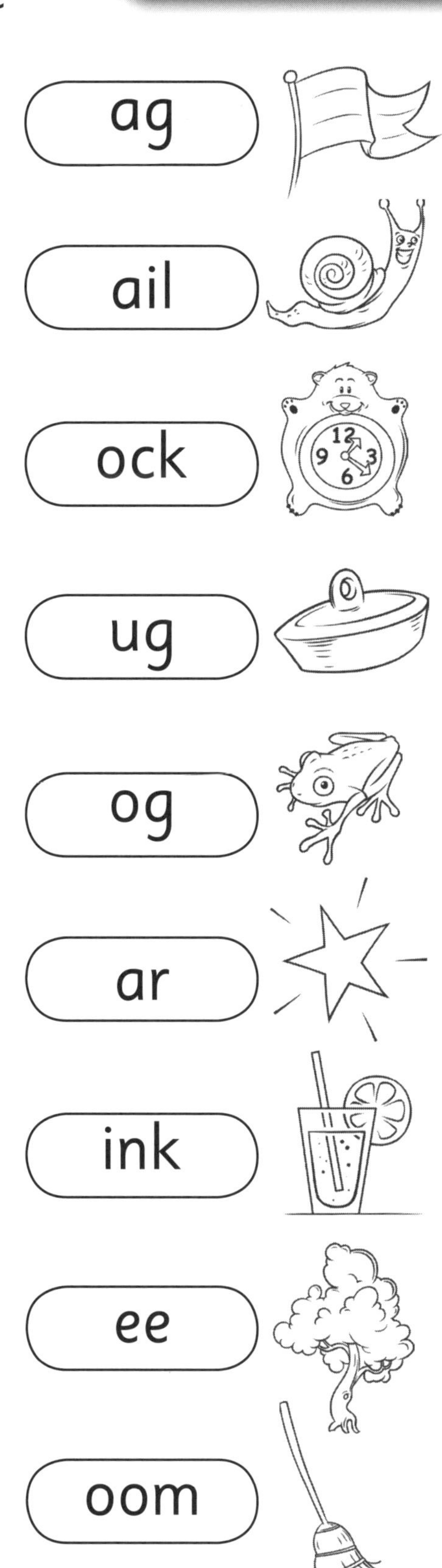

Lesson 111 blends

Learning objectives

Children will:

- review using initial blends.
- read and write words using blends.

Australian Curriculum Content Descriptions

Sound and letter knowledge

ACELA1457 replace sounds in spoken words; recognise words that start with a given sound, end with a given sound, have a given medial sound, rhyme with a given word

ACELA1458 recognise sound-letter matches including common vowel and consonant digraphs and consonant blends

ACELA1459 recognise that letters can have more than one sound; recognise sounds that can be produced by different letters

Expressing and developing ideas

ACELA1435 learn that word order in sentences is important for meaning

ACELA1438 build word families using onset and rime

ACELA1778 write one-syllable words containing known blends; learn an increasing number of high-frequency sight words recognised in shared texts and in texts being read independently; know that regular one-syllable words are made up of letters and common letter clusters that correspond to the sounds heard, and how to use visual memory to write high-frequency words

Interpreting, analysing and evaluating

ACELY1659 combine knowledge of context, meaning, grammar and phonics to decode text; recognise most high-frequency sight words when reading text

Sight words

why

Word families

blob, black, brave, Brad, clap, clean, clock, cry, crab, crack, crash, drive, flash, flower, flag, frown, friends, glass, green, grass, place, pram, prop, scoop, scar, slid, slip, slug, smart, small, snack, stuck, three, track, truck, tree, trip, try

Vocabulary words

happy

Extra assistance

Spanish speaking students may put a vowel sound in front of an initial *s* blend when reading aloud, for example, *slug* may sound like *es-lug*. Russian speakers may use a */z/* sound instead of *s*, eg *slip* may sound like *zlip*. Those from an Asian language background may confuse *l* and *r*. Give students lots of practice hearing and speaking words with a blend. Try some of these tongue twisters:

Six slimy snails slid silently by.

Brad's black bath brush broke.

Classroom activities

How Does it End?

Give students a blend each. Ask them to write as many words as they can that begin with this blend. Write some ending ideas on the board to help them extend their lists – short vowel rimes, digraphs (*ee, oo, ea, ie*), split digraphs (*a-e, i-e, o-e, u-e*) and ending with a consonant digraph (*ch, sh, th*). Discuss their words with the class.

Reading Eggs Lesson sequence	TEACH Content and skills	PRACTISE Children will:	APPLY
Hear: *Animated Lesson*	Review blends for the beginnings of words.	identify the word that has a different initial blend.	**Worksheet 1** Initial sounds
Write: *Rocket Launch, Extra Word, Write the Banner*	Identify sounds in a word and make the word. Recognise correct word order for a sentence.	select the correct onset and rime to make the word. Put the words in order and cross out the extra words.	**Worksheet 2** Vocabulary
Find: *Word Family, Squirter, Snowman, What's Missing?*	Identify the missing sound in a word. Recognise a given word.	choose the correct letter to make the word. Find the given word in a group.	**Worksheet 3** Reading
Vocabulary: *Power Words*	Build vocabulary skills: Recognise key vocabulary.	match pictures to words.	**Worksheet 4** Check
Read: *Book Ends, Book*	Read sentences using basic vocabulary. Read aloud book.	choose a word to finish the sentence. Listen, follow the reading and read along.	**Reading Eggs Story book** Brad the Crab

Classroom activities

Build a House

Put the class in two teams. Think of a word that starts with a blend. Put a series of lines on the board for how many letters are in the word. Each team takes turns guessing a letter. For every letter they get right, draw part of their house – 1 floor, 2 walls, 2 roof lines. When they get a letter right they get another guess. If they can guess the word before it is complete their house gets finished. Which team will end up with the most houses?

Related Reading Eggs Activities, Interactives, Songs and Books

Spelling Bank

Elephants

Lesson 38

Focus sound words: brag, brick, brush, crab, crisp, crop, brown

Challenge: bridge, cricket

Reading Eggs Puzzle Park

Animal Fun

Transport

Making Music

What is it?

Driving Tests

Reading Eggs Posters

Spelling strategies

Before reading

Reading Eggs Library Books

My Program Books

Teacher Toolkit

- Spelling Activities
- Grammar Lessons
- Comprehension Lessons
- Targeting Comprehension Interactively
- Targeting Text Interactively

Reading Eggs Apps

Eggy Snap

Eggy Phonics 3

Eggy Vocab

Critter Card

Brad the crab

Blends

Lesson 111 • Worksheet 1

Name

Initial sounds

1 Follow the track. Write each word you make.

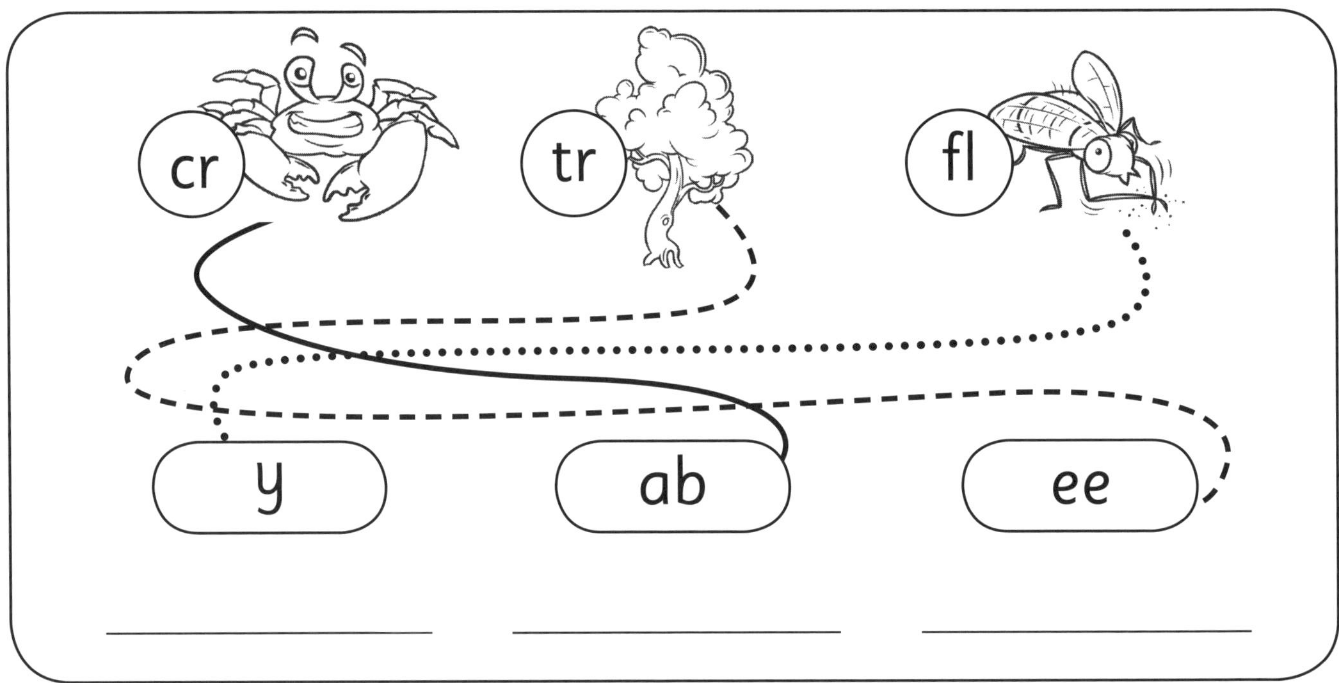

2 Complete each word with **pl**, **br** or **cl**. Draw a picture.

3 Colour **sl** words red. Colour **fr** words yellow.

frog	fridge	slug	fry
slip	slot	free	slam

Name

Vocabulary

Blends

Lesson 111 · Worksheet 2

1 Match each word to a picture.

2 Read the clue. Write the word.

I have branches and green leaves. I am a t____________.	Trains can travel on me. I am a t____________.
I have lots of wheels. I can carry heavy things. I am a t____________.	I live in the sand. I have six legs. I am a c____________.

Reading

Name

Lesson 111 • Worksheet 3

1 Read the text.

Brad is a crab. He wanted to see the world. He wanted to go on a trip. Brad the crab walked up the track.

Underline the correct answer.

2 What is Brad?

- he is a truck
- he is a crab
- he is a track
- he is a trip

3 What did Brad want to see?

- the crab
- the truck
- the world
- the friends

4 Where did Brad walk?

- to the park
- up the track
- to the trees
- on the grass

Name

Check

Blends

Lesson 111 • Worksheet 4

1 Write the words on the correct truck.

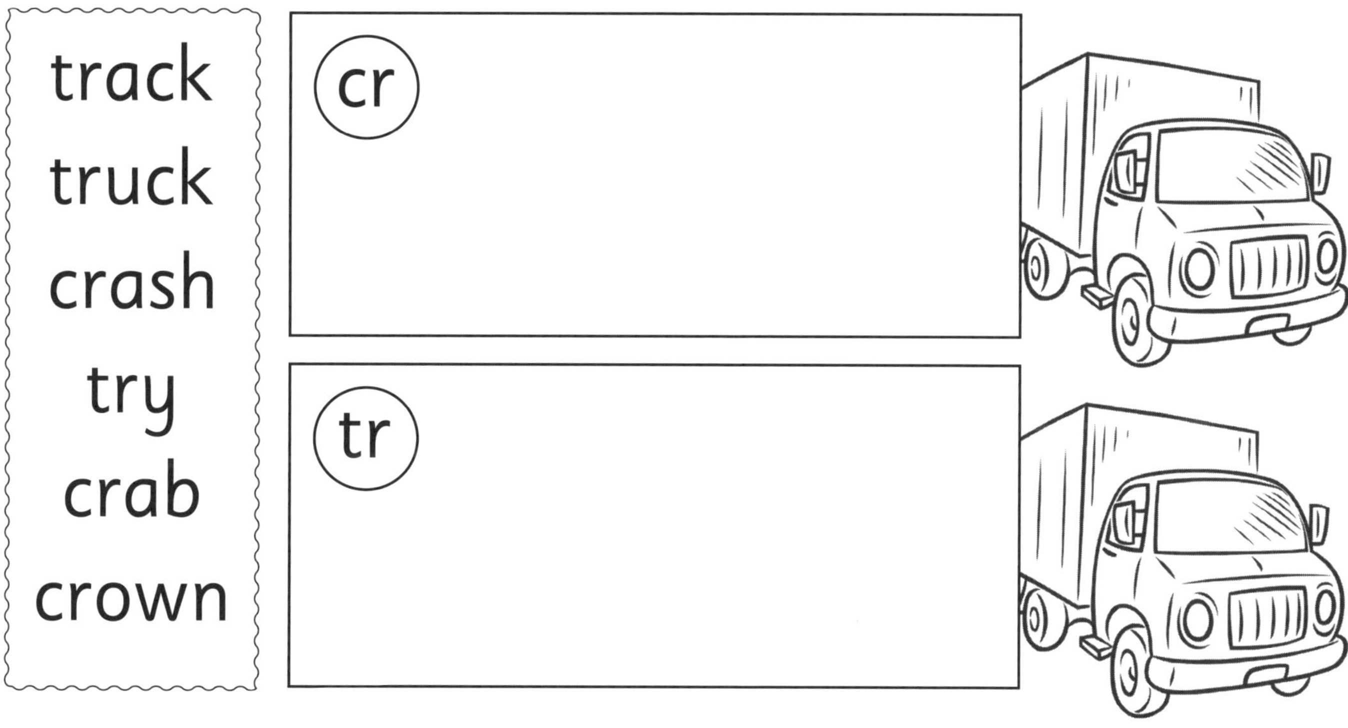

2 Complete the sentences.

friends cry truck trip

Brad wants to go on a ________.

The ________ is stuck, and so is Brad.

Brad the crab had a bit of a ________.

The three crabs are Brad's ________.

Lesson 112 syllables

Learning objectives

Children will:

- identify syllables in words.
- recognise that syllables align with vowels.
- read and write words about keeping healthy.

Australian Curriculum Content Descriptions

Sound and letter knowledge

ACELA1439 identify rhyme and syllables in spoken words

ACELA1457 recognise words that start with a given sound, end with a given sound, have a given medial sound, rhyme with a given word

ACELA1458 recognise sound-letter matches including common vowel and consonant digraphs and consonant blends

Expressing and developing ideas

ACELA1435 learn that word order in sentences is important for meaning

ACELA1455 build word families from common morphemes; use morphemes to read words

ACELA1778 write one-syllable words containing known blends; learn an increasing number of high-frequency sight words recognised in shared texts and in texts being read independently; know that regular one-syllable words are made up of letters and common letter clusters that correspond to the sounds heard, and how to use visual memory to write high-frequency words

Interpreting, analysing and evaluating

ACELY1659 combine knowledge of context, meaning, grammar and phonics to decode text; recognise most high-frequency sight words when reading text

Sight words

somewhere

Vocabulary words

healthy, clothes, exercise, home, sleep, water, food, drink, need, wear, hat, sun, keeping, enjoy, growing, eaten

Extra assistance

Here are some fun ways to teach the idea of syllables to students:

- clap for each vowel sound in a word and count the syllables.
- put your hand a little way under your chin and every time it touches is a syllable.
- speak like a robot – the pauses you naturally make define syllables.
- use a metronome to make a beat, only saying one part of the word for each click.
- write the syllables of a word into an animal outline divided into head and body; add a tail for 3 syllables.

Classroom activities

Syllable Shuffle

This is best done in a hall or on the playground. After each student has found a way to count syllables that works for them (see Extra assistance), have them sit in a group in the middle. Label four corners of the space with the numbers 1 to 4. Ask students to think of something, such as their family name, hair colour or favourite TV show. The students then count how many syllables are in this word and move to that corner.

Reading Eggs Lesson sequence	TEACH Content and skills	PRACTISE Children will:	APPLY
Hear: *Animated Lesson*	Introduce syllables and the idea that they are usually linked to the number of vowels.	clap the syllables in words. Tap on vowels to divide words into syllables. Identify the number of syllables in a word.	**Worksheet 1** Syllables
Write: *Syllable Crunch, Extra Word*	Identify syllables in a word. Recognise correct word order for a sentence.	select the correct syllables to make the word. Put the words in order and cross out the extra words.	**Worksheet 2** Spelling
Find: *Driving Trucks, Buzzy's Word Machine, Pack the Shelves*	Recognise a given word. Identify word endings. Identify the correct word to complete the sentence.	find the given word in a group. Match the word to its ending. Choose the word which completes the sentence.	**Worksheet 3** Vocabulary
Vocabulary: *Today's Topic Words, Syllable Gobbler*	Build vocabulary skills: Recognise key vocabulary. Identify the number of syllables in a word.	match pictures to words. Choose the number of syllables in a word.	**Worksheet 4** Check
Read: *How Does it End?, Q & A, Book*	Read sentences using basic vocabulary. Comprehend the meaning of a text. Read aloud book.	read a beginning and match it to an ending. Read the text and answer questions. Listen, follow the reading and read along.	**Reading Eggs nonfiction book** Keeping Healthy

Classroom activities

Which Hat?

Place three hats on the floor with the labels 1, 2 and 3. Have a pile of objects or pictures of objects that have up to 3 syllables. Each student chooses one and works out which hat it must go in. Discuss their choice with the class.

Related Reading Eggs Activities, Interactives, Songs and Books

Driving Tests

Spelling Bank

Reading Eggs Puzzle Park

Number Nuts
Vegetables
Dressing Up

Reading Eggs Posters

Syllables

Reading Eggs Library Books

My Program Books

Teacher Toolkit

- Spelling Activities
- Grammar Lessons
- Comprehension Lessons
- Targeting Comprehension Interactively
- Targeting Text Interactively

Reading Eggs Apps

Eggy Snap

Eggy Vocab

Critter Card

Coco the starfish

Syllables

Lesson 112 • Worksheet 1

Name

1 Clap the syllables as you say each word.
Write the words in the correct boxes.

cup happy eating cake
wombat hotter crab slam

1 clap	2 claps

2 Colour 1 syllable words **blue**. Colour 2 syllable words **yellow**.

flower Brad track Flossy
clam plum crying sister

Name

Spelling

Syllables

Lesson 112 · Worksheet 2

1 Write the missing syllable to complete each word.

rot   er   bit   on   ing

flow______

car______

lem______

rab______

wat______

eat______

ex______cise

sleep______

2 Join each word to the **er** machine. Write each word you make.

help

long

hard

small

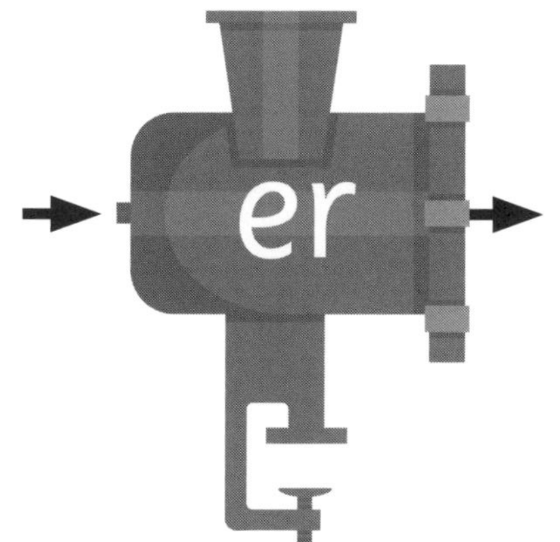

______

______

______

______

Vocabulary

Name

Lesson 112 • Worksheet 3

1 Match each picture to a word.

2 Trace and copy.

Name

Check

Syllables

Lesson 112 · Worksheet 4

1 Write the words in the correct box.

water home sleep
healthy growing food

1 syllable	2 syllables

2 Complete the sentences.

grow water clothes eat

I need food to __________.

I need __________ to drink.

Exercise helps us to live and __________.

We need __________ to wear.

Lesson 113 end blends

Learning objectives

Children will:

- identify end blends.
- read and write words with blends.

Australian Curriculum Content Descriptions

Sound and letter knowledge

ACELA1439 identify rhyme and syllables in spoken words

ACELA1457 recognise words that start with a given sound, end with a given sound, have a given medial sound, rhyme with a given word

ACELA1458 recognise sound-letter matches including common vowel and consonant digraphs and consonant blends

ACELA1459 recognise that letters can have more than one sound; recognise sounds that can be produced by different letters

Expressing and developing ideas

ACELA1435 learn that word order in sentences is important for meaning

ACELA1438 build word families using onset and rime

ACELA1455 build word families from common morphemes; use morphemes to read words

ACELA1778 write one-syllable words containing known blends; know that regular one-syllable words are made up of letters and common letter clusters that correspond to the sounds heard, and how to use visual memory to write high-frequency words

Interpreting, analysing and evaluating

ACELY1659 combine knowledge of context, meaning, grammar and phonics to decode text; recognise most high-frequency sight words when reading text

Word families

best, gold, fridge, ant, gulp, sand, ring, milk, gift, skunk, stink, pink, sink, drink, blink, stamp, ramp, lamp, lump, thump, bump

Vocabulary words

smell, flamingo, stinky, keeping, wanted, running

Extra assistance

Some students may have trouble with final blends like *nd* and *ng*. They may only pronounce the first consonant. Give them opportunities to say and hear the difference. One way to do this is with a Spelling Bee. Give students a list of words ending with blends to learn for a week. Ask students one at a time to spell one of the words from the list. They have to listen for the ending when you say it and then they have to spell it correctly and say the word clearly.

Classroom activities

Match Up

Divide the class into three groups. Give one group an initial sound or blend on a card, one group gets vowels and the other group receives an ending blend. Ask students to form a trio and make a word with their cards, (have some spare cards to swap for students who are unable to make a word at the end.) The trio should write their word on a piece of paper, then illustrate it. Each trio should present their word to the class and explain what the word means.

Reading Eggs Lesson sequence	TEACH Content and skills	PRACTISE Children will:	APPLY
Hear: *Animated Lesson*	Identify parts of words including end blends.	make words with end blends.	**Worksheet 1** Ending sounds
Write: *Syllable Crunch, Extra Word, Write the Banner*	Identify syllables in a word. Recognise correct word order for a sentence.	select the correct syllables to make the word. Put the words in order and cross out the extra words.	**Worksheet 2** Beginning, middle and ending sounds
Find: *Word Family, Bowling, Buzzy's Word Machine*	Identify the correct onset letter to complete the word. Recognise the rime in the word. Identify word endings.	choose the correct initial letter to make the word. Match a word to its rime. Select a word and its ending.	**Worksheet 3** Vocabulary
Vocabulary: *Today's Topic Words, Word Dominoes*	Build vocabulary skills: Recognise key vocabulary.	match pictures to words.	**Worksheet 4** Check
Read: *Book Ends, Book*	Read sentences using basic vocabulary. Read aloud book.	choose a word to finish the sentence. Listen, follow the reading and read along.	**Reading Eggs Story book** Frank the Skunk

Classroom activities

Rhyme Time

Write the word *best* on the whiteboard and ask the class to say as many words as they can that rhyme with it. Write these on the board. Write the words *sand*, *ant* and *ring* on the board. Ask the students to each choose a word and write as many words as they can that rhyme. Discuss responses with the class.

Related Reading Eggs Activities, Interactives, Songs and Books

Spelling Bank

Dogs

Lesson 30

Focus sound words: bump, jump, dump, pump, hump, lump, thump

Challenge: stump, crumple

Reading Eggs Puzzle Park

More Than One

Animal Fun

Do it

Describe it

Driving Tests

Reading Eggs Posters

The ng Sound

ng and nk

Reading Eggs Library Books

My Program Books

Teacher Toolkit

- Spelling Activities
- Grammar Lessons
- Comprehension Lessons
- Targeting Comprehension Interactively
- Targeting Text Interactively

Reading Eggs Apps

Eggy Snap

Eggy Phonics 3

Eggy Vocab

Critter Card

Frank the skunk

End blends

Lesson 113 • Worksheet 1

Name

Ending sounds

1 Join the words that end with **nk** to Frank.

2 Use the wheels to make words. Write the words.

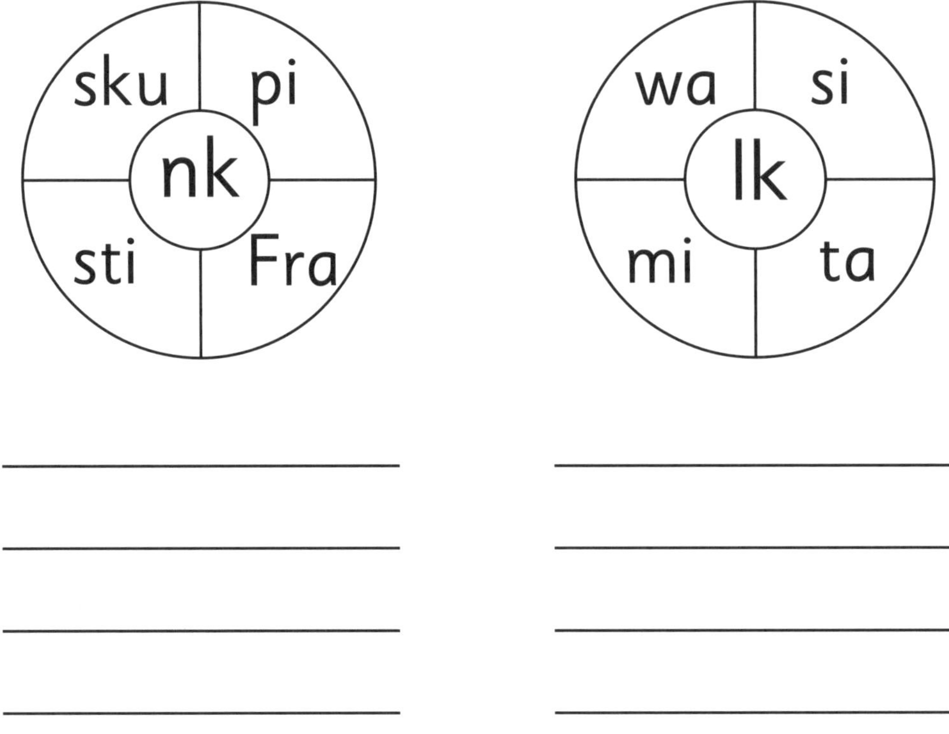

Name

Beginning, middle and ending sounds

End blends

Lesson 113 · Worksheet 2

1 Complete each word.

lk nd ng st nt ft

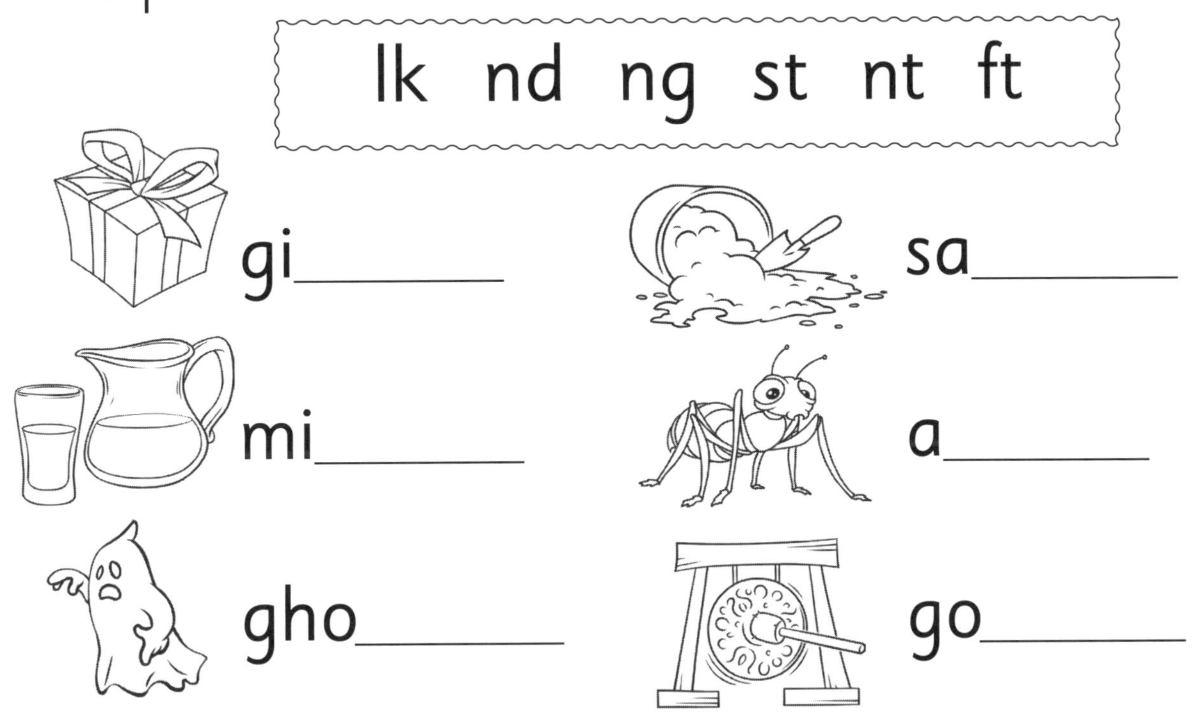

gi______ sa______

mi______ a______

gho______ go______

2 Say the name of each picture. Colour its beginning, middle and ending sound. Write the word.

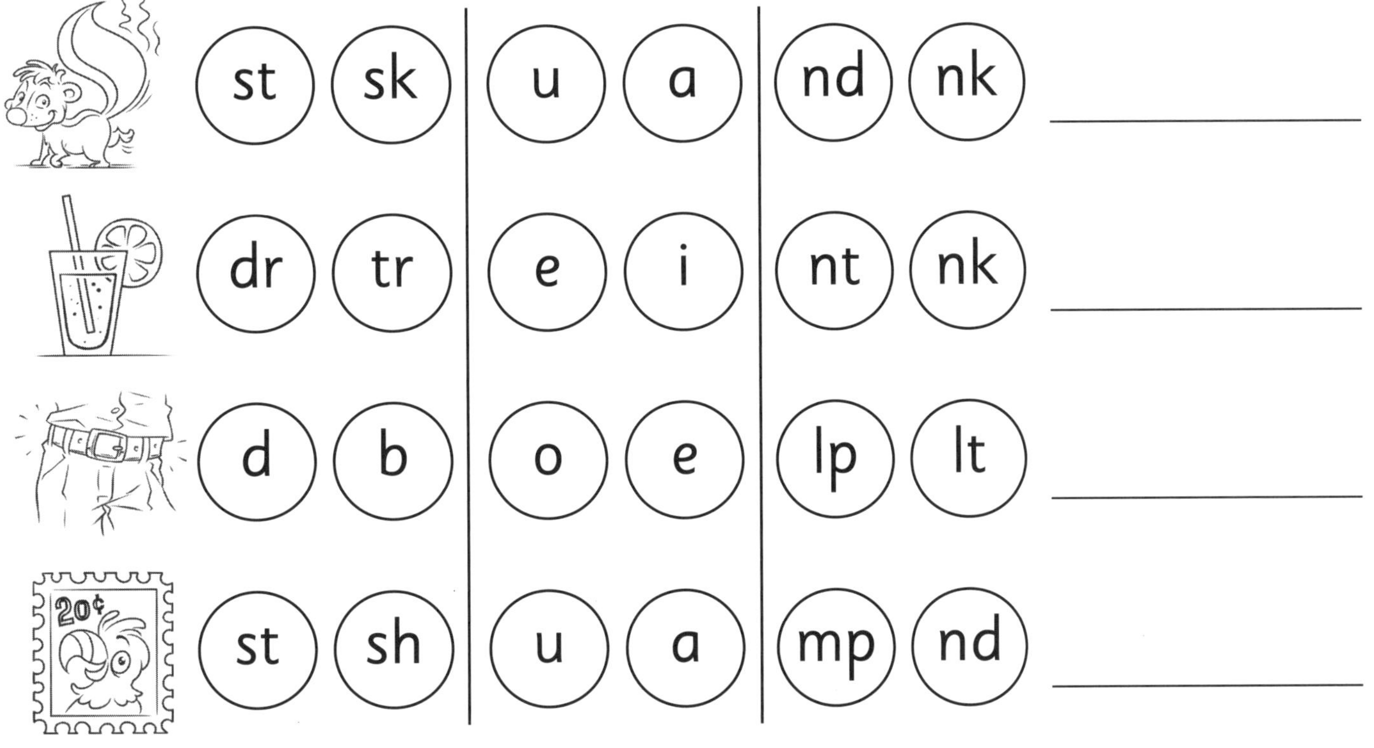

st	sk	u	a	nd	nk	______
dr	tr	e	i	nt	nk	______
d	b	o	e	lp	lt	______
st	sh	u	a	mp	nd	______

End blends

Lesson 113 · Worksheet 3

Name

Vocabulary

1 Join each word to a picture.

2 Read the clue. Write the word.

I am furry. I have four legs and I can smell bad! I am a sk__________.	I am made by cows. You can drink me. I am mi__________.
You can fill me with water and wash the dishes. I am a s__________.	I am a colour. I am made when you mix red and white. I am p__________.

Name

Check

End blends

Lesson 113 • Worksheet 4

1 Colour the correct word. Cross out the wrong word.

This is Frank the [stink] [skunk]. Frank likes to [drink] [drift] pink milk. Frank sits on the [sang] [sand]. He [gulps] [stings] the pink drink.

2 Write a sentence using Frank the skunk's word.

Lesson 114 the sound **oa**

Learning objectives

Children will:

- identify the sound oa.
- read and write oa words.
- make compound words.

Australian Curriculum Content Descriptions

Sound and letter knowledge

ACELA1439 identify rhyme and syllables in spoken words

ACELA1457 recognise words that start with a given sound, end with a given sound, have a given medial sound, rhyme with a given word

ACELA1458 recognise sound-letter matches including common vowel and consonant digraphs and consonant blends

ACELA1459 recognise that letters can have more than one sound; recognise sounds that can be produced by different letters

Expressing and developing ideas

ACELA1435 learn that word order in sentences is important for meaning

ACELA1438 build word families using onset and rime

ACELA1778 write one-syllable words containing known blends; know that regular one-syllable words are made up of letters and common letter clusters that correspond to the sounds heard, and how to use visual memory to write high-frequency words

Interpreting, analysing and evaluating

ACELY1659 combine knowledge of context, meaning, grammar and phonics to decode text; recognise most high-frequency sight words when reading text

Word families

soap, moan, loaf, oats, road, toad, roast, coast, toast, coat, boat, float, goat, soak, oak, foam, goal

Vocabulary words

picture, flowers, house, find, waterfall, thunderstorm, sailboat, raincoat, tophat, houseboat, overcoat

Extra assistance

The digraph *oa* makes the same long *o* sound as the split digraph *o-e*, for example, *boat* and *bone*. There is no rule for when to use one or the other, the individual spellings must be learned. It may help to make a divided list of long *o* sound words with *o-e* on one side and *oa* on the other, (you may want a third section for other spellings eg *toe, bow, go*) that students can refer to when writing in class.

Classroom activities

For Starters

Put the rime *oast* on the board in magnetic letters. Put all the letters of the alphabet around it. Students take turns to make *oast* words by simply changing the initial phoneme. Can anyone use a blend at the start?

Change the rime to *oat*, then *oad*, and repeat the activity.

Reading Eggs Lesson sequence	TEACH Content and skills	PRACTISE Children will:	APPLY
Hear: *Animated Lesson*	Introduce the digraph *oa* making the *long o* sound through the song *Oats wants to go to Ireland.*	identify the sound *oa* and make *oa* words.	**Worksheet 1** Phonics
Write: *Syllable Crunch, Broken Sentence, Bird Words*	Identify syllables in a word and make the word. Recognise correct word order for a sentence.	select the correct syllables to make the word. Choose the correct words to make a sentence.	**Worksheet 2** Reading
Find: *Word Family, 1, 2, 3, 4, Hairy Heads*	Identify the correct onset letter to complete a word. Identify the order of a sequence of events. Recognise a given word.	choose the correct letter to make the word. Put pictures in order to show a sequence. Find the given word in a group.	**Worksheet 3** Vocabulary
Vocabulary: *Today's Topic Words, Scrapbook, Groups*	Build vocabulary skills: Recognise key vocabulary. Identify parts of a compound word. Recognise categories of words.	match pictures to words. Choose two words to make a compound word. Match pictures to categories.	**Worksheet 4** Check
Read: *Book*	Read aloud book.	listen, follow the reading and read along.	**Reading Eggs Story book** Goat on a Boat

Classroom activities

Memory Game

Write the word *overcoat* on the board. Sound it out with the class and discuss the two words within it. Have students trace the word on someone's back or in the air with their finger. Rub out the word and write these words on the board: offcoat, overcoat, offercoat, overcote, over cot. Ask them to identify which is correct, then discuss what is wrong with the other versions.

Related Reading Eggs Activities, Interactives, Songs and Books

Spelling Bank

Spelling Bank

Goats

Lesson 55

Focus sound words: oat, coat, road, toad, soap, foam

Challenge: throat, coast

Driving Tests

Reading Eggs Puzzle Park

Animal Fun

Transport

Dressing Up

What is it?

Music Café

Oats wants to go to Ireland

Reading Eggs Posters

The oa Sound

Alternate Spellings /oa/

Reading Eggs Library Books

My Program Books

Teacher Toolkit

- Spelling Activities
- Grammar Lessons
- Comprehension Lessons
- Targeting Comprehension Interactively
- Targeting Text Interactively

Reading Eggs Apps

Eggy Snap

Eggy Phonics 3

Critter Card

Floaty boat

oa

Name

Phonics

Lesson 114 • Worksheet 1

1 Colour the boats that have an **oa** sound.

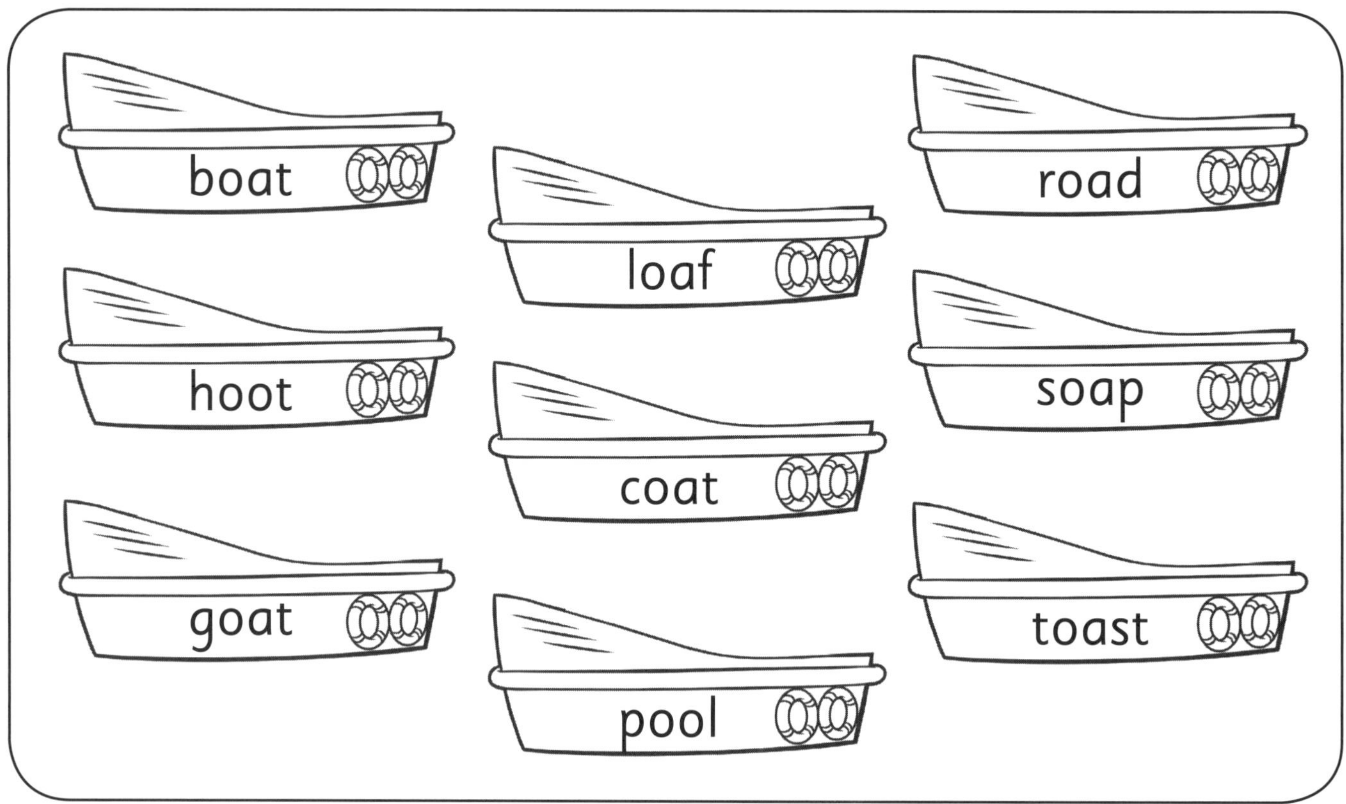

2 Use Floaty Boat's **oa** to make words. Write each word. Read each word.

l oa d

f____m

r____d

s____k

Name

Reading

Lesson 114 • Worksheet 2

1 Read the text.

> The goat has a soak in some foamy soap. “My goal today is to get on a boat,” said the goat. “I cannot miss that boat!”

Underline the correct answer.

2 Who has a soak?

- the boat
- the soap
- the goat
- the foam

3 What is the goat’s goal?

- to have a soak
- to get on a boat
- to miss the boat
- to make some foam

4 What can the goat not miss?

- the bus
- the party
- the soap
- the boat

oa

Lesson 114 • Worksheet 3

Name

Vocabulary

1 Match each word to a picture.

2 Complete the sentences.

float toast oats soap

I ate ________ and jam for breakfast.

Wash your hands with ________ and water.

Boats can ________ on the sea.

I would like a bowl of hot ________.

Name

Check

oa

Lesson 114 • Worksheet 4

1 Circle the rhyming word in each row.

goat	heat	foot	boat	part
soak	seek	sink	park	oak
goal	foal	hill	girl	fall
toast	feast	nest	roast	taste

2 Complete the sentences.

goat oats boat soak toast

The goat had a __________ in some soap.

Do you want toast or __________?

I cannot miss that __________!

He made some __________ .

The __________ missed the boat.

Lesson 115 the sound **ir**

Learning objectives

Children will:

- identify the sound made with a vowel and r as /ir/.
- recognise the combinations that make /ir/ – ar, ir, ir, or, ur.
- read and write words with /ir/ sounds.

Australian Curriculum Content Descriptions

Sound and letter knowledge

ACELA1457 replace sounds in spoken words; recognise words that start with a given sound, end with a given sound, have a given medial sound, rhyme with a given word

ACELA1458 recognise sound-letter matches including common vowel and consonant digraphs and consonant blends

ACELA1459 recognise that letters can have more than one sound; recognise sounds that can be produced by different letters

Expressing and developing ideas

ACELA1435 learn that word order in sentences is important for meaning

ACELA1438 build word families using onset and rime

ACELA1778 learn an increasing number of high-frequency sight words recognised in shared texts and in texts being read independently; know that regular one-syllable words are made up of letters and common letter clusters that correspond to the sounds heard, and how to use visual memory to write high-frequency words

Interpreting, analysing and evaluating

ACELY1659 combine knowledge of context, meaning, grammar and phonics to decode text; recognise most high-frequency sight words when reading text

Word families

car, her, sir, fur, bird, germ, turn, dollar, worm, flower, water, dirt, shirt, skirt, flirt

Vocabulary words

grow, seedling, soil, warm, sunlight, catfight, flowerpot, fingernail

Extra assistance

For pronunciation, the */ir/* sound is used for most combinations of *e, i* and *u* with *r* – *her, sir, fur*. It is sometimes used for *ar* and *or* as well – *worm, dollar*. However, *ar* and *or* can also make their own distinctive sounds, as in *far* and *for*. The choice of vowel for spelling the */ir/* words follows no rules. These spellings must just be learnt and accessed from visual memory.

Classroom activities

Mix and Match

Put the letters of the alphabet on the board in magnetic letters. Write the sounds *ir, ur* and *ir* on the board. Each student comes to the board and makes a word using *ir/ur/er* and the magnetic letters. Discuss their words with the class.

Reading Eggs Lesson sequence	TEACH Content and skills	PRACTISE Children will:	APPLY
Hear: *Animated Lesson*	Introduce the way the letter *r* changes vowel sounds.	identify the sound /ir/ made with a vowel and *r*.	**Worksheet 1** Phonics 1
Write: *Pelican Spelling*	Identify sounds in a word and write the word.	sound out a word and select letters to spell it correctly.	**Worksheet 2** Phonics 2
Find: *Word Family, Dragon Fire, Pack the Shelves*	Identify the correct onset letter to complete the word. Recognise a given word. Identify the correct word to complete the sentence.	choose the correct initial letter to make the word. Find the given word in a group. Choose the word which completes the sentence.	**Worksheet 3** Vocabulary
Vocabulary: *Today's Topic Words, Dress the Monster, Groups, Scrapbook*	Build vocabulary skills: Recognise key vocabulary. Sort words into categories. Identify the parts of a compound word.	match pictures to words and categories. Read and follow instructions. Choose two words to make a compound word.	**Worksheet 4** Check
Read: *Q & A, Book*	Comprehend the meaning of a text. Read aloud book.	read the text and answer the questions. Listen, follow the reading and read along.	**Reading Eggs nonfiction book** Caring for Plants

Classroom activities

Which Hat?

Place three hats on the floor with the labels *ir*, *er* and *ur*. Discuss the sounds. Have a pile of objects or pictures of objects that have *ir/er/ur* in their name. Each student chooses one and works out which hat it must go in. Discuss their choice with the class.

Related Reading Eggs Activities, Interactives, Songs and Books

Spelling Bank

Hippos

Lesson 63

Focus sound words: fir, bird, dirt, shirt, skirt, first

Challenge: thirsty, squirt

Driving Tests

Reading Eggs Puzzle Park

Dressing Up

Do it

What is it?

Reading Eggs Posters

The er Sound

Compound Words

Reading Eggs Library Books

My Program Books

Teacher Toolkit

- Spelling Activities
- Grammar Lessons
- Comprehension Lessons
- Targeting Comprehension Interactively
- Targeting Text Interactively

Reading Eggs Apps

Eggy Sight words

Eggy Vocab

Critter Card

Twirly bird

Name

Phonics 1

1 Join Shelly shark to the **ar words**.

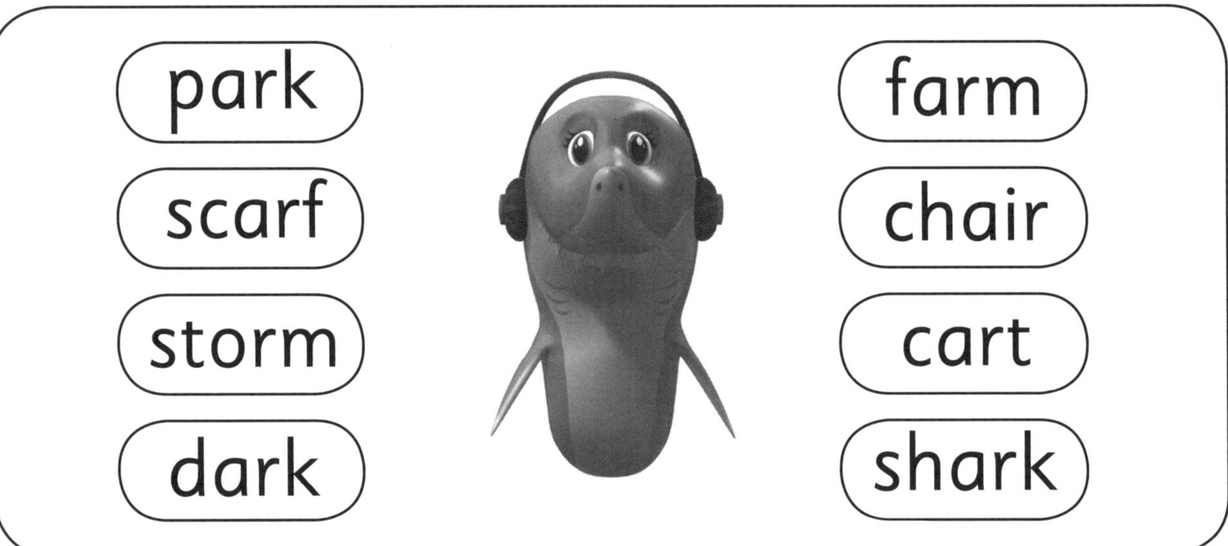

2 Write the word on the correct barn.

art
term
germ
card
herd
serve
barn
garden

er

ar

Name

Phonics 2

ir

Lesson 115 • Worksheet 2

1 Colour the **ir** words.

2 Use Roary's **ur** to make words. Write each word. Read each word.

f____

c____l

b____n

h____t

n____se

Vocabulary

Name

Lesson 115 · Worksheet 3

1 Match the words to the pictures.

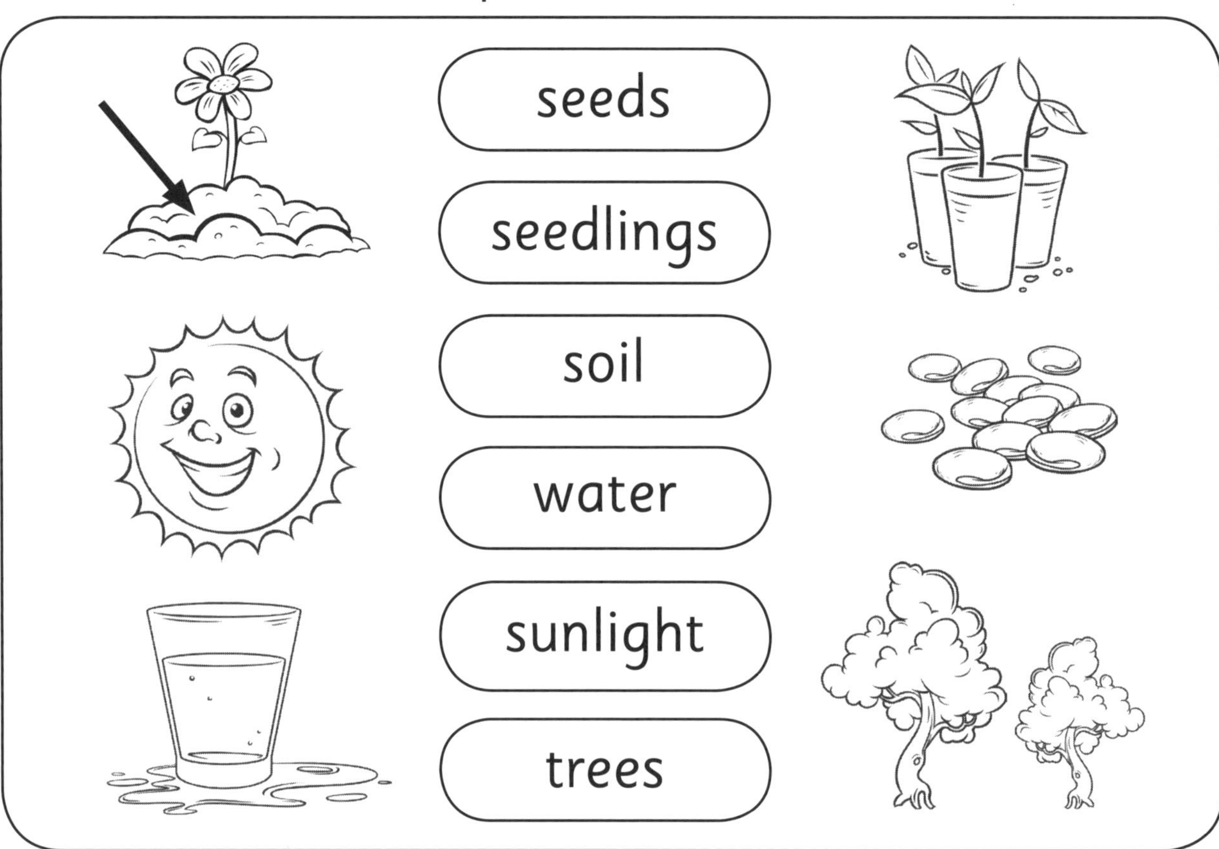

2 Read the clue. Write the word.

You plant me. I grow into seedlings. I am s____________.	I come out of a tap. You cannot live without me. I am w____________.
We can grow tall. We have branches and leaves. We are t____________.	I am sometimes called dirt or earth. Seeds grow in me. I am s____________.

Name

Check

Lesson 115 • Worksheet 4

1 Find the words. Colour **term** blue, **park** green, **bird** yellow and **hurt** pink.

p	a	r	k	h	u	r	t	t	e	r	m
b	i	r	d	t	e	r	m	p	a	r	k
h	u	r	t	p	a	r	k	b	i	r	d
t	e	r	m	b	i	r	d	h	u	r	t
p	a	r	k	t	e	r	m	b	i	r	d

2 Complete each word. ur er ar ir

c______t g______m sk______t n______se

3 Write the words in the correct order.

soil and grow. need to Flowers live

____

____

Lesson 116 the sound **igh**

Learning objectives

Children will:

- identify the letters igh making the long i sound.
- recognise words that contain igh.
- read and write igh words.

Australian Curriculum Content Descriptions

Sound and letter knowledge

ACELA1439 identify rhyme and syllables in spoken words

ACELA1457 replace sounds in spoken words; recognise words that start with a given sound, end with a given sound, have a given medial sound, rhyme with a given word

ACELA1458 recognise sound-letter matches including common vowel and consonant digraphs and consonant blends

ACELA1459 recognise that letters can have more than one sound; recognise sounds that can be produced by different letters

Expressing and developing ideas

ACELA1435 learn that word order in sentences is important for meaning

ACELA1438 build word families using onset and rime

ACELA1778 write one-syllable words containing known blends; know that regular one-syllable words are made up of letters and common letter clusters that correspond to the sounds heard, and how to use visual memory to write high-frequency words

Interpreting, analysing and evaluating

ACELY1659 combine knowledge of context, meaning, grammar and phonics to decode text; recognise most high-frequency sight words when reading text

Word families

fight, sight, might, right, night, bright, flight, tight, knight, fright, light, sigh, high

Vocabulary words

moonlight, starlight, goodnight, sandpaper, flowerpot, waterfall, icecube

Extra assistance

The long *i* sound is most commonly made with the split digraph *i-e*. The next most common spelling is *igh*. Most *igh* words end in *t*, as in *light* and *night*. There are a couple of words that don't, for example *sigh* and *high*. The *gh* is not pronounced but changes the *i* to a long vowel, as in *lit* and *light*. There is no rule for when to use *igh*. Play lots of word recognition games to learn these on sight.

Classroom activities

Bingo!

Give students a laminated board with ten squares on it. Ask them to write a word in each square from an *igh* word list (use whiteboard markers). Say words from the list. Students put a cross on that word on their board. First one to ten calls out 'bingo' and wins!

Reading Eggs Lesson sequence	TEACH Content and skills	PRACTISE Children will:	APPLY
Hear: *Animated Lesson*	Introduce the sound *igh*, a *long i*.	identify the sound *igh* and make *igh* words.	**Worksheet 1** Phonics
Write: *Extra Word, Pelican Spelling, Bird Words*	Recognise correct word order for a sentence. Identify sounds in a word.	put the words in order and cross out the extra words. Sound out a word and spell it correctly.	**Worksheet 2** Read and write
Find: *Word Family, Shooting Stars*	Identify the correct onset letter to complete the word. Recognise a given word.	choose the correct initial letter to make the word. Find the given word in a group.	**Worksheet 3** Vocabulary
Vocabulary: *Syllable Gobbler, Scrapbook*	Build vocabulary skills: Recognise the number of syllables in a word. Identify the parts of a compound word.	select the number for the syllables in a word. Choose two words to make a compound word.	**Worksheet 4** Check
Read: *How Does it End?, Book Ends, Book*	Read sentences using basic vocabulary. Read aloud book.	choose a word or phrase to finish the sentence. Listen, follow the reading and read along.	**Reading Eggs Story book** Bat and Bird

Classroom activities

Find the Sound

Give each student a card with *i-e* on one side and *igh* on the other. Say a long *i* word and ask students to listen to the end sound. They should hold up the card and show which spelling is used for the vowel sound. Use clear, recognisable words such as *light, line, night* and *nine.*

Related Reading Eggs Activities, Interactives, Songs and Books

Spelling Bank

Goats

Lesson 53

Focus sound words: sigh, high, night, fight, might, light

Challenge: alright, tonight

Reading Eggs Puzzle Park

Sense it

Describe it

Arrows

Animal Grid

Driving Tests

Reading Eggs Posters

The igh Sound

Alternate Spellings /igh/

Reading Eggs Library Books

My Program Books

Teacher Toolkit

- Spelling Activities
- Grammar Lessons
- Comprehension Lessons
- Targeting Comprehension Interactively
- Targeting Text Interactively

Reading Eggs Apps

Eggy Sight words

Eggy Snap

Critter Card

Nighty night light

igh

Lesson 116 · Worksheet 1

Name

Phonics

1 Join the **igh** words to Nighty night light.

2 Use the wheel to make words. Write the words.

3 Complete the labels.

Name

Read and write

igh

Lesson 116 · Worksheet 2

1 Complete the sentences.

night Bird high

"I like to fly," said ________.

"I can fly ________ in the sky," said Bat.

Bat can fly all ________.

2 Guess the word by its shape. Write each word in a box.

high night knight light

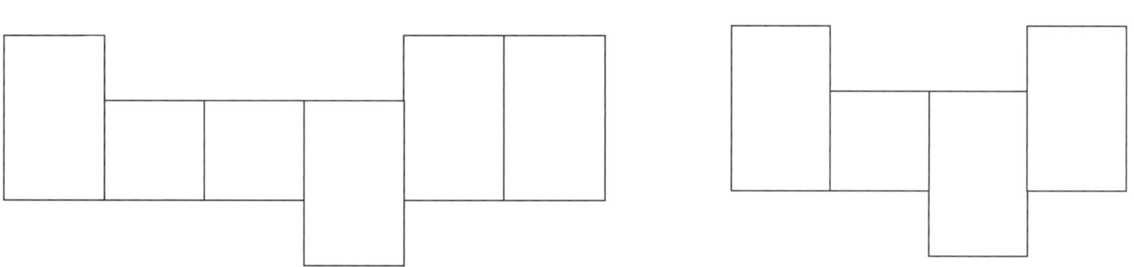

Vocabulary

Name

Lesson 116 • Worksheet 3

1 Join the two words together. Write each new word.

moon + light = ____________________

good + night = ____________________

sand + paper = ____________________

ice + cube = ____________________

2 Join each word to a picture.

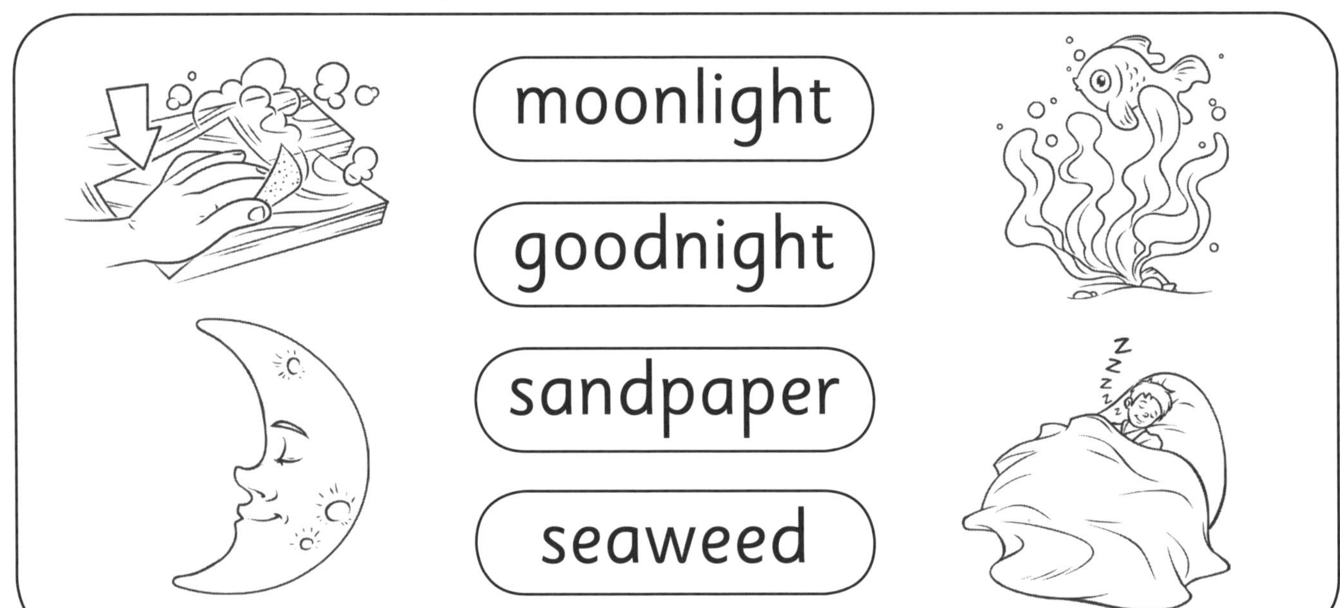

3 Make two more compound words.

Name

Check

igh

Lesson 116 • Worksheet 4

1 Circle the **i_e** words. Colour the **_igh** words blue. Colour the **_y** words red.

"I like to fly," said Bird. "I can fly high." "I like to fly high," said Bat. "The sky is mine." "Sigh," said the Moon.

Colour a cloud each time you find a word.

2 Write a sentence using Bat's word.

Lesson 117 nouns

Learning objectives

Children will:

- identify nouns and proper nouns.
- recognise that proper nouns need capital letters.
- read and write nouns and proper nouns.

Australian Curriculum Content Descriptions

Sound and letter knowledge

ACELA1439 identify rhyme and syllables in spoken words

ACELA1457 recognise words that start with a given sound, end with a given sound, have a given medial sound, rhyme with a given word

ACELA1458 recognise sound-letter matches including common vowel and consonant digraphs and consonant blends

Expressing and developing ideas

ACELA1435 learn that word order in sentences is important for meaning

ACELA1455 build word families from common morphemes; use morphemes to read words

ACELA1778 learn an increasing number of high-frequency sight words recognised in shared texts and in texts being read independently; know that regular one-syllable words are made up of letters and common letter clusters that correspond to the sounds heard, and how to use visual memory to write high-frequency words

Interpreting, analysing and evaluating

ACELY1659 combine knowledge of context, meaning, grammar and phonics to decode text; recognise most high-frequency sight words when reading text

Word families

girl, sandpit, crocodile, swing, paw, coast, thorn, raincoat, toast, lion, butterfly, tadpole, waterfall, bathroom, rowboat, tree, tiger, bird, goat, shirt, flower, light, moon, night, spider

Vocabulary words

better, loudly, caught, chew, roar, wanted, hurt

Extra assistance

Nouns are most easily explained to young children as the names of places and things, such as *home, school, pencil, girl, rabbit* and so on. Proper nouns are the names of particular people, places and things, for example *Mary, Sydney* and the *Eiffel Tower*. Play sorting games to reinforce this concept, using nouns and proper nouns, or nouns and other types of words.

Classroom activities

Collage

Give each student a piece of paper with the word *noun* written on it. Have them go through old magazines or newspapers and cut out pictures of objects, places, people and animals. They glue these on the paper and label them with a noun. Remind them to use a capital letter for proper nouns.

Reading Eggs Lesson sequence	TEACH Content and skills	PRACTISE Children will:	APPLY
Hear: *Animated Lesson*	Introduce nouns and proper nouns with capital letters.	understand what nouns and proper nouns are.	**Worksheet 1** Common nouns
Write: *Syllable Crunch, Write the Banner*	Identify syllables in a word. Recognise correct word order for a sentence.	select the syllables to make a word. Choose the correct words to make a sentence.	**Worksheet 2** Proper nouns
Find: *1, 2, 3, 4, Buzzy's Word Machine, What's Missing?, Dragon Fire*	Identify the order of a sequence of events. Select word endings. Identify the missing sound in a word. Recognise a given word.	put pictures in order to show a sequence. Match the word to its ending. Choose the correct letter to make the word. Find the given word in a group.	**Worksheet 3** Read and write
Vocabulary: *Define It, Scrapbook, Power Words*	Build vocabulary skills: Recognise words by their definitions. Identify the parts of a compound word. Recognise key vocabulary.	choose the correct word to match the definition. Select two words to make a compound word. Match pictures to words.	**Worksheet 4** Check
Read: *Book*	Read aloud book.	listen, follow the reading and read along.	**Reading Eggs Story book** Roary the Lion

Classroom activities

From A-Z

Encourage the children to list as many nouns as they can that start with each letter of the alphabet. This can be done individually, in pairs or as a whole class activity. Extend the activity by asking the children to determine if the nouns that they have written are common or proper.

Related Reading Eggs Activities, Interactives, Songs and Books

Driving Tests

Test 14

Letters and sounds: flowers, girls

Content words: bath, water

Spelling Bank

Reading Eggs Puzzle Park

Name it

What is it?

Do You Know?

Reading Eggs Posters

- Nouns
- Common nouns
- Proper nouns

Reading Eggs Library Books

My Program Books

Teacher Toolkit

- Spelling Activities
- Grammar Lessons
- Comprehension Lessons
- Targeting Comprehension Interactively
- Targeting Text Interactively

Reading Eggs Apps

Eggy Vocab

Eggy Snap

Critter Card

Roary the lion

a

Nouns

Name

Lesson 117 • Worksheet 1

Common nouns

1 Match each common noun to its picture.

2 Colour Roary's common nouns.

Name

Nouns

Lesson 117 • Worksheet 2

Proper nouns

1 Match each proper noun to its picture.

2 Write the nouns in the correct boxes. Hint! Look for the capital letters.

Monday
bird
Charlie
leaf
tooth
Africa
stick
July

common nouns

proper nouns

Nouns

Lesson 117 • Worksheet 3

Name

Read and write

1 Complete the sentences.

net cake friends drink

Roary wanted an icy cold __________.

Roary got caught in a __________.

Catty was baking a __________.

"It's good to have __________!"

2 Write a sentence using Roary's word.

Name

Check

Nouns

Lesson 117 · Worksheet 4

1 Circle the common nouns.

Roary got a thorn stuck in his paw. Then he got caught in a net. The mice chewed the rope until Roary was free.

Colour a star each time you find a common noun.

2 Give each proper noun a capital letter.

charlie likes to swing in the trees.

I went to a party on sunday.

reggie loves to read books.

kate is going on holiday to china.

Colour a star each time you write a capital.

Lesson 118 the sound **or**

Learning objectives

Children will:

- identify different spellings for the sound /or/.
- read and write /or/ words.
- recognise clothing and weather words.

Australian Curriculum Content Descriptions

Sound and letter knowledge

ACELA1457 replace sounds in spoken words; recognise words that start with a given sound, end with a given sound, have a given medial sound, rhyme with a given word

ACELA1458 recognise sound-letter matches including common vowel and consonant digraphs and consonant blends

ACELA1459 recognise that letters can have more than one sound; recognise sounds that can be produced by different letters

Expressing and developing ideas

ACELA1438 build word families using onset and rime

ACELA1778 write one-syllable words containing known blends; know that regular one-syllable words are made up of letters and common letter clusters that correspond to the sounds heard, and how to use visual memory to write high-frequency words

Interpreting, analysing and evaluating

ACELY1659 combine knowledge of context, meaning, grammar and phonics to decode text; recognise most high-frequency sight words when reading text

Word families

corn, thorn, horn, stork, fork, cork, sort, sport, short, warm, core, score, wore, store, shore, oar, boar, roar, pour, door, floor, poor

Vocabulary words

clothes, pants, boots, jumper, raincoat, T-shirt, shorts, weather, rainy, windy, snow, sunny, cloudy, hot, cold, cool, warm, dry, wet, short, long

Extra assistance

There are many spellings used to produce the /or/ sound: *or* (as in *short*), *ore* (*wore*), *oar* (*roar*), *our* (*four*), *oor* (*door*) and *ar* (*war*). When the /or/ sound is in the middle of a word, it tends to be spelt *or* as in *sport* (and occasionally *ar* as in *swarm*). The other usages are generally on the end of a word. There are very few rules and these words must just be learned and accessed from visual memory. This is where the rote learning techniques such as look, cover, write, check have their value.

Classroom activities

Mind the Gap!

Write the sentences below on the board and fill the first gap in each sentence with a weather icon, eg ☼. Give students flashcards with weather and clothing words on them. Ask them to hold up a card for each gap. Discuss their answers.

Monday was a ___ day. I wore ___.
Tuesday was a ___ day. I wore ___.
Wednesday was a __ day. I wore ___.

Reading Eggs Lesson sequence	TEACH Content and skills	PRACTISE Children will:	APPLY
Hear: *Animated Lesson*	Introduce the sound /or/ and how to write this sound with the song *Roary's dad wants to play sport.*	identify combinations of letters that make the sound /or/ - *or, ar, ore, oar, our, oor.*	**Worksheet 1** Phonics
Write: *Pack the Shelves*	Identify the correct word to complete the sentence.	choose the word which completes the sentence.	**Worksheet 2** Word family
Find: *Word Family, Days*	Identify the correct onset letter to complete the word. Recognise the days of the week.	choose the correct initial letter to make the word. Order the days of the week.	**Worksheet 3** Vocabulary
Vocabulary: *Today's Topic Words, Dress the Monster, Opposite Pairs, Words per Minute*	Build vocabulary skills: Recognise key vocabulary. Identify words whose meanings are opposites.	match pictures to words. Read and follow instructions. Select cards which are opposites.	**Worksheet 4** Check
Read: *Q & A, Book*	Comprehend the meaning of a text. Read aloud book.	read the text and answer questions. Listen, follow the reading and read along.	**Reading Eggs nonfiction book** Clothes

Classroom activities

Make Your Own Questions

Students write some of their own questions following the format:
___ will be ___. What should I wear?

They fill the gaps with the days of the week and weather conditions eg cold, hot, warm, sunny, rainy etc. Then they swap with a partner and answer each other's questions with a type of clothing using the sentence: You should wear ___.

Related Reading Eggs Activities, Interactives, Songs and Books

Spelling Bank

Leopards

Lesson 91

Focus sound words: form, sort, short, thorn, stork, torch, narrator

High frequency sight words: before, horse

Challenge: corner, uniform

Reading Eggs Puzzle Park

More than One

Dressing Up

Opposites

Driving Tests

Music Café

Roary's dad wants to play sport

Reading Eggs Library Books

My Program Books

Reading Eggs Posters

The or Sound

Alternate Spellings /or/

Teacher Toolkit

- Spelling Activities
- Grammar Lessons
- Comprehension Lessons
- Targeting Comprehension Interactively
- Targeting Text Interactively

Reading Eggs Apps

Eggy Phonics 3

Eggy Vocab

Critter Card

Milky way

or

Name

Phonics

Lesson 118 · Worksheet 1

1 Colour the **or** words.

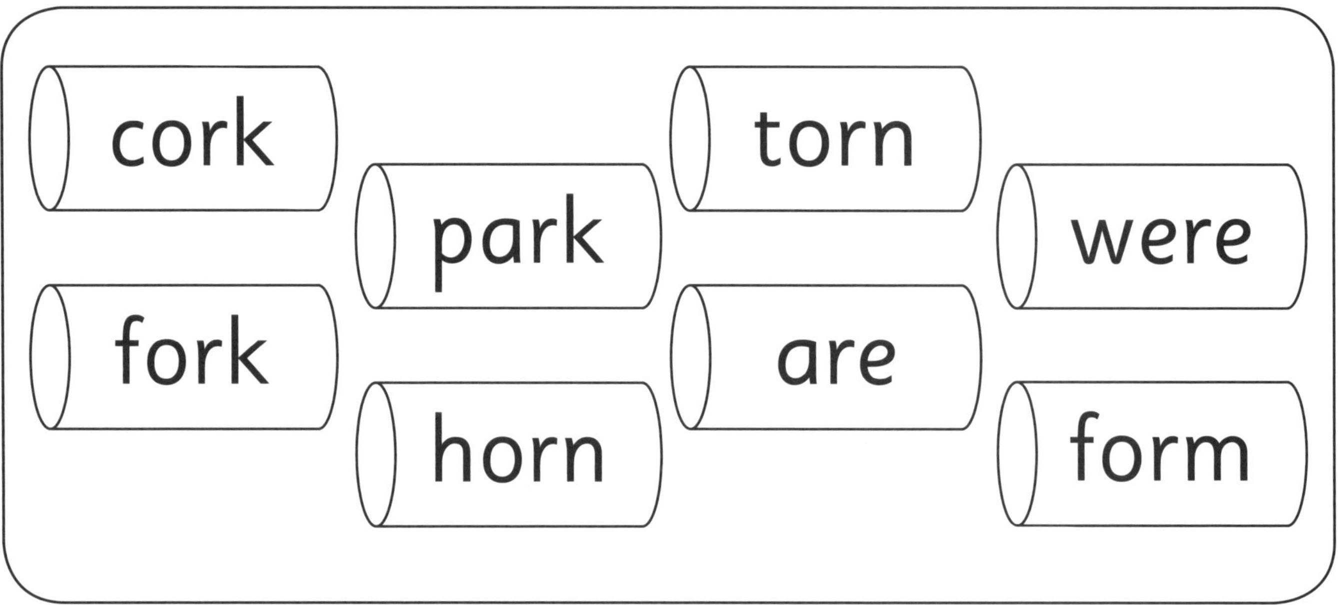

2 Use Spiny procupine's **or** to make words. Write each word. Read each word.

p_____k

st_____m

th_____n

st_____k

f_____m

Name

Word family

ore

Lesson 118 • Worksheet 2

1 Trace.

2 Complete the words. Use Roary's letters.

_____ore

_____ore

_____ore

_____ore

3 Colour the **ore** words.

bore	snore	cloud	card
chore	store	care	wore
poor	more	shore	core

Vocabulary

Name

Lesson 118 • Worksheet 3

1 Match each picture to a word.

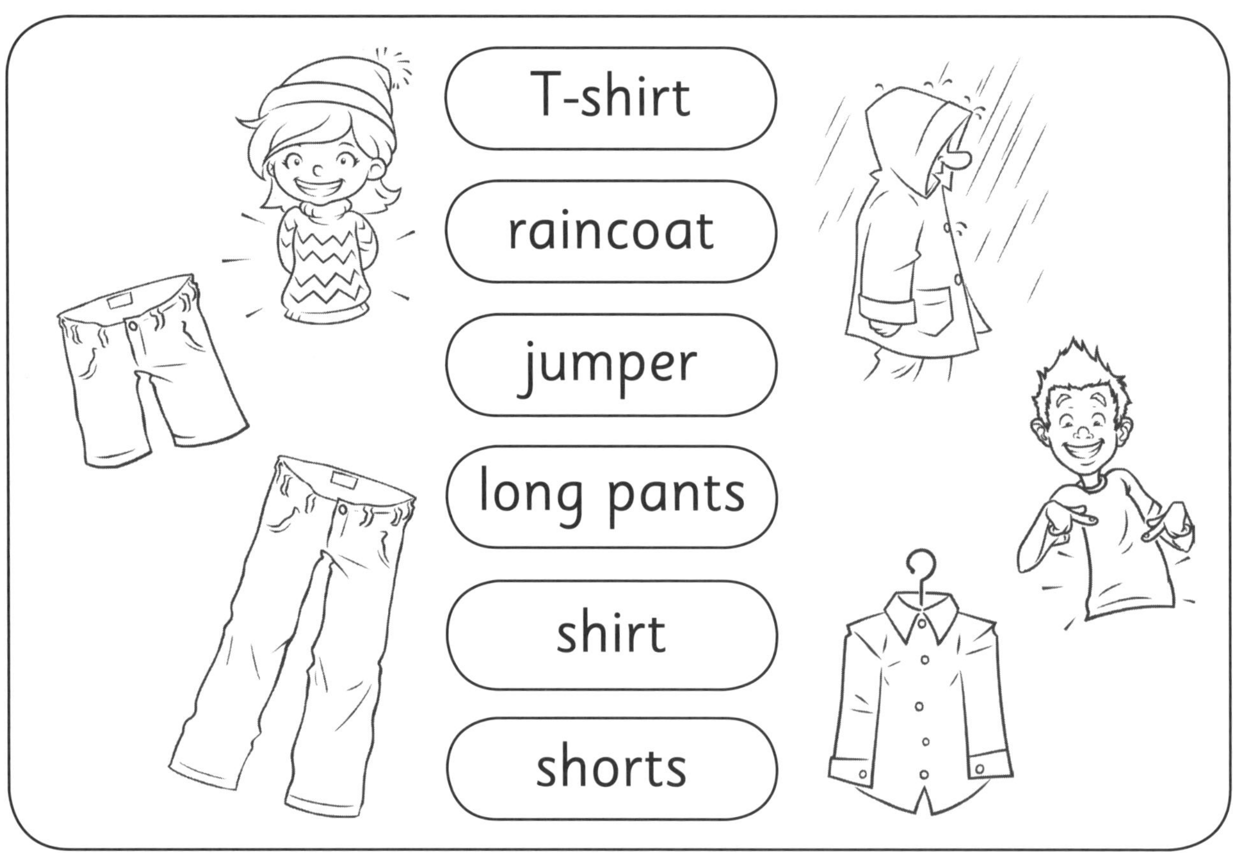

2 Trace and copy.

Name

Check

Lesson 118 • Worksheet 4

1 Circle the rhyming word in each row.

corn	can	horn	cane	seen
tore	take	time	store	wire
pork	park	pink	paint	fork
more	mine	wore	many	our
storm	steam	stem	form	team

2 Complete the sentences.

long pants raincoat T-shirt

When it is sunny, I wear a ________________.

I wear a ________________ on rainy days.

My ________________ keep my legs warm.

Lesson 119 verbs

Learning objectives

Children will:

- identify verbs as doing or action words.
- recognise that almost every sentence has a verb.
- read and write verbs.

Australian Curriculum Content Descriptions

Sound and letter knowledge

ACELA1439 identify rhyme and syllables in spoken words

ACELA1457 replace sounds in spoken words; recognise words that start with a given sound, end with a given sound, have a given medial sound, rhyme with a given word

ACELA1458 recognise sound-letter matches including common vowel and consonant digraphs and consonant blends

Expressing and developing ideas

ACELA1435 learn that word order in sentences is important for meaning

ACELA1455 use morphemes to read words

ACELA1778 write one-syllable words containing known blends; know that regular one-syllable words are made up of letters and common letter clusters that correspond to the sounds heard, and how to use visual memory to write high-frequency words

Interpreting, analysing and evaluating

ACELY1659 combine knowledge of context, meaning, grammar and phonics to decode text; recognise most high-frequency sight words when reading text

Word families

run, leap, fly, seeing, hearing, smelling, lifting, said, shout, whisper, ask, pounce, glide, wriggle, jump, imagine, remember, spray, creep, swoop, cling, squeal, scuttle, walk, crawl, stop, stomp, hiss, flap, hop, lie, roll

Vocabulary words

sideways, scared

Extra assistance

The first type of verb to introduce is the doing or action word. These are easy words for younger students to identify – words that tell what something is doing. Students can check if a word is an action verb by putting it with I – I sleep, I walk, I run. Play the game Simon Says to reinforce verb words. Play sorting games with flashcards to identify verbs amongst other words. Use flashcards to make sentences and identify the verb.

Classroom activities

Act it Out

Have a set of verb flashcards. Students take turns picking one from the pile and acting it out while the rest of the class guess what their verb is.

When everyone has a card they must write a sentence using their verb. Discuss the responses.

Reading Eggs Lesson sequence	TEACH Content and skills	PRACTISE Children will:	APPLY
Hear: *Animated Lesson*	Introduce verbs and how to use them with the song *Crash the Verb Man loves verbs.*	understand that verbs are doing or action words that are used in almost every sentence.	**Worksheet 1** Action verbs
Write: *Rocket Launch, Syllable Crunch, Bird Words*	Identify sounds or syllables in a word and make the word. Recognise correct word order for a sentence.	select the correct onset and rime or syllables to make the word. Choose the correct words to make a sentence.	**Worksheet 2** Saying verbs
Find: *What's Missing?, 1, 2, 3, 4*	Identify the missing sound in a word. Recognise the order of a sequence of events.	choose the correct letters to make words. Put pictures in order to show a sequence.	**Worksheet 3** Read and write
Vocabulary: *Word Whiz, Define It*	Build vocabulary skills: Recognise key vocabulary. Identify words by their definitions.	tap on the word being said and put it in a sentence. Choose the correct word to match the definition.	**Worksheet 4** Check
Read: *How Does it End?, Q & A, Book*	Read sentences using basic vocabulary. Comprehend the meaning of a text. Read aloud book.	match a sentence beginning and ending. Answer questions about a text. Listen, follow the reading and read along.	**Reading Eggs Story book** How Animals Move

Classroom activities

Verb, Noun or Adjective?

Place three boxes on the floor labelled verb, noun and adjective. Discuss the three types of words with the class. Have a pile of flashcards with a mix of these types of words and ask students one at a time to choose a card, read the word aloud and decide which box it should go in. Discuss their choice as a class.

Related Reading Eggs Activities, Interactives, Songs and Books

Driving Tests

Test 12

Sight words: give, stand, write, walk

Letters and sounds: dance, fly

Spelling Bank

Reading Eggs Puzzle Park

Do it

Sense it

Opposites

Music Café

Crash the Verb Man loves verbs

Reading Eggs Posters

Verbs

Suffixes -ing

Reading Eggs Library Books

My Program Books

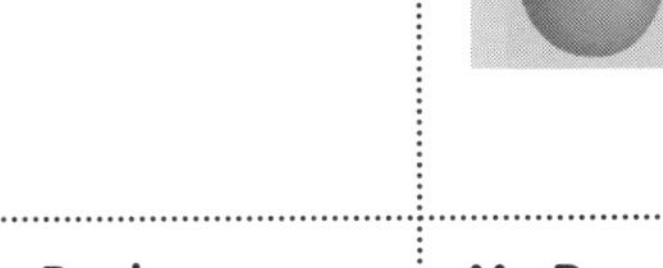

Teacher Toolkit

- Spelling Activities
- Grammar Lessons
- Comprehension Lessons
- Targeting Comprehension Interactively
- Targeting Text Interactively

Reading Eggs Apps

Eggy Sight words

Critter Card

Huggle buggle

Verbs

Name

Action verbs

Lesson 119 • Worksheet 1

1 Match the animal to the correct verb.

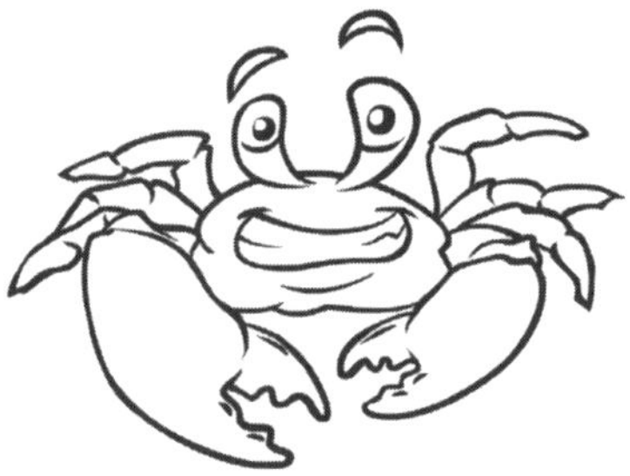

fly · hop · crawl	swoop · wriggle · creep
swim · run · fly	pounce · creep · stomp

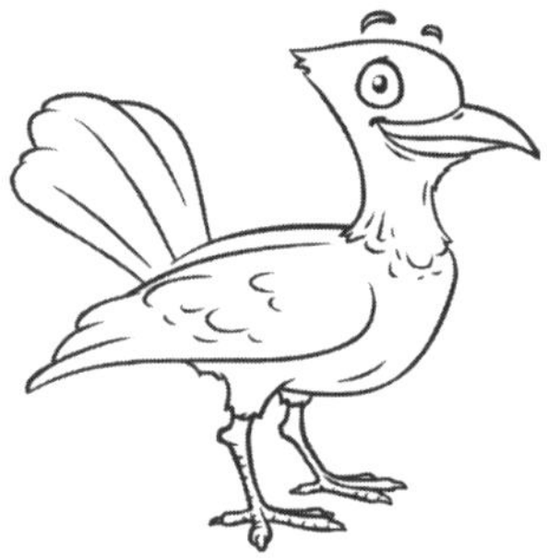

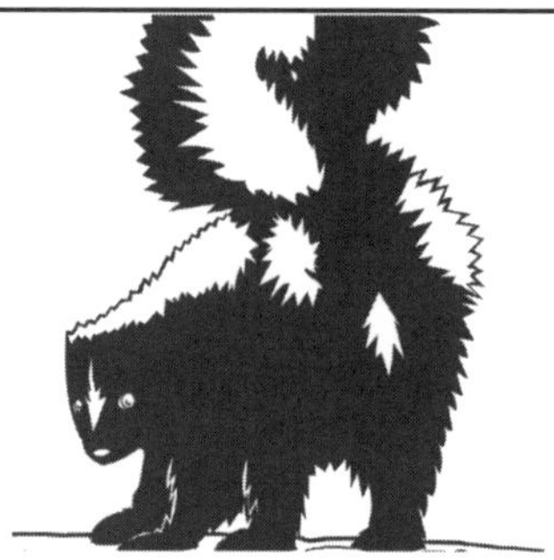

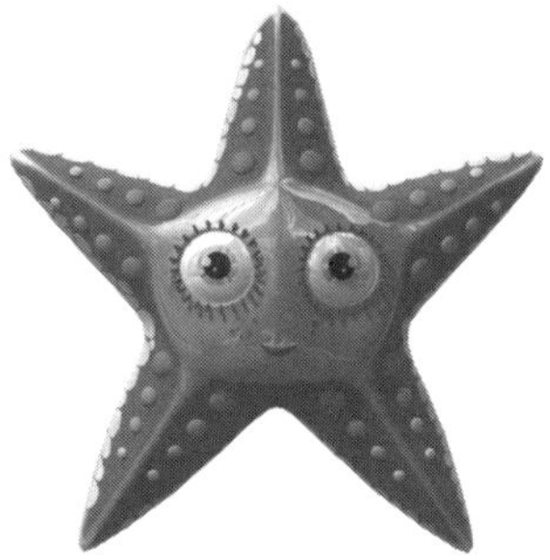

2 Colour the action verbs.

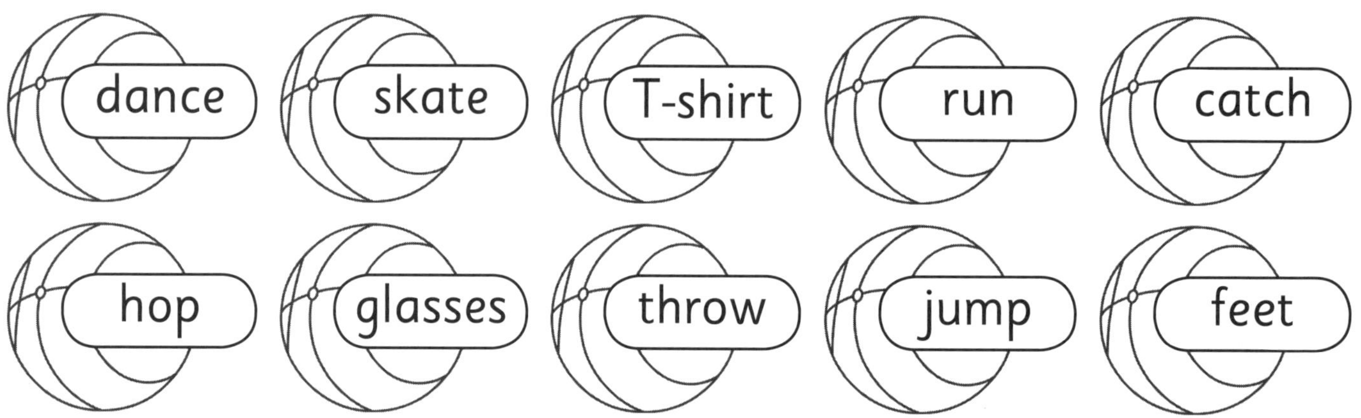

Name

Saying verbs

Verbs

Lesson 119 • Worksheet 2

1 Match each saying verb to its picture.

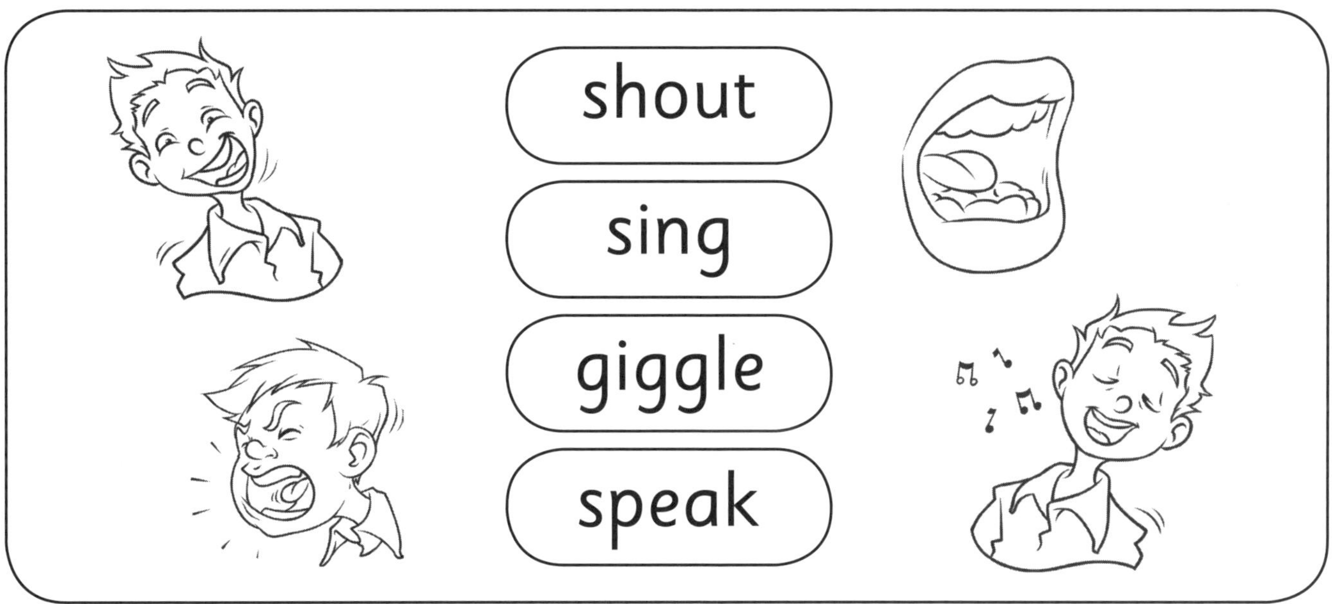

2 Cross out the word **says**. Choose a better verb from the list.

hisses barks roars asks

"What's the time?" says Tick tock clock. ______________

"I love to bake cakes," says Jake the snake. ______________

"Let's go and play!" says Tom the dog. ______________

"Vroom, vroom!" says Fast As. ______________

3 Colour the saying verbs.

shouts runs asks screams hops

Verbs

Lesson 119 • Worksheet 3

Name

Read and write

1 Circle the verbs.

Frank the skunk runs and stomps his feet. Blue wing hops along the ground and glides in the air. Brad the crab scuttles across the sand.

Colour a starfish each time you find a verb.

2 Complete each sentence.

walks pounces clings flaps

Roary the lion runs and ____________ on his food.

Coco the starfish ____________ onto rocks with her feet.

Brad the crab ____________ sideways on his eight legs.

Blue bird ____________ his wings to fly.

Name

Check

Lesson 119 • Worksheet 4

1 Circle the action verbs.

Dan plays soccer on Saturdays. He runs, jumps, kicks and scores a goal! The crowd claps and cheers for Dan.

Colour a ball each time you find an action verb.

2 Colour the right verb. Cross out the wrong one.

"I live in a lovely nest," builds sings Blue wing.

"Let's scribble a picture!" laughs draws Scribble stick.

"Shh! I need a little nap," sleeps whispers Happy nap.

"It's time to lay my egg," clucks flies Meg the hen.

Lesson 120 the sound **ay**

Learning objectives

Children will:

- identify the sound ay.
- read and write ay words.

Australian Curriculum Content Descriptions

Sound and letter knowledge

ACELA1439 identify rhyme and syllables in spoken words

ACELA1457 replace sounds in spoken words; recognise words that start with a given sound, end with a given sound, have a given medial sound, rhyme with a given word

ACELA1458 recognise sound-letter matches including common vowel and consonant digraphs and consonant blends

ACELA1459 recognise that letters can have more than one sound; recognise sounds that can be produced by different letters

Expressing and developing ideas

ACELA1435 learn that word order in sentences is important for meaning

ACELA1438 build word families using onset and rime

ACELA1778 write one-syllable words containing known blends; know that regular one-syllable words are made up of letters and common letter clusters that correspond to the sounds heard, and how to use visual memory to write high-frequency words

Interpreting, analysing and evaluating

ACELY1659 combine knowledge of context, meaning, grammar and phonics to decode text; recognise most high-frequency sight words when reading text

Word families

Sunday, today, birthday, midday, stay, hooray, play, hay, clay, spray, tray, bay, lay, say, stray, sway, stay, day, okay, way

Extra assistance

The spelling *ay* is another form of the long *a* vowel sound also produced by the digraphs *a-e* and *ai*, as in *tale* and *tail*. This form of the sound */ae/* is nearly always used on the end of a word, for example *today*, *stray*, *way*. Exceptions include compound words made with an *ay* word first (eg *daytime*) and the use of suffixes (eg *layer*). Most words ending with the */ae/* sound are spelled *ay*.

Classroom activities

Run to it!

This is best done in a hall or on the playground. Label four corners or areas with signs saying *ay, igh, or* and *oa*. The students stand in the middle and when the teacher calls out a word containing one of these sounds, they must run to the matching corner. Try harder words, with more than one syllable, for example *birthday*, *boatload* or *sighing*.

Reading Eggs Lesson sequence	TEACH Content and skills	PRACTISE Children will:	APPLY
Hear: *Animated Lesson*	Introduce the sound *ay* with the song *May the Jay's birthday.*	identify the sound *ay* and make *ay* words.	**Worksheet 1** Word family
Write: *Rocket Launch, Pelican Spelling, Broken Sentence*	Identify sounds in a word and make the word. Recognise correct word order for a sentence.	make a word using onset and rime. Select letters to spell a word. Choose the correct words to make a sentence.	**Worksheet 2** Reading
Find: *Word Family, Days*	Identify the correct onset letter to complete the word. Recognise the days of the week.	choose the correct initial letter to make the word. Put the days of the week in order.	**Worksheet 3** Vocabulary
Vocabulary: *Syllable Gobbler, Dress the Monster, Bingo Stars*	Build vocabulary skills: Identify the number of syllables in a word. Recognise key vocabulary.	choose the number of syllables in a word. Read and follow instructions. Tap on the word being said.	**Worksheet 4** Check
Read: *Book Ends, Book*	Read sentences using basic vocabulary. Read aloud book.	choose a word to finish the sentence. Listen, follow the reading and read along.	**Reading Eggs book** Word families for igh, ay, ir, or, oat, oad

Classroom activities

Bingo!

Give students a laminated board with ten squares on it. Ask them to write a word in each square from the list of *ay* words (use whiteboard markers). Say words from the list. Students put a cross on that word on their board. First one to ten calls out 'bingo' and wins!

Related Reading Eggs Activities, Interactives, Songs and Books

Spelling Bank

Goats

Lesson 49

Focus sound words: play, tray, stay

High frequency sight words: away, say, today

Driving Tests

Reading Eggs Puzzle Park

More than One

What is it?

Do You Know?

Music Café

May the Jay's birthday

Reading Eggs Posters

The ay Sound

Alternate Spelling /ai/

Reading Eggs Library Books

My Program Books

Teacher Toolkit

- Spelling Activities
- Grammar Lessons
- Comprehension Lessons
- Targeting Comprehension Interactively
- Targeting Text Interactively

Reading Eggs Apps

Eggy Sight words

Eggy Snap

Eggy Vocab

Critter Card

Oats the billy goat

ay

Lesson 120 · Worksheet 1

Name

Word family

1 Trace.

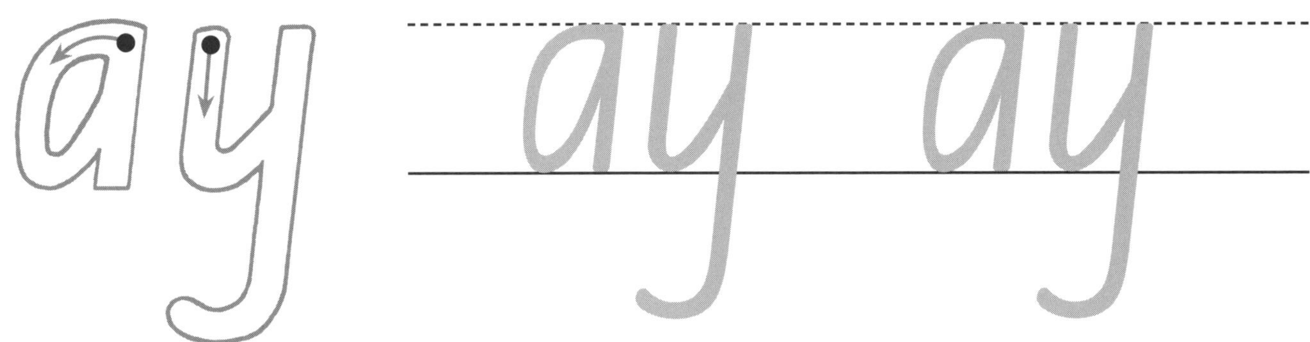

2 Use the wheel to make words. Write the words.

3 Colour the **ay** words.

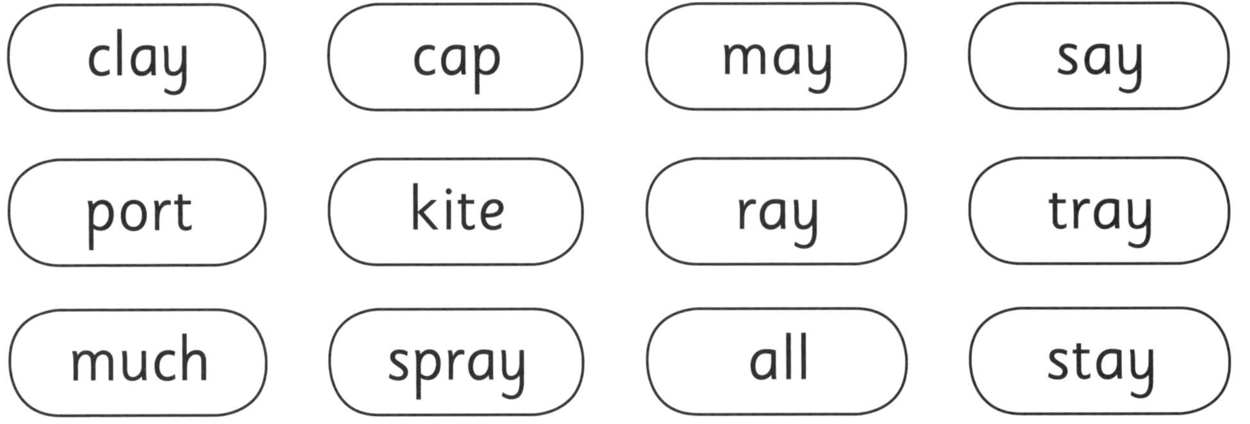

Name

Reading

Lesson 120 • Worksheet 2

1 Read the text.

Brad is a crab. Crabs walk sideways. Frank is a skunk. Skunks can hiss, squeal and spray very smelly stuff. Roary is a lion. Lions run and pounce on their food.

Underline the correct answer.

2 Who is a crab?

- Frank
- Roary
- Brad
- Coco

3 What noise do skunks make?

- roar
- hiss
- bark
- squeak

4 Which animals pounce on their food?

- starfish
- lions
- crabs
- horse

Lesson 120 · Worksheet 3

Name

Vocabulary

1 Match each picture to a word.

2 Read the clue. Write the word.

I have wings. I can fly up high. I am a b______________.	I have four legs. I live in a stable. I am a h______________.
I help you to see things when it is dark. I am a l______________.	I float on water. I carry things and people across the sea. I am a b____________.

Name

Check

Lesson 120 • Worksheet 4

1 Join Milky way to the **ay** words.

2 Guess the word by its shape. Write each word in a box.

light oats bird tray

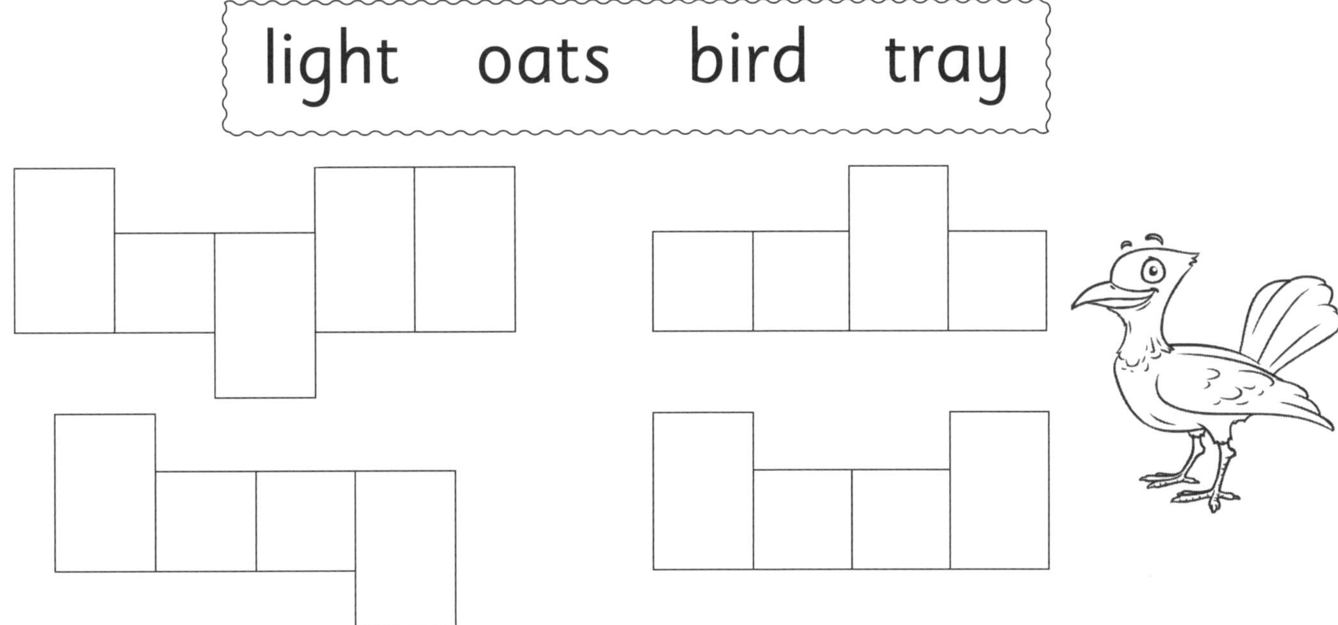

3 Write a sentence using the word **play**.

Reading Eggs Posters

In meeting the demands of the Australian Curriculum we have created a poster series as a teaching tool. These full colour, engaging posters can be used on Interactive Whiteboards and tablets as well as printed for classroom use. The series covers the broad scope of curriculum outcomes including language, literature and literacy.

Here is a sample from the series that address reading comprehension.

Purpose

To provide a resource for early readers to apply comprehension techniques to their reading.
The posters address strategies for reading with comprehension and activities for consolidating students' comprehension of a text. There are techniques to be applied before, during and after reading a text which will focus on reading for meaning. There are strategies to help students and teachers summarise what they have read and posters which focus attention on particular aspects of reading texts.

Australian Curriculum Content Descriptions

Responding to literature

Discuss characters and events in a range of literary texts and share personal responses to these texts, making connections with students' own experiences (**ACELT1582**)

Text structure and organisation

Understand that the purposes texts serve shape their structure in predictable ways (**ACELA1447**)

Teaching notes

- Print the Reading and Spelling Strategies posters in A3 format to put up on the wall. Refer students to the strategies during writing and reading activities to build independence.
- Use the posters for approaching a text before, during and after reading in small reading groups or on whole class texts. Making Predictions, Retelling, Summarising and Sequencing are all ways in which students can show their comprehension of the text.
- Posters explaining Story Elements can be helpful starting points to lead students into discussions of aspects of literature upon which they can base personal opinions.
- Comprehension rests on the connections readers make between the text and themselves, their world and other texts they have read. The Making Connections series of posters can generate interesting discussion amongst students who may have different world views and backgrounds.
- The posters explaining common types of texts are designed to support the teaching of how texts fit a certain genre and how to identify what type of text students are reading. They can narrow it down from a broad category such as Narrative to a particular type of narrative, for example, Fairytale.
- Encourage students to examine texts they have read with the Compare and contrast and Differences posters. It can be interesting to discuss two texts that fit the same genre and text type but are very different.

The posters

Reading strategies

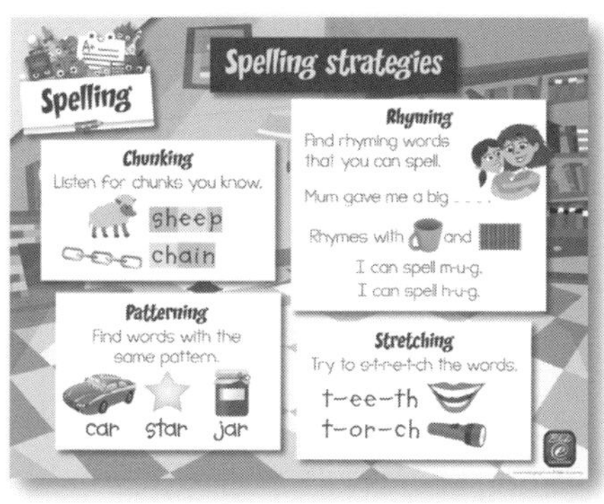

Spelling strategies

Story elements

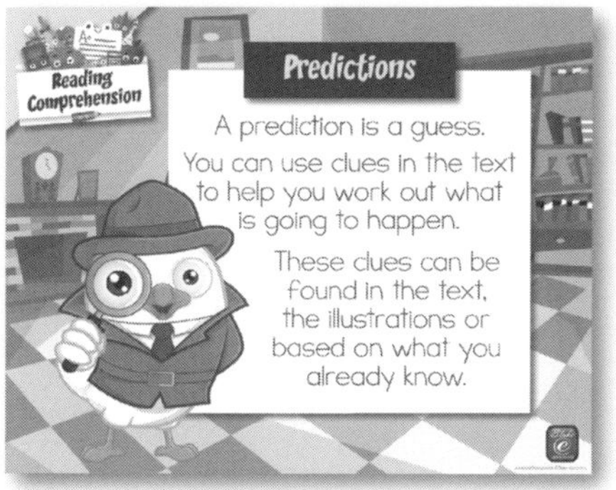

Predictions

Retelling

Making connections

Narrative structure

Fairytales

Compare and contrast

Skills Checklist Lessons 91-120

Name

Lesson	Skills	Check
91	Recognises and writes *soft c* words. Identifies and writes theme words – bicycles. Writes number words one to five and matches to numerals. Completes sentences.	
92	Recognises -ice, -ime and -ipe words. Writes -ite, -ine, and -ime words. Identifies and writes compound words. Completes and reads sentences using *long i* words.	
93	Recognises and writes *soft g* words. Writes and recognises sight words – Saturday, today, day. Writes -age words and identifies -ice and -age words. Completes sentences using *soft g* words.	
94	Recognises and writes -ake and -ate words. Reads and comprehends sentences. Identifies the words rooster and duck. Completes sentences.	
95	Writes *long a* word families. Recognises *long a* words. Identifies theme words – cake baking. Reads and comprehends sentences.	
96	Recognises and writes -ace and -ice words. Identifies theme words – space. Reads and comprehends sentences. Write and read the words above and higher.	
97	Differentiates between vowels and consonants. Writes and reads compound words. Identifies theme words – verbs and space. Uses vowels correctly.	
98	Differentiates between short and long vowels. Reads and comprehends sentences. Completes and writes sentences. Writes and recognises theme words – craft.	
99	Recognises and writes words using *ee*. Identifies and writes words that end in -y. Writes and recognises theme words – circus. Completes sentences.	
100	Identifies which sound completes a word. Completes sentences. Writes -ake, -ice and -ape words. Recognises words used in previous lessons.	
101	Recognises and writes *short oo* words. Reads and comprehends sentences. Writes and recognises theme words – cakes. Completes sentences.	
102	Recognises and writes *long oo* words. Reads and comprehends sentences. Writes and completes sentences. Identifies rhyming words.	
103	Recognises and writes *long o* words. Writes and recognises theme words – animals. Reads and comprehends sentences. Completes sentences.	
104	Writes and recognises *long o* words. Reads and comprehends sentences. Recognises theme words – tadpole race. Completes sentences.	
105	Recognises cl-, pl-, sl- and sh- words. Completes sentences. Identifies which sound completes a word. Writes words with a blend at the beginning.	

Name

Skills Checklist Lessons 91-120

Lesson	Skills	Check
106	Writes words with a blend at the beginning. Identifies which sound completes a word. Reads and comprehends sentences.	
107	Writes and recognises *ea* words. Reads and comprehends sentences. Differentiates between *ea*, *ee* and *e* words.	
108	Writes and recognises *long u* words. Completes sentences. Identifies rhyming words.	
109	Writes and recognises -er words. Completes sentences. Writes their own sentence. Reads and comprehends sentences.	
110	Recognises and writes words with a blend at the beginning. Reads and comprehends paragraphs. Recognises and writes adjectives. Completes sentences.	
111	Identifies which beginning blend completes a word. Recognises words with a blend at the beginning. Reads and comprehends sentences and paragraphs. Completes sentences.	
112	Identifies the number of syllables in a word. Recognises missing syllables. Writes words that end with -er. Recognises and writes theme words – healthy things.	
113	Recognises and writes words with a blend at the end. Reads and comprehends sentences. Completes sentences. Writes their own sentence.	
114	Writes and recognises *oa* words. Reads and comprehends paragraphs. Completes sentences. Identifies rhyming words.	
115	Writes *ar*, *er* and *ur* words. Recognises *ar* and *ir* words. Identifies theme words – gardening. Reads and comprehends sentences.	
116	Writes and recognises *igh* words. Completes sentences and writes their own. Writes and recognises compound words. Identifies *long i* words.	
117	Identifies common and proper nouns. Differentiates between common and proper nouns. Completes sentences. Writes their own sentence.	
118	Writes and recognises *or* words. Writes and recognises *ore* words. Recognises and writes theme words – weather and clothes. Completes sentences.	
119	Recognises action and speech verbs. Identifies verbs in a paragraph. Completes sentences.	
120	Writes and recognises *ay* words. Reads and comprehends sentences and paragraphs. Recognises words used in previous lessons. Writes their own sentence.	

READING ASSESSMENT
Lessons 91-120

Name

Read the text.

On Monday, Frankie had a long tail.
On Tuesday, Frankie had pointy ears.
On Wednesday, Frankie had big, webbed feet.
On Thursday, Frankie had great, big bug eyes.

Underline the correct answer.

1 When did Frankie have a long tail?
- Monday
- Tuesday
- Wednesday

2 What did Frankie have on Tuesday?
- bug eyes
- webbed feet
- pointy ears

3 What were Frankie's eyes like?
- webbed
- big
- pointy